Discovering intimacy

Relating to God and Others
as Single Adults

David & Teresa Ferguson
Bruce & Joyce Walker

Great
Commandment
Ministry
RESOURCES

RELATIONSHIP PRESS

Discovering Intimacy

David and Teresa Ferguson
Bruce and Joyce Walker

Relationship Press
P.O. Box 201808
Austin TX 78720-1808
1.800.881.8008
Fax 512.795.0853
U.K. 01.926.421.004
www.GreatCommandment.net
www.NeverAlone.net

ISBN 1-893307-01-8

First Edition: January, 1999
Second Edition: September 2000
Third Edition: November 2002

Contents

Acknowledgments

When God said to Adam in the Garden of Eden, "It is not good for you to be alone," He was referring to more than the introduction of a marriage relationship. He was unveiling the essence of what it means to be created in the image of God—we are relational. That truth is just as applicable to the single adult as it is to the married couple or family. That is why we are deeply grateful to God and privileged to introduce Discovering Intimacy as a resource to help churches equip single adults to experience Great Commandment love in relationships.

This project would not have been possible apart from the contributions of a number of people who co-labored with us in a variety of ways. Particular thanks go to Patrice Sampley, Leah Springer and the singles ministry team at Restoration Church in Euless, Texas, and Dan and Lois Coutcher who head the Navigator ministry at North Carolina State University. These two groups served to field test the most recent versions of the resource. At several points along the way, they provided extensive input which is now part of the finished work. David and Jeannie Ware from Irving Bible Church in Irving, Texas also contributed input to the process as they led small groups, Bible study classes, and retreats through the preliminary versions of the material.

Jim Walter of the Intimate Life staff in Austin was a constant companion and encourager, particularly during the times when too many projects were competing for too few hours in the day. Alister and Christine Mort provided an international perspective and validated the need for such a resource in the United Kingdom. Dr. Don McMinn and Wayne and Terri Snead offered constructive edits that helped polish the final product. Dr. Marcia Wiinamaki and Daniel Jensen deserve special acknowledgment for putting together the original manuscript of Discovering Intimacy. Cindy McCoy was especially helpful in our work, giving input from the perspective of a professional counselor and single parent mother.

We are indebted to the staff of the Intimate Life Enrichment Center who kept the ministry functioning while some of us slipped away to write. These contributors include Dr. Lewis Alexander, Robert Hart, Joe Maddox, Barry Metz, Terri Snead, Sarah Taylor,

Jim Walter, Joella Waters, and Kerry Williamson. Their support and encouragement remove a great deal of our aloneness in these projects.

Finally, but significantly, we want to thank Drew Walker who gave up some of his time with Dad to support the final push toward completion.

David and Teresa Ferguson   Bruce and Joyce Walker

Beginning the Journey

Welcome! You are about to begin a journey toward a richer, fuller, deeper relationship with God and with others. Such relationships are a significant part of the abundant life promised through Jesus Christ (John 10:10). We trust that your experience will be fulfilling as well as challenging. Our desire is to introduce you to life-changing biblical principles about relating to God and to one another in meaningful ways. Our hope is that you will apply these principles in your life from now on.

Discovering Intimacy is a book about people and relationships. You may be a person who has never married or someone who has experienced the end of one or more marriages through death or divorce. You may have several children or none at all. You may, in fact, be a married person who works in some capacity with single adults. Nevertheless, there is one thing we can justifiably assume about you—it is not good for you to be alone!

Please understand us clearly. We are not talking about occasional solitude when we speak of aloneness. We are not suggesting that it is wrong to get away from the crowd, or the kids, or the stress of performing your work now and then. Even Jesus needed and sought solitude by retreating from the throngs of people who sought Him almost constantly, demanding His time and attention. When we refer to aloneness, we are talking about being disconnected or estranged, misunderstood, unsupported, rejected, disrespected, and unable to communicate with others meaningfully by sharing what is on your heart and theirs. In these ways, it is not good for you to be alone!

While we are at it, let us clarify something else. This is a book about your need for intimacy regardless of your marital status. It is *not* a book that assumes you will marry or remarry some day. If you do marry, the principles that you experience as you proceed through this material will prove useful. But these principles are applicable in any and all relationships—those with friends, parents, children, co-workers, fellow believers, and God Himself. It is a book that will teach you about removing aloneness—in yourself and in others, for it is not good for you to be alone!

The format for this material is somewhat unique also. We do not think it sufficient to merely acquire more biblical truth. Knowledge in and of itself has a tendency to bloat the ego rather than develop godly character. It is necessary instead, that we *experience* truth and live it day after day. Consequently, we have designed this course to be experiential. Therefore, as you take this course, you will need a relationship in which to implement these principles. One way for this to be done is to complete the material with one or two close friends whom you already know well. Some of you may be working through the book as part of a discipleship class or fellowship group and may not know the other people well at first. In this case, we recommend the formation of small groups for the experiential exercises. Whether you complete the workbook with existing friends or assigned partners, these relationships will be a vital part of your *Discovering Intimacy* journey.

How to Make Best Use of This Workbook

Discovering Intimacy is a course about people and relationships. But developing close personal relationships in today's society can be challenging, if not risky, even within the church. This book will help you *experience* biblical principles about intimacy and integrate them into your lifestyle, making a positive impact on your relationships with God and others. But, relationships, by definition, require interaction with others. And since *Discovering Intimacy* is intended to build relationship skills, you will learn best if you have a relationship in which to apply these principles as you take the course. Listen to the testimony of a single woman in England who completed a study of the Intimate Life principles with two of her friends.

I was introduced to the intimacy principles at a conference and subsequently completed the workbook with two other women. As we completed the exercises and shared together in our small group meetings, I came to know that it really is okay to have needs that are met through relationships. I began to realize that my neediness does not derive from my being single. I used to think that my married friends never felt the same things that I did, for example, about security, approval, or attention. But I learned from a person in my small group who is married, that we are more similar in the needs we have than I had ever imagined. I now feel released from the pressure that, as a single person, I should be totally self-sufficient emotionally lest I feel a failure. It is okay to need both my relationship with God and close relationships with others.

You may have begun reading *Discovering Intimacy* on your own, with a friend, as part of a Bible study class, or in a small fellowship group. Whatever the context, we strongly encourage you to experience the material with another person or persons.

Each chapter of *Discovering Intimacy* will provide several opportunities for you to reflect on your life experiences and to write down some of your thoughts and feelings related to the principles being presented. At the end of each chapter, we have included material to help you apply the principles that have been presented. There are passages of Scripture that you can use to deepen your relationship with God. These exercises will help you know the heart of the Father in a deeper way.

There are also two "Experiencing Intimacy" sections for use in a small group or with one or two "journey-mates"— friends who have agreed to work through the course together.   Plan a regular time each week to meet with your group or journey-mates to discuss the questions provided in these sections. The goal for these meetings is to experience the biblical principles covered in each chapter. The discussion questions refer to the information presented and the questions completed in each chapter. These meetings are a significant part the *Discovering Intimacy* experience, so we urge you to begin now by enlisting a journey-mate or organizing a small group of friends to complete the workbook together. When you meet for the first time, you may want to review the "Guidelines for Sharing with a Journey-mate or Small Group" that follow.

1. General Guidelines for Discussions

Read the chapter and complete all the written exercises prior to meeting with your group or journey-mates. When discussing the chapter or your answers to the exercises, be as specific as possible. Avoid long storytelling about events or experiences you have had. Focus instead on your thoughts, feelings, and responses. Allow each person an opportunity to share a response to each question before moving to the next one. As people share, reflect upon how they were impacted emotionally by their experiences. Be sure to honor each person by keeping the discussions confidential. Avoid giving advice, minimizing the impact of their experiences, or abruptly changing the focus to another subject or person. Convey genuine concern and comforting words if the one sharing discusses a emotionally painful experience.

Listed below is a covenant understanding for each journey-mate or group member to endorse.   The guidelines included in the covenant are to be discussed when you meet the first time to review the first chapter of the workbook.

Course Covenant for Discovering Intimacy

1. I will set aside time each week to complete the individual exercises in the workbook.

2. I will set aside time for meeting with my journey-mate/small group each week and give these meetings priority.

3. I will participate in the giving and receiving of support and care with the other participants of these meetings.

4. I will be open and willing for God to teach me about my relational needs and areas for growth and change in relationships with Him and other persons.

5. I will maintain the confidentiality of my journey-mate/group members. Therefore, I will not relate what I hear or observe about my journey-mate/group members to anyone else.

6. I will purpose to be quick to listen attentively, honoring and respecting each person, and avoid giving advice or trying to solve the problems of my fellow participants. I will offer constructive feedback and suggestions only when invited to do so.

7. I will pursue other counseling or support services if I discover problems or concerns that require more time or care than my journey-mates/group members are able to provide.

Name: _____ Date: _____

II. Caring for Others By Meeting Intimacy Needs

One of the greatest blessings from completing the *Discovering Intimacy* workbook with others comes in the giving and receiving of caring concern at points of relational neediness. You may want to refer periodically to the following list of relational needs that can be met during your small group or journey-mate encounters. These needs are explained in Chapter Two.

Acceptance
Receiving another person willingly and unconditionally, especially when the other's behavior has been imperfect; being willing to continue loving another in spite of offenses (Rom. 15:7)

Affection
Expressing care and closeness through non-sexual physical touch, carefully respecting the boundaries of the other person; saying "I love you" (Rom. 16:16; Mark 10:16)

Appreciation
Expressing thanks, praise, or commendation. Recognizing accomplishment or effort (Col. 3:15b; I Cor. 11:2)

Approval (Blessing)
Building up or affirming another; affirming both the fact of and the importance of a relationship (Eph. 4:29; Mark 1:11)

Attention
Conveying appropriate interest, concern, and care; taking thought of another; entering another's "world" (I Cor. 12:25)

Comfort
Responding to a hurting person with words, feelings, and touch; to hurt with and for another's grief or pain (Rom. 12:15b; Matt. 5:4; II Cor. 1:3-4; John 11:35)

Encouragement	Urging another to persist and persevere toward a goal; stimulating toward love and good deeds (I Thess. 5:11; Heb. 10:24)
Respect	Valuing and regarding another highly; treating another as important; honoring another (Rom. 12:10)
Security (Peace)	Harmony in relationships; freedom from fear or threat of harm (Rom. 12:16, 18)
Support	Coming alongside and gently helping with a problem or struggle; providing appropriate assistance (Gal. 6:2)

We are confident that God is at work in every believer performing His work of grace until the day Christ returns in glory (Phil. 1:6). We trust that God will bless you with a greater sense of abundant life in Christ as you learn and apply the principles of intimacy contained in this book. *Discovering Intimacy* is a tool to help you experience this abundant life through relationships that remove aloneness and glorify God. We trust that this journey will be rewarding and life changing for you. We are honored that you would journey with us part of the way.

Chapter One

——— ◆ ———

MADE FOR INTIMACY
Relational by God's Design

*The Lord God said, "It is not good
for man to be alone..." Genesis 2:18*

Having grown up in a small rural town in Oklahoma, I (Bruce) will never forget my first impressions of New York City. I had taken a job in a nonprofit organization located in the heart of Manhattan. I remember walking to work along Fifth Avenue that first morning. There were thousands of people on the sidewalks moving in both directions. I was looking at a virtual sea of humanity. Everyone seemed focused and intent on getting somewhere. As I made my way to the office, a profound thought struck me. I was totally anonymous! I could have stood on my head in the middle of the sidewalk and the flow of bodies would have continued. Though surrounded by people, no one knew me. There was no meaningful interaction. As far as I could tell, no one cared whether or not I existed. There were lots of people, but no relationships. I realized that more than ever before, I was alone.

As the 21st century dawns, we find ourselves in a world that produces unbelievable advances in technology, using products that were the stuff of science fiction only a decade or two before. Though technologically advanced, we are relationally challenged. We can communicate electronically anywhere on the globe, but struggle to connect emotionally with someone in the same room. In touch with the world, we remain disconnected in our closest relationships. That may explain why over 70 percent of Americans described themselves as lonely in a recent survey. This pervasive loneliness is related to the systematic breakdown of committed, trust-based relationships in our society. For example, a pattern of marriage failure is weaving itself throughout the very fabric of American society, becoming institutionalized and expected. For several decades now, divorce rates have hovered at 50 percent for all marriages. The prognosis for second and subsequent marriages is even worse, with approximately 70 percent ending in divorce. Studies have shown that divorce "begets" divorce, as children of divorced parents have a higher expectation and probability to experience divorce in their own marriages. It is predicted that more than two-thirds of our children will spend at least some part of their childhoods in a single-parent home.

These trends suggest that generations of young adults have never experienced relationally healthy and enduring family environments. How have these people been coping with their loneliness? Have they given up on relationships completely? Well, only a few have entered monasteries or retreated to Antarctica! But, increasing numbers are choosing to marry at later ages than their parents did, living with someone before making a permanent commitment, or putting off marriage altogether. Many have already experienced the pain of divorce. Some of these will marry again, though not all. Overall, these trends have resulted in declining confidence in the stability and durability of relational commitments. And no wonder, for the blueprint for relationships left behind in recent decades has been faulty at best. Not only has the disruption of relationships become ingrained in our culture, the ability to develop relational intimacy has become a lost art.

We would like to think that Christians have done much better in their trust-based relationships. However, that has not been the case. The statistics for divorce, teenage pregnancies, drug and alcohol abuse, and other social problems are not much different for Christians than they are for the general public. Unfortunately, membership in a church does not automatically remove our loneliness or insulate us completely from relational difficulties.

Can aloneness be God's desire for us? Are we really supposed to move further and further toward autonomy and self-sufficiency? Do we even acknowledge our genuine need for meaningful fellowship with other human beings? Will we settle for polite, superficial friendships? Will fear of intimacy keep us from enjoying more genuine relationships that include honest, heart-to-heart disclosure of our needs, feelings, and boundaries? Are we "stuck" not knowing how to remove the emptiness of aloneness? Do God's instructions concerning relationships seem irrelevant in our technological age?

We have good news for you. There is light at the end of this tunnel—God's light. Churches around the world are refocusing on the principles of Scripture that show us how to restore Great Commandment love in our relationships with God and others. Here is an example of what that looks like.

Ray entered the worship center of a church in his city on a Friday night to find a crowd of people spread throughout the room in pairs and small groups. Some were talking quietly while others were weeping together. Curious, Ray walked over to a man standing in the back by himself and asked what the group was doing. The man in the back was Dr. David Ferguson. He explained to Ray that the people were comforting each other as they shared past and present hurts that they had experienced. Ray could sense the relevance of the moment. These people were experiencing genuine intimacy. They were relating to each other on a level he had only imagined possible. He turned to Dr. Ferguson and said, "That's what I need." Later, he would share that he had just gone through a broken engagement, his job was in jeopardy, and he had recently placed his mother in a nursing home. These events had left him defeated and devastated. He was in pain and had been facing that pain alone. But what Ray observed in the church that night gave him hope.

Ray became much more aware of his need for God and others as he encountered significant challenges and hardships. How about you? How aware have you been of your own need for meaningful relationships. How comfortable are you with the idea that God has created you with an innate need for intimacy with Him and other humans?

Write down what you are currently thinking and feeling about your own relational neediness:

_____
_____
_____
_____
_____
_____

<u>Aloneness</u>
Mankind's First Dilemma

No one would argue that we all have *physical* needs for food, water, sleep, air, and even touch. Christians certainly know that we also have *spiritual* needs for eternal life, peace of mind, and the presence of God. But how comfortable are you with this idea that you were intentionally created with needs that are relational? Let's look further at our need for intimacy with God and others. Let's examine the Genesis 2 account of the first human who experienced life as a single adult—Adam.

*What a life! Though formed from the dust of the ground, God has provided Adam luxurious accommodations in which to live. The temperature is pleasant enough that clothes are unnecessary. The foliage is resplendent with variety and color. There is no pollution, no traffic jams, no taxes, no conflicts, and NO SIN! It is truly a **perfect environment**. Even work, as we know it, has not been deemed a necessity. What a place to kick back and hang out!*

*In addition, thanks to God's kindness and blessing, Adam **possesses everything** to make life comfortable and easy. Food is abundant and good to eat. The Garden is the original convenience store without the high prices. Adam is at the top of the food chain with no competition for a place to pitch his tent.*

*Furthermore, God has established Adam in an **exalted position**. He is Chief Executive Officer of the Garden. He gets to look after things, assign all the titles, and decide who gets the sunny spot next to the creek. And, he doesn't even have to work up* *through the ranks. Above all, Adam has a direct line to the Creator. He is in communication with God Almighty. He has an unhindered, free and open relationship with the Father because there is, up to this point, no sin to get in the way.*

Adam shouldn't need anything or anyone else, right? He is in fat city, experiencing the American dream, living high on the hog. Life is good! It's good, that is, except for one thing. For you see, Adam is ALONE! And Adam is about to hear from the Creator of the Universe that it is NOT GOOD for him to be alone (Gen. 2:18). Adam's aloneness was not a mistake by a God who is sovereign and all-knowing. Instead, God's declaration is evidence that being created in the image of God includes being relational. God has designed us with an inherent need for intimacy with Him AND with other persons who are significant to us.

Did God say that it was not good for people to be *single?* No. He said it was not good for us to be *alone.* The condition of aloneness is not established by a person's marital status. It is not limited to single adults. Aloneness is not a character flaw or a sign of inferiority. And, it can be experienced *after* you have come to know the Lord. An awareness of aloneness is evidence that your God-given relational nature is operative within you. When you sense that it is not good to be alone you are identifying with an aspect of who God is—a relational being. Therefore, it is okay to be single and to want to be meaningfully connected with God and others in ways that remove your aloneness and bring glory to Him.

We, too, are relational beings. Therefore, it is natural and normal, even as Christians, to want to remove our aloneness through meaningful relationships with others. God agrees with that. He is the one who declared that it was not good for Adam to be alone and then made provision for his need. Consequently, single adults can embrace their need for close, meaningful relationships with God *and* others.

Aloneness

Complete the statements that follow. If you cannot remember specifics, write down how you remember that things were in general.

Describe specific times in your life when you have experienced significant aloneness:

_____
_____
_____
_____
_____
_____
_____
_____

Describe, for each specific time identified above, how other people responded to you during those times of aloneness:

_____
_____
_____
_____
_____
_____
_____
_____

Later, as you have opportunity to do so, share your responses with your journey-mate or small group. This will be one of many opportunities offered in this course to know and be known by some trusted friends. Even if you do not have someone with whom you think you can share your comments, continue to write them down and pray for God to provide such a journey-mate. If you have not already done so, we would encourage you to disclose this need to your pastor.

Lonely AND Whole

Several frustrating courtships and a broken marriage had left Pat feeling empty and disillusioned about the whole business of close personal relationships. The fact that he and his former spouse were Christians only heightened the frustration. The persons that he most expected to understand and meet his needs, his Christian friends and relatives, had repeatedly disappointed him. Though often surrounded by people at church and work, Pat usually felt empty and isolated. He began to think that his constant longing for relationship was a sign of spiritual immaturity. If only he could do what many had told him to do and be completely satisfied by his relationship with God. His friends assured Pat that God would somehow enable him to "rise above" his relational dilemmas such as loneliness and rejection. In essence, they were suggesting that the solution to his emptiness and pain was keeping a spiritually stiff upper lip.

What does it mean to be spiritually healthy as a single with regard to relationships? Is spiritual maturity equated with needing God alone? Are we inadequate in some way if we long for meaningful companionship with others? All too often, we have been taught that humans can function "quite well, thank you," as long as they have God. Some would say that the more spiritually mature you are the less you will need other people. They suggest that to long for meaningful human companionship is a sign of spiritual weakness. That response does not encourage the lonely. Instead, it heaps condemnation on persons who are simply reflecting the relational blueprint of the Creator. Nowhere is the pain of that accusation more damaging than among the single adult population in our society, particularly within the church.

Single her entire life, Kathy was attending one of Dr. Ferguson's conferences on relationships due to her work as a ministry consultant. Included in the conference was a discussion of the Genesis 2 account of Adam's dilemma—aloneness. At the end of that session, Kathy shared with David that loneliness had been her frequent companion. Engagements had been broken and close friends had moved to other parts of the country. Kathy had been faithful to God in all her relationships. Nevertheless, she had felt guilty and inadequate for not shaking her desire for a close, personal relationship with someone. Some of Kathy's friends told her that she should really only need God. Therefore, she concluded that the presence of the longing meant that she was spiritually deficient. After hearing God's declaration about Adam's aloneness and understanding that God chooses to meet many of our needs through other human beings, Kathy began to rejoice. She no longer confused her feelings of loneliness with her condition of wholeness or maturity in Christ. The truth that God Himself had declared that we are relational beings who have an innate need for intimacy with others had set her free.

Pat's struggle was made "unsolvable" by the assumption that it is wrong or immature to feel lonely or to long for human companionship. Kathy's conclusion that her faith was lacking due to the presence of lonely feelings limited her freedom and peace of mind. In truth, Pat, Kathy, and other Christians who have trusted Jesus for their salvation and life itself, can be complete and mature in Christ, and simultaneously experience aloneness and a longing for human companionship. Some use the bold declaration of the apostle Paul, "And my God will meet all your needs according to his glorious riches in Christ Jesus" (Phil. 4:19), to justify a form of self-reliance. But, it is clear in the preceding verses that Paul knew God often chooses to involve others to meet our material, relational, and emotional needs. He says in verse 14 of the same passage, "Yet it was good of you to share in my troubles." Why would Paul say this if it was better for us to remain independent of others?

Relational Intimacy
God's Antidote for Aloneness

You might be asking why God, who is all-knowing, all-present, and all-powerful, created us with a need for others rather than for Him only? Why didn't He just enable us to be totally self-sufficient? What prompted God to include this interdependency dynamic in the makeup of the human race? Could it be, that when God said in Genesis 1:26, "Let us make man in our image, in our likeness..." it was His desire to let us experience the oneness with Him and with others that He experiences with the Son and the Holy Spirit? Therefore, He made us with the need and the capacity for relationship that goes far beyond a superficial coexistence to a dynamic called intimacy. Could it be that He had tasted the pain of aloneness already, when in His unfathomable eternal presence, He knew a time when He was separated from His Son between the Crucifixion and Resurrection? And, having experienced this, God knew firsthand that it was not good!

We can learn a lot about living abundantly in our relationships by carefully studying and emulating the ways of our Lord. How did Jesus experience intimacy and deal with aloneness while on earth? He lived His earthly life as a single person. Jesus understood that it was not good to be alone. Yet it was not the will of the Father for the Christ to experience marriage other than to His bride, the church. For Jesus, there was no "right person," other than God, but there were right relationships.

Jesus encountered thousands upon thousands of people, was acquainted with many, and lived and traveled with a group of His disciples. But, he had special friendships with a select few, including Peter, James, and John among the disciples. He also experienced relational intimacy within a network of believing friends—His own "singles network" of Mary, Martha, and Lazarus. Jesus entrusted these close associates with the deeper struggles of His life and entered their worlds as they had need.

Though fully divine, He was also fully human and experienced everything that we as humans experience, including aloneness, abandonment, rejection, and even betrayal. There were times when even His closest disciples let Him down, such as the night before the Crucifixion. In those times, Jesus depended upon the love of the Heavenly Father without denying the difficulty of His situation.

Take time now to reflect upon the compelling love of Christ that found Him facing the pain of the cross for you and me. Consider that as physically painful as crucifixion was, the emotional and spiritual pain may have been even greater. He was ridiculed, shamed, and humiliated in the hours leading up to His death. Most significantly, He took our sin upon Himself that we might live. For our sake, He experienced a depth of aloneness we never have to experience as believers. He experienced separation from God. Who could claim to have been more alone than Christ as He hung on the cross, uttering the words, "My God, my God, why have you forsaken me?" (Matt. 27:46) He truly knows the pain of aloneness that we encounter. Can you appreciate the price He paid for you *because He loves you?* What feelings stir up within you as you consider such love? Write them here, along with an expression of your gratitude to Him.

_____

_____

_____

_____

_____

The Meaning of Intimacy

Intimacy in relationship with God and other persons is the antidote for aloneness. But, what is intimacy? In our society, the meaning of the word is often distorted and misapplied. Many assume that intimacy refers only to physical or sexual encounters. Intimacy has a much broader and deeper meaning. It is primarily about knowing and being known for the right reasons and with the right motivations. Furthermore, intimacy is God's idea. It can be experienced in every dimension of our being—spirit, soul, and body. Intimacy includes knowing someone, allowing that person to know you, and seeking to be caringly involved in one another's lives.

But what does intimacy look like? How do we actually experience it in relationships, especially as single adults? Several words in the Old Testament relate to our need for intimacy with God and others. A review of these words will provide valuable insights into this central aspect of human longing and motivation.

1. Intimacy includes knowing another deeply.

YADA — to know deeply. One Hebrew word that relates to intimacy is transliterated, YADA, and comes from a root meaning "to know." It refers to having a **deep personal awareness and understanding** *of another*. This word appears in one of the saddest passages in the Old Testament, Job 19:14, where Job laments, "All my intimate friends detest me!" What makes the story of Job so sad is that he had come to feel so estranged from the very people who should have known him best, friends who were in position to remove some of his aloneness brought on by a variety of tragedies. Surely God knew us first and knows us best. He knew us from our mothers' wombs (Jer. 1:5), and is acquainted with our every thought, emotion, and motivation (Psa. 139:1-4). This kind of deep knowing of the heart and mind goes far beyond the mere sharing of facts, ideas, and opinions so common in many relationships. It is this kind of knowing that helps us understand what "oneness" requires in a marriage.

The New Testament also has a term for this type of deep knowledge of one another, *koinonia*, which translated from the Greek, means *fellowship.* This word speaks of a close partnership among people who share things in common. In I John 1:3, this *koinonia* describes the relationship among the Christians AND with God, "We proclaim to you what we have seen and heard, so that you also may have fellowship with us. And our fellowship is with the Father and with His Son, Jesus Christ."

Thus, intimacy is a desired standard in our human and divine relationships.

Deep personal awareness and understanding go far beyond the superficiality so common in many of our relationships today. The same word for close, personal knowing of another referenced in the book of Job is also used in Genesis 4:1 (KJV) which states, "Adam *knew* his wife Eve, and she conceived and brought forth Cain." Here, the same word for intimacy was used to represent their sexual union, intended by God to be a special expression of intimacy reserved for husbands and wives. In this book we will show you how to experience intimacy in ways that honor God and meet one another's need to not be alone.

2. Intimacy includes letting someone know you.

SOD — to reveal or disclose. Another Hebrew word that refers to the concept of intimacy is transliterated as SOD. It refers to *revelation or disclosure of one to another.* This reference is even more startling than the first. It is used in Proverbs 3:32 (NASB), which states, "God is *intimate* with the upright." The same verse in the NIV says that the Lord, "...*takes* the upright *into His confidence."* This amazing and wonderful statement shows that the Creator of the universe chooses to disclose Himself to us, the created. We find the ultimate revelation of His self-disclosure in the coming of Jesus Christ, as, "The Word became flesh and made his dwelling among us" (John 1:14). Thus, God allows us to experience intimacy with Him. If God did not reveal Himself to us, we would know little about Him, much less, know His heart. Also, in the New Testament passage often referred to as His high priestly prayer, Jesus speaks about the eternal significance of this intimate knowing, when He boldly declares, "And this is eternal life, that they may *know* Thee, the only true God and Jesus Christ whom Thou hast sent" (John 17:3).

In a similar manner, we must practice vulnerable communication in order for intimacy to develop in our relationships. This would include sharing the more personal aspects of ourselves, such as our hopes, aspirations, dreams, fears, regrets, and losses. We would see communication that goes far beyond the sharing of thoughts and opinions that require much less risk taking. In our communication with our Heavenly Father, our prayers need to be open, inviting God into our confidence and trusting Him to treat us caringly and faithfully.

3. Intimacy includes caring involvement.

SAKAN — to be of use to. The third Hebrew word we will refer to, transliterated SAKAN, speaks of *"beneficial or caring involvement."* In many ways, this concept suggests the motivation behind the mutual knowing that should exist in intimate relationships. Why do you think that God wants to know us so intimately, and to let us know Him? Does He use His knowledge to hurt us when we are most sensitive and vulnerable? Absolutely not! Psalm 139:1-3 (NASB) portrays God's intimate knowledge of each person. It says, the Lord is "...*intimately acquainted* with all my ways." He reveals the *motive* for this intimacy a few verses later, where the Psalmist records that the Heavenly Father knows us intimately in order to guide us and make us secure (Psalm 139:10).

God's motive for intimate relationships is active, engaging, caring love. His expression of loving care is part of His very nature. He cares even though He knows all about our actions and thoughts that are far from perfect. In fact, God cares so much that He even gives sacrificially to us while we are in rebellion against Him (Rom. 5:8).

God's knowledgeable, caring involvement in our lives beautifully portrays the liberating motivation that we need for our human relationships. Why should we seek to enter into our friend's world? Why should we prioritize time for our loved ones? Why give sacrificially to others in the church? It should be because we care, and then choose to be *caringly involved in their lives*! It is not because of duty or obligation, and certainly not to manipulate or take for our own benefit. Such selfless, other-centered giving is not natural. Instead, it is supernatural, coming from God in Christ, who said, "freely you have received, freely give" (Matt. 10:8b).

Genuine intimacy is motivated by a desire for caring involvement with each other. Self-serving attitudes, on the other hand, wound others as they become vulnerable. Many adults fear intimate relationships because they were hurt as children by someone who knew them well, but used that knowledge to abuse or take advantage of them. We can allow God to build that desire within us.

Personal Application
Intimate Encounters

Reflect on your childhood for a minute. Think of someone who demonstrated one of the three aspects of intimacy described above—deep knowing of you as an individual, appropriate and honest disclosure of his or her thoughts and feelings, or demonstrating genuine concern for you through some form of active involvement. This person might be a parent, a sibling, or even a teacher who invested in your life. Write the name of the person below and describe some ways he or she demonstrated one or more of these intimacy characteristics.

_____

_____

_____

_____

_____

Describe the feelings that his/her actions evoked within you then (or even now as you ponder it):

_____

_____

_____

_____

_____

Intimacy with God

Isn't it incredible that the Creator of the universe would want you to know Him personally? Isn't it gratifying to realize that He already knows you and wants only what is best for you? Don't you feel honored to be asked to join His family and be included in His mission on earth? Or could it be that these thoughts are still difficult to grasp or embrace? Maybe you can identify with Joyce's journey.

As I grew up, I saw God as a demanding, critical ruler who kept score of all my good and bad deeds. I felt a pressure to perform in order to be acceptable to Him. Though my family took me to church almost every week of my life then, I had a distorted picture of whom God is and how He loved me. At the age of 29, I came to see my sinful nature for what it was—rebellion against the God who truly loved me more than I could imagine. For the first time in my life, I knew that Jesus Christ had died sacrificially for ME, that my sin might be forgiven and my relationship with God restored. I admitted that I needed God's forgiveness for my sins, and committed myself to the Lordship of Christ. Immediately, I sensed within that He loved me right where I was. My walk with God really began then. Now, I am learning how to know the heart of God and to love Him in return.

Intimacy with God begins when we take care of the offenses that have broken our relationship with Him—the sins that we have inevitably committed (Rom. 3:23) against God. He already loves us before we admit that we need Him (Rom. 5:8). But to fellowship with Him, we must resolve the break in our relationship caused by our rejection and rebellion against God. The good news is that the God of the universe has promised to forgive us if we turn to Him through faith in Jesus Christ. We can then relate to God in a personal way, just as we might with a very close friend for whom we hold utmost respect. We cannot earn that relationship through good deeds. It is received through believing that Christ paid the penalty for our sins and that God loves us and adopts us as His own children when we turn back to Him (Isa. 53:6; Eph. 2:8-9; Rom. 8:15-17, 23).

Once a person is restored to fellowship with God, what does it look like to experience intimacy with Him on a daily basis? Let's return to the three Hebrew words that we used to define intimacy.

Deep knowing (YADA) — As we journey with God, we need to know his *ways*, not just His *deeds*. That means discerning the very heart of God—what He feels as well as what He says is truth. The Holy Spirit can lead us to such discernment if we give sufficient opportunity for communication with God. Reflections of coming to deeply know God would include memorizing and meditating on God's word, reflecting on what Jesus must have felt as we read about His ministry on earth, paraphrasing Scripture and journaling how it is relevant today in your life, and asking God in prayer how He might be trying to change or grow you, particularly in relationship to others.

Vulnerable disclosure (SOD) — We know that God has deeply known us from the time we were conceived (Psa. 139:3,13,16). But how vulnerable are you with God? In Psalm 51:6, David writes, *Thou dost desire truth in my innermost being.* Do your prayers express your contrition, your gratefulness, your dependency, or even your anger with God? Is there a humility that acknowledges God is in control but also trusts that He knows what is best for you? Can you admit to Him when you struggle to trust Him that way? Are you willing to ask the Creator to bring to your mind ways that He wants you to change? Are you willing to make yourself accountable to some trusted friends about these change areas? Admitting to God your need of Him and others and your present imperfections is essential for experiencing the joy of intimacy.

Caring involvement (SAKAN) — For most of Jesus' ministry on earth, His disciples were simply *with Him.* They were learning and being blessed by their relationship with Him. Eventually, however, He gave them opportunity to become involved in His work to save a lost world. He gave them a Great Commission (Matt. 28:18-19) that was to be motivated out of a Great Commandment heart (Mark 12:30-31). If we are intimately involved with someone, we will care about what they are about and become involved in some way. We will not remain aloof to His purposes. Such involvement may take many forms, just as there are many motivational gifts of the Spirit. Ultimately, we will be trying to discern what God is doing in our midst and become a part of it.

Relational Intimacy
for Single Adults

When God created us with an innate need for intimacy with others, He also made provision for that need. He gave Adam the companionship of a wife and subsequently provided a family which could experience fellowship together. Later, Christ would establish His church, all those who would come to believe on Him. Though His followers would differ in talents, abilities, and personality, He gave them one Spirit that they might fellowship with the Father and each other (John 17:20-21; Eph. 4:4). Thus, the church offers a larger community for intimate relationships.

Many singles, however, feel cheated or disadvantaged when it comes to experiencing godly intimacy with others. They have not been on the receiving end of much deep knowing, vulnerable disclosure, or caring involvement that was healthy or genuine. The same may be true for many married adults with regard to relational intimacy on an emotional level. But, an invalid perception or stigma adds to the dilemma of single adult aloneness in a couples-oriented world. Our society often regards single adults as "less than," or in a state of "limbo" that denies personal fulfillment.

Being Single—Blessing or Curse

How do you feel about your single status? We invite you to take a few moments to survey your own thoughts, feelings, and attitudes about being single in a culture where over 90 percent of the population eventually marry. Circle your answers.

Agree Disagree   1. I am very satisfied at this time being single rather than being married.
Explain: _____

Agree Disagree   2. I am very comfortable talking to others about the fact that I am single.
Explain: _____

Agree Disagree   3. I have close friends or relatives who know how I feel about being single.
Explain: _____

Agree Disagree   4. I enjoy dating and spending time alone with people of the opposite sex.
Explain: _____

Agree Disagree   5. I want to know and be known deeply by someone of the opposite sex.
Explain: _____

Agree Disagree   6. I have same-gender journey-mates who know me and let me know them.
Explain: _____

Agree Disagree   7. I like the way my singleness is regarded by most married persons.
Explain: _____

Agree Disagree   8. I would like to be married (or married again) eventually.
Explain: _____

Agree Disagree   9. I like the way singleness is regarded by my church and/or other Christians.
Explain: _____

How did you feel as you completed this questionnaire? Would it surprise you to know that many single adults find it difficult, even painful, to discuss their singleness? In one study, a single woman stated, "Since it hurts to talk about singleness, I choose to appear strong, in control." Another remarked, "You wouldn't understand and I don't want to appear desperate." In addition, many singles report ambivalent feelings about being unmarried. They enjoy the freedom and autonomy but often experience a sense of loss if there is no one readily available with whom to share interests, concerns, joys and sorrows. It is also common for singles to feel hurt and frustration because they are sometimes regarded as failures, particularly if they have experienced divorce. Thus, many singles carry painful emotions about singleness that they are facing alone.

It shouldn't surprise us that there is often pressure from within and from others for singles to "fix" their aloneness problem by finding a marriage partner. That, in our opinion, would be the wrong motive for anyone to marry. Instead, we would encourage singles, whether widowed, divorced, or never married, to develop a *lifestyle* of relational intimacy with God and trustworthy friends as a prerequisite to serious male-female engagements.

God has not forgotten single adults when it comes to their aloneness. For them, the resources available from God for meeting relational needs include families, church communities, and close personal friends. Sadly, our candidates for relational intimacy often fail us (and we them) in the meeting of these needs. This leaves us disillusioned and hurt. Often, in our frustration and fear, we settle for counterfeit forms of intimacy that never truly satisfy our longing for genuine relationship with others. Counterfeits of genuine intimacy are readily available. They often emphasize physical intimacy to the exclusion of relational and spiritual intimacy. In fact, the need for spiritual intimacy may be minimized or ignored altogether. In God's design, however, the priority is just the opposite. The condition of the spirit, one's relationship and walk with God, is the most defining part of a person, and the primary criteria for adult attachments (II Cor. 6:14).

Every manifestation of intimacy, whether of the spirit, soul, or body, should honor God and respect His commandments and principles. Soul intimacy, relating meaningfully on an emotional, psychological, and intellectual level, is something we should develop carefully with conscious effort. Physical intimacy, in the form of appropriate affectionate touch, is also important, though sexual intimacy is specifically reserved for the husband-wife relationship alone. In subsequent chapters, we will describe what each of these dimensions of intimacy looks like for single adults whose desire is to experience God's abundance in relationships.

Remember Pat and Kathy? They, like most of us, had come to regard their loneliness and desire for genuine intimacy with others to have been a sign of spiritual immaturity. They had been led to believe that if they were just spiritually strong enough, they would *only* need a relationship with God. They had acquired a limited and distorted understanding of the nature of relational neediness. They had not been taught how to experience real intimacy in relationships in ways that honor God. God would not want us to live lives based upon lies and distortions. In this chapter, we have focused on the truth, recorded in the Scripture, that God created us with a need for relationship with Him *and* with others. We have made it clear that this neediness was not related to mankind's fallenness, but was instead part of God's intentional design for humankind to be relational even as He is. In the chapters that follow, we will discover more about our relational needs and identify practical ways to experience intimacy in relationships.

Encountering God in His Word

"A God Who Lets Us Know Him"

Genesis 18:1-33 (focal passage: Genesis 18:16-19)

Read this passage and note how the Lord takes Abraham into His confidence, saying, "Shall I hide from Abraham what I am about to do?" (Gen. 18:17) Can you imagine this? The Creator of the universe is ready to administer judgment on the wickedness of Sodom and Gomorrah, and stops to advise a mere mortal of His plans. Put yourself in Abraham's shoes. Can you think of a time when someone in a powerful or prestigious position let you in on her plans or even sought your counsel? But, this is the character of God, according to Proverbs 3:32 which says, "...He is intimate with the upright." (NASB), or "...the Lord...takes the upright into his confidence."

◆ Why do you think God chose to include Abraham in His plans and deliberations?

_____

_____

_____

_____

_____

◆ What would you feel inside if God chose to bring you into His "board room?"

_____

_____

_____

_____

_____

◆ Rewrite or paraphrase Proverbs 3:32 in your own words:

_____

_____

_____

_____

_____

◆   As you apply Proverbs 3:32 to yourself personally (that God would really share His thoughts and heart with you as you walk with Him), what do you sense inside?

_____
_____
_____
_____
_____
_____

◆ Write your response here to God's offer to relate to you on such an intimate level:

_____
_____
_____
_____
_____
_____
_____
_____

God already knows you intimately— your every thought, word, and deed, and wants you to know Him in the same way. Encourage one another daily to walk with Him that you might know Him.

Group Dialogue

If you do not have a designated group leader, choose some-one in the group who will serve to facilitate the discussion. Begin by briefly reviewing the discussion guidelines.

Discussion Guidelines

◆ Allow everyone an opportu-nity to share thoughts and feelings
◆ Avoid long story telling
◆ Be quick to listen with empathy

◆ Be slow to give advice
◆ Speak the truth in love
◆ Say what you mean and mean what you say
◆ Protect the confidentiality of every person

Discussion Suggestions for Chapter One

1. Unless you have met previously, introduce yourselves and tell about the place you grew up.

2. Share something you like or dislike about the work or activity you do most.

3. Discuss what you think about the guidelines for these dis-cussions.

4. State what you hope to gain by completing *Discovering Intimacy.*

5. Tell about your own experience with loneliness and how people close to you have typically responded to your loneli-ness.

6. Describe a person in your life who truly joined you at a point of loneliness or sadness and was an encouragement to you. Tell what we would have observed this person DOING that was most helpful to you at that time in your life. Which of the three dimensions of intimacy (deep knowing, vulnerable disclosure, caring involvement) was being displayed?

7. Close your time together by asking a volunteer to pray for the development of intimacy with God and others throughout the duration of the course.

Journey-mate Encounters

The Journey-mate Encounter exercises at the end of each chapter give you an additional opportunity to experience biblical principles about relational intimacy at a deeper level. These exercises encourage personal and relational growth. Since growth means change, there is some degree of tension or anxiety present. Sharing this process of change with a trusted friend or partner removes your aloneness and encourages perseverance. As you begin your meetings, you may want to review together the Guidelines for Discussions on page *x*. Here are a few reminders for your Journey-mate Encounters.

◆ Set aside one to two hours for the meeting to give ample time for each person to share.
◆ Select a meeting location that minimizes distractions or interruptions.
◆ Read the chapter and complete all the written exercises *before* meeting to discuss them.
◆ Purpose to start on time and complete each exercise, staying focused on the material.

Suggestions for Journey-mate Encounter #1

1. Begin by talking about what each of you hopes to gain by completing the *Discovering Intimacy* material and experiencing the principles in your journey-mate relationships.

2. Next, list any fears or concerns that you may sense concerning your journey-mate discussions. Share your lists with each other.

_____

_____

_____

3. To learn more about each other, take turns sharing a positive memory that you recall from your adolescence that your journey-mates do not already know.

4. Now, tell about your own experiences with loneliness and how people close to you typically respond to your loneliness. (For example, teased, ridiculed, comforted, offered advice, etc.)

5. Take turns sharing from page 14 about people who modeled godly intimacy during your youth.

6. Complete the *Intimacy Inventory for Single Adults* (Appendix A) and discuss your results with each other. Focus on deepening your *understanding* of yourselves and one another.

7. Close with prayer for each other, particularly for God to increase your intimacy with Him as you go through this process.

Hiding the Word in Your Heart
Genesis 2:18a

Write the verse here: _____
_____
_____
_____
_____
_____
_____
_____
_____
_____

Repeat the verse from memory each day for several weeks. Using the space below, you may want to journal ways that God has allowed you to experience the verse as you have hidden it away in your heart. _____
_____
_____
_____
_____
_____
_____
_____
_____
_____
_____
_____
_____
_____
_____
_____

Check the box at the right when you have committed the verse to memory. Continue to repeat the verse daily for at least three weeks. ☐

Chapter Two

— ◆ —

MEETING INTIMACY NEEDS
The Powerful Process for Removing Aloneness

"...according to the need of the moment..."
Ephesians 4:29 (NASB)

Meet Elise. She's a thirty-something bundle of energy setting records as a consultant in the telecommunications industry. Elise could probably retire now by managing her investment portfolio carefully. She put herself through law school to get the edge she needed to compete successfully. Elise is known for delivering hard-hitting proposals that make sense to the executives who develop long-term strategies for their corporations. Her independence and positive attitude are a far cry from the memory of an impish, subservient mother who had been unable to stand up to her hateful, demeaning, and abusive step-father. Though Elise had rarely been the target of his angry outbursts, she had often been sickened by what she saw him do to her less determined siblings. She swore then that she would never leave herself vulnerable to any form of dependency on others, especially men. As a child, she had hated the fact that she needed her parents to survive and looked forward to the day when she would outgrow her neediness. Today, however, as she reflected in her study, Elise sensed a vague longing to connect with someone who would know her as well or better than she knew herself.

Is Elise just having a weak moment? Is she just in need of a friend with whom she can enjoy the latest opera or skiing vacation? Does she just need a change of pace to reduce her stress? No. Elise has just been confronted with an aspect of her being that is as natural and ingrained as the color of her eyes. She was born for relationships that go far beyond having a regular tennis partner or an occasional romantic fling. Elise is a person created in God's image with a need for relational intimacy. She needs to experience godly relationships that are motivated by caring involvement, developed through vulnerable disclosure, and characterized by deeply knowing and being known by one another. But understandably, she had assumed that needing others emotionally was dangerous and undesirable. She regarded such neediness like facial blemishes, something one outgrew when adolescence departed. Many of her assumptions, like many of ours, were wrong.

In this chapter, we will see that relational intimacy is experienced through the meeting of relational needs, which we also refer to as *intimacy needs.* We will look together at our need for relational intimacy in the context of our total being—spirit, soul, and body. We will consider the purpose for our neediness in God's design for image-bearers. You will have an opportunity to better define your own intimacy needs. We will also identify the most common obstacles that can limit your ability to give or receive intimacy. That's a lot of ground to cover, so let's get started!

Dimensions Of Neediness

God, in His infinite wisdom, chose to create us as three-dimensional beings. He gave us a physical body for navigating this earthly environ, a soul comprised of mind, will, and emotions, and a spirit that was breathed into Adam by God Himself. His design of our human being included neediness in all of these dimensions. None of us can survive, much less live abundantly, apart from His provisions for the body, soul, and spirit. Yet, out of His love for us, God designed provisions for each of our needs.

No one would argue that we have **physical** needs, such as air, water, food, or sleep. God provided us a world with provision for such needs. We take these for granted until they show up lacking, as in an extended drought. However, just as our physical bodies have needs, so do our spirits and souls. Yet, many of us minimize the importance of these needs or completely deny that they exist.

Spiritually, we need to be connected with the Creator of the universe, to God Himself. Our **spiritual** neediness is revealed when we realize that God truly exists and that we are separated from Him by our sin and rejection of Him. We have failed to *be* whom He created us to be—His children who faithfully know Him, love Him, and out of that love, live as He teaches us to live. Just as with physical needs, God has not left us without provision spiritually. He has made a way for us to be acceptable to Him again. God's forgiveness of our sin, necessary to restore our relationships with Him, is readily available to all who turn from their own ways and receive the gift of eternal life through faith in Jesus Christ, the Son of God (Isa. 53:6; John 1:12). Therefore, our spiritual need for oneness, communion, and peace with God, cannot be met or secured alone. It *requires* a relationship with God.

The needs of the soul cannot be met in a vacuum either. They are **relational** needs, met or not met in the context of a relationship. These needs include acceptance, approval, encouragement, support, affection, security, attention, comfort, respect, and appreciation. They will often be referred to as *intimacy needs* in this book. But, how do we determine what our intimacy needs are and whether or not they are being met? A physical need for water is recognized by a sensation of thirst. It is satisfied or quenched by drinking liquid. Similarly, unmet intimacy needs may be revealed by the presence of unpleasant feelings and subsequently satisfied by meaningful person-to-person interactions.

Understanding Our Neediness

Aloneness is removed through person-to-person interactions that address unmet intimacy needs effectively. You may be asking if some of your intimacy needs can be met on your own. For example, isn't it good to give yourself encouragement? We would agree that it doesn't hurt to think positively and to eliminate condemning self-talk. But, have you noticed that encouraging words take on added meaning when they come from someone you esteem? That added value cannot be duplicated or created on your own. Therefore, any time a relational need is met, some of our aloneness is removed. We cannot remove aloneness without a relationship and we cannot meet our relational needs alone. We cannot manufacture by ourselves the intangible value that is realized when another person imparts his or her life to us by unselfishly giving to meet a need that we have. This is especially true when the other Person is God and when we have not deserved the investment He makes in us (Rom. 5:8).

One of the nicest gifts I (Bruce) received in recent years was a visit by a fellow minister who came to my father's funeral. In addition to my need for comfort in a time of loss, this man met a great need that I had for attention, for he went well out of his way to enter my world and say that I mattered to him. You see, my colleague didn't just drive across town. He and his wife had to travel over ten hours in bad weather to be with me. He had given up his Saturday in order to be present with me at an important time in my life. I felt loved and cared for and grateful to God and my friend for this unconditional gift. This need could not have been met without him knowing my need and making an effort to meet it.

This example of an intimacy need being met in a relationship glorifies God, for He loved first. Now, let's take a further look at some characteristics of intimacy needs.

1. Intimacy needs are cross cultural and independent of history.

Asians, Africans, Latins, Anglos, and Indians are all relational beings and thus require community and fellowship with others, just as they all need food and forgiveness. Intimacy needs are not a function of a particular era of time, either.

Adam, Abraham, Pilate, Attila the Hun, Mozart, Lincoln, Ghandi, and Kruschev all had something in common. They had needs that could not be met without the help of others and God. Thus, intimacy needs are not strictly twentieth-century phenomena. Every person who has ever lived or will ever live needs it.

2. Intimacy needs continue throughout life.

Like your physical need for air and sleep, you never outgrow your intimacy needs. These needs may modify to some degree, but they do not disappear when we enter adulthood. The need to be meaningfully related to others is endless, beginning at birth and continuing through old age. Let's look at some examples of intimacy needs occurring in different stages of life.

◆ Imagine a newborn baby coming home from the hospital. He exhibits a need for **attention** if left alone for too long a period of time, even when fed.
◆ When a toddler falls, he looks around to see if someone has noticed, and may cry if no one responds, demonstrating a need for **comfort**.
◆ When a parent is ill and confined to bed, it is not uncommon for a pre-schooler to want to rest on the parent's arm, revealing a need for **affection**.
◆ A grade school child may cringe at the thought of reciting a poem before her class, suggesting a need for **encouragement** to overcome this anxiety.
◆ Watch a teenage athlete seek **approval** by glancing to the grandstands to see if Dad was watching when she hit that off-balance, buzzer-beating game-winner.

But notice also how adults also demonstrate intimacy needs.

◆ Witness the sadness of the efficient secretary who hears no words of **appreciation** for her consistent contributions to the success of the company.
◆ Observe the frustration of the single parent who struggles to secure the **support** of his ex-wife to honor his desire for

the children to not be exposed to R-rated television when they visit her house.

◆ Notice the dejection in the eyes of a fifty-year-old man whose company has let him go rather than value or **respect** the contributions he has made and continues to make.

◆ Hear the pain of the elderly woman in the nursing home who longs for the **attention** of her children who seem too busy to visit.

3. Intimacy needs must be met on a continuing basis.

Since intimacy needs continue throughout life, it would be nice if we could "store up" some of the supply for these needs. For, though we can *survive* periods of time when they are not met, we suffer, whether we have recognized our dilemma or not. Our needs for attention, support, appreciation, respect, and others must be replenished repeatedly, much like our physical needs of water, sleep, and air.

The Need for Neediness

Why would God insist on creating us so needy? Couldn't we save Him some maintenance work if He didn't have to invest so much time nurturing and supplying us? Aren't we supposed to grow up spiritually so that we need Him (and others) less? Didn't He say in Philippians 4:19 that He would supply *all* our needs? If so, why do we need other people?

As you ponder those questions, think about what it would be like if you DIDN'T need any help, involvement, or interaction with God or anyone else. Could it be that we are created as needy people so that we will be drawn to Him and to others. The condition of neediness requires that we look beyond ourselves for that which we need, learning to love and trust in the process. It means that we learn the very essence of relationship, even as the Father experiences it with the Son (John 17:21). If we could meet all of our own needs, we might miss the blessing of relational oneness.

To acknowledge that we have needs is not an admission of weakness, it is a confession of our humanity (Matt. 5:3). We need God and we need one another. That is the way God made us. So, when we reveal our need for relationship with others, we are agreeing with God, accepting that His design and purpose for our lives includes a need for community. Unfortunately, the Christian community often suggests in subtle but erroneous ways that the more mature we become in Christ, the fewer needs we will have that require other people. The truth is, these God-given relational needs prompt us to look to God, humbly allowing Him to minister to our need through others, while freely and unselfishly meeting the needs of others (II Cor. 1:3-4; Matt. 10:8).

If we didn't have needs, we would be like robots on an assembly line, unaware of anyone else around us. God could have chosen to meet all our needs directly Himself. However, His ways, which are above our ways, include using people to meet the needs of other people. Similarly, He chooses to use people to communicate the Good News of Jesus Christ to others. His word frequently tells us to invest in people in positive ways, building up one another. Therefore, God's design for humanity calls for each of us to develop a fellowship of "back-scratchers" who aren't caught up in keeping track of the score. When the back scratching is mutual, both persons feel loved, cared for, and significant. Then, the relationship experiences a wonderful dimension we call intimacy!

The Priority of Needs

Although every intimacy need we have listed is common to everyone, the *priority* of those needs differs from one person to another. Your greatest need may be for affection, while your best friend's greatest need may be for security. One child may have an acute need for comfort, another child, encouragement. Respect may be at the top of the list for your neighbor, whereas your boss may need approval most.

If we are not careful, we will treat everyone the same as if they all had the same priority of needs. Furthermore, we may unconsciously try to meet the needs of others based upon our *own* priority of needs. In other words, we will see their neediness through the filter of our own, giving us a distorted picture. For example, if you have a great need for affection, you may gallantly and sincerely inundate a discouraged friend or dating partner with affection without realizing that it may be at the bottom of her priority list. You might then feel indignant if your friend does not seem grateful for your affection. Your behavior was well-intended, but was not according to the need of the moment. It missed the mark.

An important aspect of learning to love people well is taking time to know them and to discover what their priority needs are. With adults, it is not uncommon to discover that their most important needs are those which were either *not met* in childhood or those which were *met generously*, reinforcing their value. For example, if I had no security growing up, I'll probably need a lot of it as an adult. On the other hand, if I experienced security regularly in my childhood, I will continue to value that need having become accustomed to feeling secure.

What are your priority needs? Let's take time to identify them and give you an opportunity to join with others to begin conscientiously meeting one another's needs in ways that glorify God.

Identifying Your Intimacy Needs

Which needs are you aware of at this time in your life? On the following page, you will find a list of the most commonly identified intimacy needs. There are many more reflected in Scripture, but these ten will let you begin to examine the areas of greatest need in your own relationships, whether in the work place, at church, within your family or among friends.

Take a few minutes to review the list of *Ten Key Intimacy Needs*. Read the definitions carefully. Then select the three areas of greatest need for you at this point in your life. Write those three needs here and think of ways that other people could respond effectively to those needs.

Priority Needs   **What Others Can Do To Meet These Needs**

1. _____   _____
                         _____
                         _____

2. _____   _____
                         _____
                         _____
                         _____

3. _____   _____
                         _____
                         _____
                         _____

You may wish to share your priority intimacy needs with a journey-mate or group members who are also completing this workbook. Remember that an essential ingredient of relational intimacy is to know one another deeply. Identifying our intimacy needs and vulnerably disclosing them to persons we trust is a significant step in developing healthy relational intimacy. A more detailed assessment of your needs can be made using the *Intimacy Needs Assessment Tool* in the appendix.

Ten Key Intimacy Needs

Instructions: Select three needs which you sense are most important to you at this time in your life. Then select three needs that you believe to be most important to one or two of your friends or relatives at this time in their lives. Later, discuss with these individuals why each of you chose the needs that you did. Then, discuss specific ways that each of you could meet the others' needs.

Myself	Intimacy Needs	Friend #1	Friend #2
☐	**Acceptance** - receiving another person willingly and unconditionally, especially when the other's behavior has been imperfect; being willing to continue loving another in spite of offenses (Rom. 15:7)	☐	☐
☐	**Affection** - expressing care and closeness through non-sexual physical touch, carefully respecting the boundaries of the other person; saying, "I love you" (Rom. 16:16; Mark 10:16)	☐	☐
☐	**Appreciation** - expressing thanks, praise, or commendation; recognizing accomplishment or effort (Col. 3:15b; I Cor. 11:2)	☐	☐
☐	**Approval (Blessing)** - building up or affirming another; affirming both the fact of and the importance of a relationship (Eph. 4:29; Mark 1:11)	☐	☐
☐	**Attention** - conveying appropriate interest, concern, and care; taking thought of another; entering another's "world" (I Cor. 12:25)	☐	☐
☐	**Comfort** - responding to a hurting person with words, feelings, and touch; to hurt with and for another's grief or pain (Rom. 12:15b; Matt. 5:4; II Cor. 1:3-4; John 11:35)	☐	☐
☐	**Encouragement** - urging another to persist and persevere toward a goal; stimulating toward love and good deeds (I Thess. 5:11, Heb. 10:24)	☐	☐
☐	**Respect** - valuing and regarding another highly; treating another as important; honoring another (Rom. 12:10)	☐	☐
☐	**Security (Peace)** - harmony in relationships; freedom from fear or threat of harm (Rom. 12:16,18)	☐	☐
☐	**Support** - coming alongside and gently helping with a problem or struggle; providing appropriate assistance (Gal. 6:2)	☐	☐

Obstructing Intimacy

Jesus said that we are to love one another, and that such love will be a witness to all people that we are His disciples (John 13:34-35). But, what would that love look like? Would it be limited to meeting one another's physical needs? Or could this love include the way that we relate to one another on an emotional level? Perhaps we will see an increasing number of churches where the relationships within the fellowship are typified by deep knowing, transparency, and caring involvement in one another's lives.

Sounds good, doesn't it? Or does this message trigger some uneasiness within you? Could it be that you, like many of us, hear an inner message that says, "That's all well and good for you, but I can do quite well by myself, thank you." Or, have you been hurt by revealing needs and feel anxious as you contemplate being emotionally vulnerable with other people? Have you sensed a tendency to charge through relationships, taking what you need and wondering why others were upset by your actions and attitudes? In this section, we will take a closer look at three common obstacles, reinforced daily in our culture, that limit our ability to experience godly intimacy in our relationships with others AND with God.

What blocks us from expressing more of the love we have from God? What hinders and limits our relationships, keeping them superficial and disengaged? What tendencies do you see in yourself that have caused relationships to be stifled or disrupted? Three of the most damaging obstacles to intimacy are self-reliance, self-condemnation, and selfishness.

1. Selfishness

A person hindered by selfishness is exalting his needs, demanding that they be met or selfishly taking what he needs. Underlying this attitude is a belief that, "I will not be okay unless my needs are met and I must take matters into my own hands." We might see this tendency revealed by a person who talks constantly and at great length about herself without asking about others. This behavior suggests an unmet need for attention. Rather than trust the others to inquire of her, she "demands" their attention by dominating the conversation. In a more subtle way, selfishness may be at work in someone who works excessively, compulsively seeking approval through a variety of achievements. The tragedy of selfish taking is that we end up securing only a counterfeit of that which we really want—unconditional love demonstrated through the meeting of relational needs.

In Philippians 2:3-4, we are exhorted to, "Do nothing out of selfish ambition or vain conceit, but in humility consider others better than yourselves. Each of you should look not only to your own interests, but also to the interests of others." Failure to recognize and put away this tendency can cause us to miss out on the true joy of giving to meet others' needs (Acts 20:35). It can cause us to forfeit God's blessing related to giving (Luke 6:38) or fail to grasp God's principle of contagious giving (Matt. 10:8). In addition, we may experience rejection as others are repelled by our self-centered behavior (Jas. 3:14).

2. Self-reliance

Self-reliance is another obstacle to genuine intimacy in relationships. Self-reliance reflects a denial of our neediness and stems from a core belief that, "I don't have any needs that cannot be met on my own." Though some who might say this would claim to "only need God," they would be opposing the truth that God created them to need other people as well. The danger of denying our need for others is that prideful self-reliance can develop hardness of heart and cause us to blindly forfeit the "glorious riches" that God had intended to bestow on us through others (Phil. 4:19). Consider the attitudes of the church at Laodicea. Before inviting the people there to renew an intimate relationship with Him, God inspired the apostle John to pen some pretty harsh words to those whose self-sufficiency had cost them their "first love."

You say, 'I am rich; I have acquired wealth and do not need a thing.' But you do not realize that you are wretched, pitiful, poor, blind and naked. (Rev. 3:17)

Not only does self-reliance blind us from the truth of our neediness, it also inhibits our ability and willingness to meet the needs of others. We will either minimize the needs of others (since we refuse to validate them in ourselves) or "minister" to them out of our own strength. For example, when people are hurting or troubled, we need to comfort them with the same comfort we ourselves have received from God (II Cor. 1:4). But if we deny our own need for God's comfort and therefore have not received it, how can we pass it along to others? What we "give" may be a counterfeit. However, when we begin to understand and face our own neediness, we become more understanding, sympathetic, patient, caring, and respectful. Self-reliance, often borne from painful neglect or wounding in the past, serves only to increase aloneness. It may help you "survive," but limits the abundance and richness in life that God supplies through intimacy with Himself and others.

3. Self-condemnation

The third obstacle to intimacy is self-condemnation. This tendency reflects a condemnation of our neediness and reveals an underlying belief that, "There must be something wrong with me because I am needy. I'm either inadequate or I'm being selfish." Here, the presence of neediness is admitted, but condemned. It might appear in a person apologizing because she cried in your presence. You may also see self-condemnation at work if a friend apologizes for "making an issue" of the disappointment felt when you failed to call or drop by for several weeks.

The truth is, relational needs are normal and a part of God's design, so to have them is not sin or shortcoming (though our manner of responding to our needs could be). While on earth, Jesus taught that such neediness is a source of blessing (Matt 5:3) and even revealed that He had such needs. For example, when He was in the Garden of Gethsemene the night before His crucifixion, Jesus wanted the support of Peter, James, and John (Matt. 26). Jesus was not only a sinless Savior, but a person who expressed a need to relate intimately with His Father and with others. Clearly, He does not look upon our neediness disapprovingly, for, "...there is no condemnation for those who are in Christ Jesus" (Rom. 8:1).

Most of us are unaware that these three obstacles to intimacy in relationships are at work within us. Just like the people in the church at Laodicea, we may be blind to our own tendencies. Few of us awoke one day and decided to begin being self-condemning or selfish or self-reliant. We gradually developed these tendencies without conscious awareness. Self-reliance, for example, may develop as a result of years of neglect or wounding by others in positions of trust. A pattern of self-condemnation may have been modeled before you at a young age, or even visited upon you through the condemnation of others. Selfishness often develops following a history of neglect or excessive indulgence in childhood. Once we recognize these tendencies, we can begin to discard them in favor of God's ways of relating (Eph. 4:22-24).

Personal Application
Identifying Your Obstacles to Intimacy

Consider how your relationships have been affected by self-reliance, self-condemnation, and selfishness. Though each of us has probably demonstrated all three at one time or another, we will probably demonstrate one more than the others. Identify the one that you seem to employ the most and describe how it shows up in your behavior.

The obstacle I see most in my own behavior: _____
_____
_____

Behavior you would see when this tendency is active: _____
_____
_____
_____

How has this obstacle affected your significant relationships?
_____
_____
_____

How has this obstacle blocked your intimacy with God? _____
_____
_____

Removing Aloneness
by Meeting Intimacy Needs

When relational needs are acknowledged and met unselfish-ly, aloneness is removed and intimacy left in its place. This is a far cry from the surface level relationships common in our society, and those that are typified by selfish taking, demean-ing condescension, or disengagement. God intended for our lives to be meaningfully connected with Him and others. Instead of relationships that are distant, indifferent, formal, removed, limited, or destructive, He guides us to experience those that are close, personal, deep, caringly affectionate, sup-portive, and respectful.

How are these meaningful relationships established and nurtured? They develop and grow when two or more people draw upon God's unlimited resources and meet one another's needs. But note that the provisions that meet the needs of the soul are not commodities that can be stocked up in a storm shelter. They are living dynamics that must be experienced and imparted over and over again. Jesus Christ is the fabric that holds it all together, and the source that keeps it alive.

Were humans truly on their own, life would be meaningless and empty. Any satisfaction would be temporary at best. But just as God developed a blueprint that included neediness, He supplied the provision for meeting the needs. Man's dilemma of aloneness is matched by God's provision of relationship with Himself and relationship with others, particularly our families, fellow believers that make up Christ's church, and for most of us eventually, spouses. The unconditional perfect love of God, whether received directly from Him or communicated by others, removes our aloneness and lets us experience the abundant life promised in Christ Jesus.

The Zaccheus Principle
Seeing the Need Beneath the Deed

The Zaccheus Principle comes from the Gospel accounts about a tax collector who had been stealing from the people (Luke 19:1-10).

> Jesus entered Jericho and was passing through. A man was there by the name of Zaccheus; he was a chief tax collector and was wealthy. He wanted to see who Jesus was, but being a short man he could not, because of the crowd. So he ran ahead and climbed a sycamore-fig tree to see him, since Jesus was coming that way. When Jesus reached the spot, he looked up and said to him, "Zaccheus, come down immediately. I must stay at your house today." So he came down at once and welcomed him gladly. All the people saw this and began to mutter, "He has gone to be the guest of a 'sinner.'" But Zaccheus stood up and said to the Lord, "Look, Lord! Here and now I give half my possessions to the poor, and if I have cheated anybody out of anything, I will pay back four times the amount." Jesus said to him, "Today salvation has come to this house, because this man, too, is a

son of Abraham. For the Son of Man came to seek and to save what was lost."

The Pharisees and Jews looked upon tax collectors hatefully because they used their power to take advantage of the poor. However, Jesus reached out to Zacchaeus without condemnation, even going to his house for dinner. The Messiah looked beneath the "deeds" and saw the "needs" Zacchaeus had for forgiveness, acceptance and salvation. Jesus' initiative to give resulted in Zacchaeus taking responsibility for his own shortcomings and giving beyond what the law required!

As we seek to increase giving in our relationships, we may find it difficult to look beyond the *behavior* of our friends to see their *needs* that we can begin serving. The temptation will be to focus on sin or fallenness, rather than need or aloneness. Jesus calls us to take responsibility to work on our own shortcomings (Matt: 7:1-6) and to give attention to the needs of others, not only our own (Phil. 2:3-4).

Personal Application

Applying the Zacchaeus Principle

Think about the negative behavior you sometimes observe in your friend or journey-mate. Isn't it possible that underneath the negative behavior, there might be significant unmet needs? Make a list below of some of this behavior and the possible underlying needs associated with it. (For example, *a behavior of an uncontrolled temper might be prompted (not justified) by a need for security, to feel adequate in all of his circumstances.*)

Behaviors I See in My Friend: **Possible Unmet Needs:**

_____   _____

_____   _____

_____   _____

_____   _____

Behaviors I See in My Friend:	Possible Unmet Needs:
_____	_____
_____	_____
_____	_____
_____	_____
_____	_____
_____	_____

Now, reflect on what you've written about your friend's behavior and the needs that might have prompted them. Can you identify some ways you can give to your friend to help meet these needs? Write your thoughts in the space provided below.

(For example, *When my friend gets angry and upset over cir-cumstances, I can assure him of my loyalty and concern for his well-being.)* _____

_____

_____

_____

_____

Now that you have identified some possible ways you can give to your friend, verbalize your commitment to God in a prayer of faith such as this one: *"Dear Lord, make me sensitive to my friend's needs and help me be a part of Your plan to meet these needs. I especially want to be available to meet his/her need for* _____
Keep reminding me of how you give to me unconditionally and prompt me to give in the same way to my friend. Amen."

Encountering God in His Word
"A Savior in Need"
Matthew 26:36-46 (focal passage: Matthew 26:39-40)

Read the passage in Matthew about Jesus' ordeal the night before He was to be crucified. Try to see the depth of the pain and anguish that Christ is in at this time. Notice how He vulnerably approaches His closest disciples for support. Then, see how He must face the disappointment of their response—falling asleep again. If you have ever had difficulty admitting that you needed others, see if God will use this passage of Scripture to help you to receive from others according to your need. If the Savior had need of others on earth, maybe it would be okay if you and I do.

◆ Describe the situation that Christ was facing in the coming hours. What would He be anguishing about? _____
_____
_____

◆ As you read the passage, list some of the feelings that Jesus must have had on this night.
_____
_____

◆ Review the list of *Ten Key Intimacy Needs* on page 38. Write down some of the things that Jesus must have been needing from his disciples on this difficult night. _____
_____
_____

◆ Describe a time when you needed others to stand beside you but were left alone instead, as Jesus was in the Garden of Gethsemene. _____
_____
_____
_____

◆ Think about what it means to you to know that your Lord understands that type of abandonment. Express your thoughts and feelings to Him here.

_____

_____

_____

_____

Your Heavenly Father has promised that He will never leave you nor forsake you (Hebrews 13:5), even though your friends and family might. Purpose to be emotionally present for other believers.

Group Dialogue

If you do not have a designated group leader, choose someone in the group who will serve to facilitate the discussion. Begin by briefly reviewing the discussion guidelines.

Discussion Guidelines

◆ Allow everyone an opportunity to share thoughts and feelings
◆ Avoid long story telling
◆ Be quick to listen with empathy

◆ Be slow to give advice
◆ Speak the truth in love
◆ Say what you mean and mean what you say
◆ Protect the confidentiality of every person

Discussion Suggestions for Chapter Two

1. Share how each of you feel about having needs that can only be met by others.

2. Identify the top three priority needs each of you selected from the *Ten Key Intimacy Needs* worksheet on page 38.

3. Share why you think the needs you identified are most important to you at this time in your life. Reflect upon how these needs were met/not met during your childhood. (For example, *After Kim's mother died when she was nine, she missed having someone at home with whom she could talk. Her need for attention—for others to enter her world—is still very important to her today.*)

4. Identify ways that the group members can meet one of your priority needs during the remainder of this course.

5. Share which of the three obstacles to intimacy (self-reliance, self-condemnation, or selfishness) you exhibit most, and what it looks like when you do.

6. Ask a volunteer to close the group time with prayer.

Journey-mate Encounters

◆ Set aside one to two hours for the meeting to give ample time for each person to share.

◆ Select a meeting location that minimizes distractions or interruptions.

◆ Read the chapter and complete all the written exercises *before* meeting to discuss them.

◆ Purpose to start on time and complete each exercise, staying focused on the material.

Suggestions for Journey-mate Encounter #2

1. Complete the *Intimacy Needs Assessment Tool* in the appendix at the back of this book. Share with your journey-mates the three needs with the highest scores.

2. Compare the results from the *Intimacy Needs Assessment Tool* with your own perception of your priority needs recorded on page 37. If they are different, discuss why. Invite your journey-mates to give you their impressions.

3. Discuss reasons each of your priority needs is of such importance to you now. Reflect upon how each need was met or not met during your childhood. (For example, *Hunter hates conflict and acts quickly to make peace with his friends, at times taking the blame when he is innocent just to restore harmony. His need for security in relationships today may have a lot to do with the years of arguing and yelling between his parents prior to their divorce.*)

4. Next, share the ways you identified on page 37 that others might meet these needs today. The goal of this discussion is to increase your understanding of how to best meet the priority needs of your journey-mates.

5. In the coming weeks, make a serious attempt to meet a different need of your journey-mate(s) each week, and try to meet that need in a way that he or she said would be preferred.

6. End your time together by praying about the specific needs identified by each person, and asking God to empower you to meet their needs using His resources.

Hiding the Word in Your Heart
Ephesians 4:29

Write the verse here:_____
_____
_____
_____
_____
_____
_____
_____
_____
_____

Repeat the verse from memory each day for several weeks.
Using the space below, you may want to journal ways that God
has allowed you to experience the verse as you have hidden it
away in your heart. _____
_____
_____
_____
_____
_____
_____
_____
_____
_____
_____
_____
_____
_____
_____
_____

Check the box at the right when you have committed the
verse to memory. Continue to repeat the verse daily for at
least three weeks.

Chapter Three

——— ◆ ———

EMOTIONAL RESPONDING
Communicating Heart to Heart

"Rejoice with those who rejoice.
Mourn with those who mourn." Romans 12:15

Lynette was one of those "fortunate" children blessed with natural beauty and charm. Even as a little girl, she would command a lot of attention without meaning to do so. When she was seven, her parents died in a car accident and Lynette went to live with her aunt. Aunt Missy provided well for her and took Lynette to church every Sunday. She was a compliant child and therefore, required little discipline. However, if she ever began to cry, especially about her deceased parents, Lynette was told to "hush up" and to remember that, "Your folks are in heaven, now, so you should be happy." When people at church showed Lynette attention and she would start to laugh and giggle, Aunt Missy would scold her for being a "flirt." Lynette became very anxious and tentative around others, not knowing what she should be feeling.

No wonder Lynette is confused! When she hurts over the loss of her parents, she is told essentially to "not feel." When she is enjoying the interaction of other people, she is told in no uncertain terms that those feelings are inappropriate, even immoral. Lynette will grow up with her emotions under close internal scrutiny. She may even feel guilty or condemn herself for being "self-centered" when others delight in her. Can you relate to her discomfort? Did God make us emotional beings in order that we might be *enslaved* by our feelings?

When God created us in His image, He chose to make us relational—having an innate desire for fellowship with Him *and* other human beings. The intimacy needs defined in the previous chapter reflect the relational aspects of our nature. We are not only relational, but spiritual, physical, mental, *and* emotional. Our emotionality plays a vital part in our journey on earth with other persons. It may be one of the least understood aspects of our being...and God's!

Emotionality
Part of the Image of God

Emotionality is a normal and necessary part of being created in the image of God. Our emotions alert us to perceived changes in our environment and motivate us to respond. You might think of emotions as signal lights on the dashboard of a car, warning us that the vehicle is low on fuel or overheating, or sounding an alarm when a door has been left ajar. Emotions act in much the same way. If you see someone threatening your nephew, a feeling of indignation might prompt you to intervene. A sense of fatigue is an indicator that you need rest. Emotions are internal signals that are based upon our senses and our perceptions.

But, what role do our emotions play in relationships? In a positive way, they serve to motivate us to engage or connect with others. If we did not experience such feelings as joy, sadness, pain, love, anger, or fear, we might have little motivation to engage others for comfort, attention, respect, security, or other intimacy needs. Without emotions, we would be content as self-sufficient automatons, rather than actively engaged in meeting one another's needs. So emotions are essential to our humanity. However, because we can feel, we can hurt, and the capacity to experience painful emotions alerts us to potential problems in our relationships. For example, when your need for attention or support is not met by a close friend, you may feel sad or disappointed. This chapter is intended to enhance your ability to respond effectively to emotions that occur within the context of your relationships.

Increasing Your Emotional Vocabulary

Yes, God created us not only as spiritual, physical, and intellectual beings, but also as emotional ones. Yet, where did you get trained to understand and relate to your emotions? Who taught you to be aware of your feelings? Where did your attitudes about your emotionality get formed? If you are like many of us, the training was limited at best.

Most of us were programmed from an early age to focus on performance and achievement, not emotional development. Young children are commonly taught how to tie their shoes and brush their teeth, but are seldom helped to identify times when they feel sad, frustrated, or happy. School-age children undertake a myriad of activities such as sports, music lessons, and scouting, but are rarely shown how to work through the disappointments or rejections that inevitably accompany these activities. The result of such conditioning is that many of us enter adulthood with a limited "feeling vocabulary" and limited emotional responding skills to use in our relationships. Is it any wonder that so many relationships stay superficial and lack genuine closeness? We don't know the *language* of relational intimacy.

Let's look at a familiar passage of Scripture as a means for enhancing our abilities to recognize and label emotions. Turn to the Gospel of Luke in the New Testament and read the story of the Prodigal Son (Chapter 15:11-32) several times. Pay close attention to the characters and their feelings. You may wish to refer to the chart of "feeling faces" on the next page to help identify the emotions of the characters during this family crisis. Then, answer the following questions.

1. How would you describe the father's *feelings* as he watched his youngest son gather his belongings and leave home, perhaps forever (verse 13)?

_____

(For example, *"My heart is heavy as I realize that I may never see my son again. It grieves me to see this day arrive. I worry over what will become of him."*)

_____ **Emotional Responding**   **57**

2. How did the son who left home *feel* after spending all his money and finding himself destitute in a famine-plagued country, forced to grovel and eat scraps left for pigs (verses 14-16)?

_____

(For example, *"I had such big dreams, and now I've lost every-thing. I feel sick, disillusioned, and ashamed, and afraid."*)

3. How did the father *feel* when, at long last, he spotted his wayward son, dusty and disheveled, making his way up the winding road, returning home (verse 20)?

_____

(For example, *"This is incredible! I have never known such joy! I am filled with gratitude and overcome with love for my son!*)

4. How did the older son *feel* when he heard the news of his brother's homecoming (verses 25- 30)? Answer as if you were the older son.

_____

(For example, *"No matter how faithful I am, my father still favors my brother who has never shown appreciation or respect. This makes me angry! I feel overlooked and cheated.*)

We assume that as you emotionally stepped into the hearts of each of these characters and articulated their feelings, the story of the Prodigal Son became significantly more real to you. Did you notice that each character felt a variety of emotions? If you will view your own life situations with similar awareness of the complexity and nuances of your emotions, you will enhance your life experience and gain a more complete perspective.

Emotions . . . How Do You Feel?

 Afraid   Angry   Anxious   Apologetic   Ashamed   Bored

 Confused   Depressed   Disappointed   Disgusted   Embarassed   Enraged

 Frustrated   Grateful   Grieving   Guilty   Happy   Hopeful

 Hurt   Insecure   Insignificant   Jealous   Joyful   Lonely

 Loved   Misunderstood   Nervous   Overwhelmed   Pressured   Regretful

 Rejected   Relieved   Resentful   Sad   Sympathetic   Unappreciated

 Unimportant   Unloved   Used   Violated   Vulnerable

Personal Application
Emotional Awareness

Read through the list of emotions that follow. Circle any of these feelings that you would consider to have been common-place for you growing up, either during early childhood or adolescence. Then, in the space provided, write down two or three specific instances that brought about these emotions. Next, write down the feelings and thoughts that you experience *now* as you recall those times.

angry	content	happy	fearful
depressed	hopeful	calm	intimidated
ashamed	scared	enthusiastic	relaxed
guilty	insecure	significant	elated
joyful	frustrated	lonely	unimportant
excited	bitter	challenged	satisfied
hurt	hostile	secure	sad

Describe specific instances when you felt the circled emotions:

_____

_____

_____

_____

Describe feelings and thoughts you are sensing now as you recall these times: _____

_____

_____

During the next few days, practice identifying the emotions you feel throughout the day. Then, before you go to bed each night, take time to recount the day's events in your mind, being careful to use your new "feeling vocabulary" to express your emotions related to those events. Write down a summary of your feelings about the day. Such "journaling" can be an important means of developing emotional awareness and responding skills.

The Emotional Impact
of Relationships

I remember standing in a remote section of Colombia looking at the unusual site—an enormous tower of rock over 200 feet high. Scientists believe the elliptical mass was a meteor that imbedded itself halfway into the earth. The majestic "El Peñol" made a beautiful picture, with black and gray stone framed within the teeming green jungle. I felt awestruck and the first thing I wanted to do was share my excitement with someone else. It was simply not enough to experience it alone!

Relationships have unlimited potential for joy and meaning. When our relationships with God and others reflect the intimacy described in the first chapter (deep mutual knowing for the purpose of caring involvement), the oneness we experience can be highly fulfilling. But sadly, not many have experienced that level of intimacy. Conflict and disengagement are more common.

Perhaps you have noticed. Conflicts in your relationships are inevitable, though not always visible! The easy give-and-take you expected rarely exists. Opposing viewpoints, contradicting agendas, gender differences, and poor communication all contribute to hurt, disappointment, anger, and frustration in relationships. If these conflicts are not properly resolved, negative emotions will accumulate and congeal into bitterness and resentment. As the negative feelings smolder and fester inside you, the positive feelings of happiness, joy, and contentment will be crowded out. Eventually, the love that once existed may grow cold. The same relationship that had generated pleasant emotions may now be producing pain.

See if you can recall a relationship that ended badly for you. What feelings were present for you at that time? Write them here. _____

_____

_____

_____

_____

It would not be surprising if you listed feelings such as hurt, grief (a sense of loss), sadness, disappointment, or anger. **Hurt** develops because we have experienced pain when we expected blessing. We received a wound when we hoped to receive a gift. Instead of the joy of togetherness and fellowship, we found ourselves experiencing loss and loneliness. Yet, our hurt is not always visible or even acknowledged, and like an undiagnosed cancer, will not be healed until it is identified and treated.

Anger is an emotion familiar to all of us that some have called the "self-preservation emotion." Anger serves as a defense against further hurt or loss. It often masks other emotions like hurt and fear which leave us feeling vulnerable. Because it is painful to focus on our inner hurts, we hide our vulnerability and pain by unleashing anger at something or someone, even if that someone is us. For many of us, anger is so automatic that we never consciously experience the hurt feelings that prompted the anger. Research indicates that the emotion of anger is accompanied by increased production of a multitude of hormones and enzymes that prepare the body for battle or flight. Our adrenalin and blood sugar levels increase, and even our white blood cell count goes up immediately to ward off potential harm from infection. We are fearfully and wonderfully made, are we not!

But in close, personal relationships, anger serves to diminish rather than enhance emotional intimacy. Anger has many "faces." It may show up as impatience, irritability, a quick temper, or raging. It may prompt other emotions such as jealousy, suspicion, or even depression. Some people may display anger in passive-aggressive manners such as silence, cynicism, sarcasm, withdrawal, or even procrastination. But regardless of the outward manifestation, some form of hurt or other vulnerable feeling lies beneath the anger. Imagine a "tree of pain" with leaves and branches that display anger, sarcasm, jealousy, sleep disturbances, perfectionism, addictions, and ulcers, but with roots made up of hurt, loss, and fear. Anger, stemming from underlying hurt, is a common product of unmet intimacy needs.

Unmet needs can also lead to **fear**. For example, if you greet a visitor at your church and he responds by immediately walking away, fear of further rejection may prompt you to be less assertive in approaching others. A favorable reception (acceptance) would have produced a different outcome. Ridicule from co-workers for a poorly-delivered presentation might produce immediate embarrassment as well as a fear of future failure. Consolation and urging you forward toward your objective (comfort and encouragement) might have motivated you to keep trying. In other words, *yesterday's pain prompts today's fear about tomorrow.*

So, what does fear look like in people? Fear, like anger, can be manifested in many forms including avoidance, withdrawal (minimizing the opportunity to be further rejected), perfectionism (reducing opportunities to be found deficient), controlling (limiting the chance others might have to hurt you), and addictions (numbing the anxiety or insecurity with a mood- altering substance or behavior). Fear opens the door for the evil one to steal the joy God intended for you. The meeting of underlying intimacy needs can displace that fear.

Often, when people are hurt in relationships, they react or retaliate against the other person in hurtful ways such as aggression, criticism, slander, or abandonment. Such inappropriate responses eventually add **guilt** (feelings associated with actual or perceived wrongdoing), or **shame** (a sense that one is inferior or inadequate) to the hurt that already existed. As with the underlying hurt, the roots of these painful feelings are unmet intimacy needs.

Thus, a "cycle" of negative emotions may repeat with the root being unmet intimacy needs.

Unmet Need→Hurt→Anger/Fear/Guilt/Shame

As we accumulate painful emotions, we experience symptoms of one form or another. These symptoms produced by unresolved emotions, become the focus of our relational difficulties and rob us of our joy. Our hope for resolving these struggles lies in a biblically-based process that *respects*, rather than ignores or exalts, the hurtful feelings we carry inside.

Emotional Capacity
What's Filling the Cup?

To better understand how relational pain can have a cumulative effect on us, imagine that your brain has a small cup inside that contains your emotions. The cup represents your "emotional capacity." The cup can hold only so much emotion before some of it spills out. A cup filled with positive emotions will overflow with love, joy, and peace—the fruits of the Spirit. But, make note of this. The same portion of your brain processes both the positive and the negative feelings. Therefore, a cup filled with negative, unhealthy emotions such as hurt, anger, guilt, fear, bitterness, and shame can limit or even prevent you from experiencing positive feelings. The symptoms induced by a cup filled with painful emotions may include fatigue, stress, difficulty concentrating, appetite and sleep disturbances, depression, rage, ulcers, or even escapes into drugs, illicit relationships, eating disorders, or workaholism. The diagram on the following page shows the effects of a pain-filled cup.

Now, let's take a look at an example of how the concept of the emotional cup relates to everyday relationships. As you read the following case study, think about the emotions that might be filling up the emotional cups of the persons described.

Laura had been working at an investment firm for the past three years. Her production was well ahead of her colleagues who had joined the firm at the same time. Despite her success and hard work, Laura's manager continued to pressure her to increase the amount of business she was bringing into the firm. He would do this by putting her down with derogatory comments such as, "Laura, I don't believe you're working up to your potential since you were such a "hot shot" when you started at the firm," or, "If you would be more aggressive with your clients and not spend so much time holding their hands and reassuring them, your numbers would improve."

When Laura was growing up, her father was extremely critical and wielded high standards for the behavior and academic success of his children. Because she desperately wanted to please her father, Laura excelled in school by studying hard

Symptoms of a *"Full Cup"*

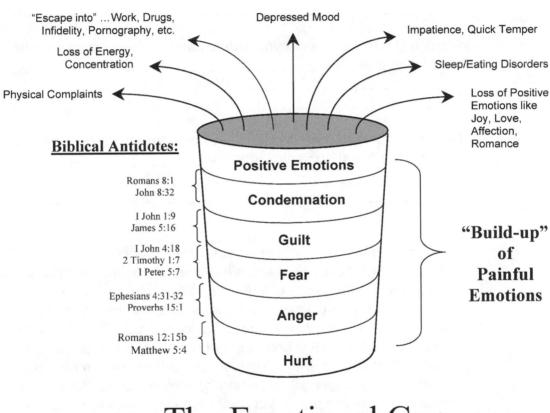

"Escape into" ...Work, Drugs, Infidelity, Pornography, etc.

Loss of Energy, Concentration

Physical Complaints

Depressed Mood

Impatience, Quick Temper

Sleep/Eating Disorders

Loss of Positive Emotions like Joy, Love, Affection, Romance

Biblical Antidotes:

Romans 8:1
John 8:32

I John 1:9
James 5:16

I John 4:18
2 Timothy 1:7
I Peter 5:7

Ephesians 4:31-32
Proverbs 15:1

Romans 12:15b
Matthew 5:4

Positive Emotions

Condemnation

Guilt

Fear

Anger

Hurt

"Build-up" of Painful Emotions

⸺ The Emotional Cup ⸺

every week. While other teens attended sports events and par-
ties, Laura spent her evenings and weekends holed up in her
room diligently striving to earn her father's approval. Laura
brought this background with her when she went to work at the
investment firm.

What emotions do you suppose are filling Laura's cup right now? (see page 59) _____

_____

_____

What intimacy needs do you think Laura misses most at this time? (see page 38) _____

_____

_____

How was Laura's childhood experience "preparation" for her current relational struggles at work?_____

_____

_____

Larry is a 41-year-old single parent who teaches high school
in New England. As the oldest sibling in his family, Larry decid-
ed to throw a retirement party for his father. Because Larry lived
several states away from his parents, the arrangements were
made through the mail and long-distance phone calls. The party
was to be held at a nice hotel in his hometown, and he expected
about 100 of his parents' friends, co-workers, and relatives to
attend. His younger siblings had offered to assist him in the
preparations for the party, but their own busy lives left little time
to follow through on the tasks he had delegated to them. As a
result, Larry was left alone to struggle with the bulk of the work.
The day of the party arrived, and everything went off without
a hitch. Because the names of the three children had been print-
ed on the invitations, Larry's parents assumed that all of the
them had been equally instrumental in arranging the party.
Toward the end of the evening, Larry's father stood up and
praised his children for the sacrifices they had made organizing

his retirement party. Larry's siblings, though embarrassed by the praise, said nothing to their father or to Larry to give him credit for the lion's share of the event's success.

What emotions do you suppose are filling Larry's cup right now? (see page 59) _____

_____

_____

What intimacy needs do you think Larry misses most at this time? (see page 38) _____

_____

_____

Did you conclude that if Laura's manager had expressed appreciation for the good work she was doing, she would have felt respected, valued, and motivated to work even harder? Could it be that she would have continued to develop loyal clientele because of the extra attention she gave to their accounts? Does it make sense to you that she would still be missing approval as she had when she was a child? Did you determine that Larry probably felt abandoned and used, not to mention taken for granted? Would his need for respect and appreciation be left wanting?

Did you identify with these scenarios? We've all experienced unmet intimacy needs and the resulting disappointment, loss, or other painful emotions. The principle is clear: *When our basic emotional needs are met, we experience intimacy, but when our needs go unmet, we experience painful emotions such as hurt, loss, anger, fear, guilt, and shame.*

What Is Filling Your Emotional Cup?

Examine your own emotional cup, using the diagram and lists provided on the next page.

1. First, circle any of the *emotions* listed on either side of the cup diagram that you seem to experience a lot. What emotion do you experience most often?

   _____

2. Now, circle any *symptoms*, such as escaping into work, that have robbed you of abundant life. What symptom is most likely to surface when your cup is full? _____

   _____

3. Next, draw a horizontal line on the cup diagram to reflect the *balance* of positive and negative emotions that *typically* fill your cup. For example, if you believe you experience negative emotions three times as often as positive emotions, you should draw the horizontal line high on the cup, indicating that your emotional cup is filled predominantly with negative feelings.

4. Finally, write on the cup the *names* of the emotions you typically experience, putting the positive emotions *above* the line you drew and the negative emotions *below* the line.

   As you look at this representation of what typically fills your cup, describe below what you are sensing right now. ___

   _____

   _____

Emptying the Cup

Whether you carry hurt from childhood, from previous marriages, or from current relationships, God has a provision for your pain. Even if your struggles are serious and your under-

What Is Filling Your Emotional Cup?

Symptoms

Depressed Mood
Anxious Mood
Irritable Mood
Uncontrollable Anger
Loss of Energy
Chronic Fatigue
Loss of Concentration
Loss of Positive Feelings

Escape Into:
   Work
   Pleasure
   Drugs or Alcohol
   Pornography
   Illicit Sex
Obsessive/Compulsive:
   Thoughts
   Behavior/Rituals

Sleep Disturbances
Appetite Disturbances
Frequent Headaches
Chronic Indigestion
Other Physical Problems
Chronic Low Self-esteem
Controlling Behavior
Manipulative Behavior
Self-degrading Behavior

Emotions

Afraid
Angry
Anxious
Ashamed
Contented
Confused
Creative
Delighted
Depressed
Disappointed
Disgusted
Embarrassed
Excited
Frustrated
Grateful
Guilty
Happy
Hopeful
Hurt
Insecure
Inspired
Insignificant

Emotions

Jealous
Joyful
Lonely
Loved
Misunderstood
Nervous
Optimistic
Overwhelmed
Pressured
Regretful
Rejected
Relaxed
Relieved
Resentful
Sad
Satisfied
Successful
Unappreciated
Unloved
Violated
Vulnerable
Worried

Emotional Cup of_____

lying hurt and pain is extensive, there is hope in the healing power of God's grace. The healing process involves emptying the negative feelings that have accumulated in your emotional cup within the context of a safe, secure, Christ-centered relationship. Even when marriages and extended families fail to provide such an environment for God's grace to flourish, the Body of Christ can and should serve as a healing community for God's work of restoration within us.

But, why would we continue to carry negative emotions in our cups? Why would experiences that may be decades old still hold the power to produce anxiety, hurt, and shame today? The answer to these questions is revealed in the manner we have responded to our pain in the past. Many of us carry a bundle of hurts that we've never even tried to identify. We may have been taught that "time heals all wounds." Or, we may have been told that we should live in the present, ignoring what we have been through in the past. Though offered with good intentions, this advice misses the mark. It discounts the fact that we are created to be emotional beings according to God's design.

Another reason that our emotional cups carry a lot of pain is that we have a hard time putting into words what we feel or what seems to be wrong. Some of us consciously "stuff" or suppress pain, fearing that others would regard us as weak or immature. Yet, deep within, we sense our pain and frustration and we know that what we have been doing to resolve it has not succeeded.

Now, let's see how to empty one another's emotional cups by *responding to the emotions* that we and others carry. In subsequent chapters, we will talk more specifically about healing unresolved pain from childhood, displacing the fear of intimacy caused by previous hurtful experiences, and resolving conflicts in current relationships.

The Bible tells us in many areas that we are to respond to the hurt and pain that others carry by offering comfort (Matt. 5:4; Rom. 12:15). Yet, all too frequently, Christians view grieving and mourning as signs of weakness and exalt denial of pain as spiritual maturity. The fact is, God cares about what we are feeling. He is not responding to our hurt by saying, "Buck up,"

"Never let them see you cry," or "Keep a stiff upper lip." Those messages often project condemnation, adding shame to the hurt a person is already feeling. Instead, God instructs us to get some of *His* grace into circulation by offering some of *His* comfort to others who are hurting.

> "...the Father of compassion and the God of all comfort, who comforts us in all our troubles, so that we can comfort those in any trouble with the comfort we ourselves have received from God." (II Cor. 1:3-4)

Christ Jesus was frequently moved with compassion and grieved about the suffering of others (John 11:33-35; Luke 19:41; 22:41-45). He could admit His own pain, even reaching out to His most trusted disciples when facing the reality of His impending crucifixion (Matt. 26:36-46). Yet, who among us would call Jesus weak? He faced his pain and that of others. He was able to reveal it instead of denying it. And, He could give an emotional response to the emotional needs of others. Clearly, experiencing hurt and pain is an inevitable part of living in an imperfect world. Our *response* to that pain, whether it is in us or in others, needs to be like that of our Savior and Lord.

Most of us were "programmed" to respond in non-emotional ways to the emotional needs in ourselves and others. Our thinking as well as our behavior would suggest that the emotion is either invalid, inappropriate, or unimportant. We may have developed a pattern of responding to emotion (our own or that of others) by rationalizing it, attacking it, superseding it, or ignoring it. We may have responded to our emotions by "escaping" them in work, play, or even ministry. *The key to effectively emptying the pain from one another's emotional cups is to get more of God's empathy and compassion into circulation.* We do this by learning to deeply comprehend the feelings of another and lovingly respond to them as Christ would do. We do this well when we remain close to the Father of compassion (II Cor. 1:3), and abide in the One who has experienced pain and suffering for us all (John 15:15).

Unproductive Responses
to the Pain of Others

Can you think of an individual who seems to be able to understand and care about what you are going through in life and how it is affecting you? Write the person's name here and describe what he or she would do that conveyed such loving concern to you. _____

_____

_____

A study of that person's behavior may give you some clues about effective responses to the hurt, pain, or fear of others. But first, let's look at some *unproductive* responses to emotional needs. These include responding to emotion with logic, criticism, complaints of your own, or neglect.

Julie arrived at the apartment forty-five minutes after the other members of her Bible study group. They had eaten out at a Chinese restaurant and Julie had gotten involved in a discussion with Mike, a young man from her college who had been trying to get her to go out with him. The group had decided to play a joke on her by sneaking out and letting Julie find her own way home. Having nothing but a credit card, Julie had ended up "bumming" a ride with Mike. She sat down on the sofa with tears in her eyes, and said, "I was hurt and humiliated by your actions, leaving me stranded with someone I have been trying to politely avoid."

The responses Julie got from the group to her vulnerable disclosure were varied, yet they all missed the mark of responding to Julie's emotion with emotion.

Mary replied, "You know, Julie, you could have called a cab and used your credit card. They have cabs that take those, you know." (Facts/Logic/Reason)

Rhonda snapped, "You're so sensitive! Get a life, would ya? We wouldn't have done it if you hadn't taken so long to get rid of him." (Criticism)

Christine quipped negatively, "Well, you complain about him trying to take you out. Think about how some of us feel who don't get asked out very often. When was the last time you showed any concern for me?" (Complaint)

Nikki, looking uncomfortable, added, "Can't we just drop it? Let's get started with our study. It's getting late." (Neglect)

Do any of these responses sound familiar? Have you heard others (or yourself) make similar comments to someone who was obviously hurting? What would you have felt if you had been Julie and your friends responded to your statements this way? Write your answer here:

_____

The common thread in all four of these responses is that they all missed the mark. They did not develop intimacy among these friends. None of them responded in a way that valued, validated, or even acknowledged the emotion that Julie had expressed. *Learning to respond emotionally begins with recognizing inappropriate, ineffective ways that we may already be responding to our friends, loved ones, and co-workers.*

So, let's practice. After reading each of the examples below, **circle** the type of unhealthy response that is being given.

1. You were supposed to have dinner with a friend, but you've kept her waiting for over an hour. When you finally arrive, you can see that she is angry. Your first words are, "I'm sorry. I just couldn't get away, and didn't even have time to call you. The traffic was terrible."

Type of response: Facts/Logic/Reasons Criticism Complaint Neglect

2. After you and your brother have finished the evening meal, he says, "I'm feeling really sad about not seeing you any more than I do." You answer, "Yeah, well, let's get going so we can get to the game on time tonight."

Type of response: Facts/Logic/Reasons Criticism Complaint Neglect

3. You walk in the front door to find your roommate sitting alone in the living room, obviously upset. You snap, "What's wrong with you now?"

Type of response: Facts/Logic/Reasons Criticism Complaint Neglect

4. As you leave work with one of the members of your car pool, she announces, "I am just worn out and frustrated about my day." You remark, "I know what you mean. You wouldn't believe how bad things were in my department today!"

Type of response: Facts/Logic/Reasons Criticism Complaint Neglect

The correct answers for the preceding exercise are:
1) Facts/Logic/Reasons; 2) Neglect; 3) Criticism; and,
4) Complaint.

To achieve emotional closeness in our relationships, we must first learn to avoid these types of responses. They miss the mark and leave us feeling empty, hurt, and alone. How do you typically respond to emotion in yourself or others? Which one of these ineffective responses do you find yourself using most often? Write your answer here. _____
Now, let's see what kinds of responses actually serve to heal hurts and remove our aloneness.

Helpful Emotional Responding

For emotional closeness to develop, two people have to relate emotionally, communicating with feelings. But, what do we mean by emotional responding? Simply stated, **emotional responding means to relate directly to the feeling(s) that are present, acknowledging and validating their importance.** Emotional responding looks like focused listening, gentleness, empathy, expressed concern, reassurance, and sometimes, confession or forgiveness. Effective emotional responding "hits the mark," bringing understanding, healing, clarification, fulfillment, respect, and closeness.

Remember Julie? Let's recall her vulnerable disclosure to her friends who had left her at the restaurant without a way home, and see how another member of the group responded.

She (Julie) sat down on the sofa with tears in her eyes, and said, "I was hurt and humiliated by your actions, leaving me stranded with someone I have been trying to politely avoid."

Michelle came over and sat next to Julie on the sofa. She made eye contact with her and said, "Julie, I don't like seeing you hurt like this. It saddens me to think that we put you in such an embarrassing position, much more awkward than we had anticipated. I can imagine it was very hurtful to be stranded by your friends without explanation. It was wrong of me to have done that to you. Please forgive me for the part I had in the prank. I do care about your friendship and your happiness.

If you were Julie, how would you have felt after hearing Michelle's response? Write your answer here. _____

_____

_____

Now, let's practice the right way to respond to the emotional needs of others. Remembering that emotion needs emotion, write out new responses to the same situations presented earlier. Begin by trying to see the situation through your friend's eyes. Imagine what your friend would be feeling, given that perspective. Then, think of a way to respond that conveys understanding, care, concern, and empathy. One possible response is provided as an example. Think of an alternative to write in the blank provided.

1. You and your friend were supposed to have a quiet dinner alone, but you've kept her waiting for over an hour. You say:

_____

_____

_____

_____

_____

_____

2. After you and your relative have finished having dinner, he says, "I'm feeling really sad about not seeing you any more than I do." You answer:

_____

_____

_____

_____

_____

3. You walk in the front door to find your roommate sitting alone in the living room, obviously upset. You comment:

_____

_____

_____

_____

_____

4. As you leave work with one of the members of your car pool, she announces, "I am just worn out and frustrated about my day." You remark:

_____

_____

_____

_____

_____

Like Julie, we are all going to experience emotional pain, such as disappointment, loss, sadness, rejection, guilt, or condemnation. If we are not keeping our emotional cups emptied with the help of trusted friends our pain will accumulate and eventually be expressed in symptoms like chronic irritability, stress, drivenness, or even some form of addiction. We can demonstrate the love of God by learning to respond emotionally to one another, removing aloneness and helping to heal and restore the years the locusts have eaten (Joel 2:25). The chart on the following page summarizes the intimacy principles related to emotional responding.

Developing Intimacy Skills...*Emotional Responding*

Unproductive Responses

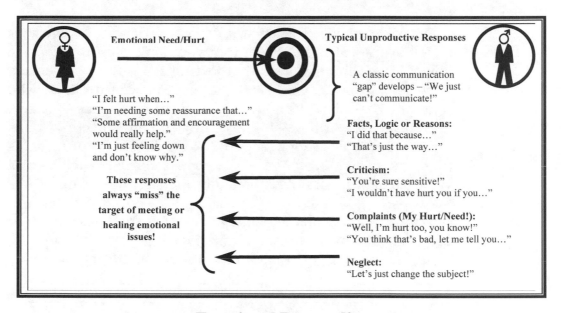

Emotional Need/Hurt

"I felt hurt when..."
"I'm needing some reassurance that..."
"Some affirmation and encouragement would really help."
"I'm just feeling down and don't know why."

These responses always "miss" the target of meeting or healing emotional issues!

Typical Unproductive Responses

A classic communication "gap" develops – "We just can't communicate!"

Facts, Logic or Reasons:
"I did that because..."
"That's just the way..."

Criticism:
"You're sure sensitive!"
"I wouldn't have hurt you if you..."

Complaints (My Hurt/Need!):
"Well, I'm hurt too, you know!"
"You think that's bad, let me tell you..."

Neglect:
"Let's just change the subject!"

Emotional Responding

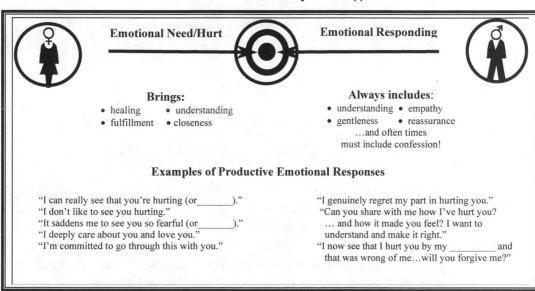

Emotional Need/Hurt   **Emotional Responding**

Brings:
- healing
- fulfillment
- understanding
- closeness

Always includes:
- understanding
- gentleness
- empathy
- reassurance
...and often times must include confession!

Examples of Productive Emotional Responses

"I can really see that you're hurting (or_____)."
"I don't like to see you hurting."
"It saddens me to see you so fearful (or_____)."
"I deeply care about you and love you."
"I'm committed to go through this with you."

"I genuinely regret my part in hurting you."
"Can you share with me how I've hurt you?
 ... and how it made you feel? I want to
 understand and make it right."
"I now see that I hurt you by my _____ and
 that was wrong of me...will you forgive me?"

Rejoice With Those Who Rejoice

Have you noticed when you have experienced a victory or a significant accomplishment that you don't want to celebrate alone? The Bible suggests that joyful times are to be shared. The first part of Romans 12:15 states, "Rejoice with those who rejoice." That might look like a hearty handshake or shouts of joy. It may be a more subdued, but equally sincere, "That's great! I am really happy for you!" Regardless of your style, as much as it is within your ability to do so, share in the joys and victories of others and let them join in with your own.

Think of a time in childhood when you experienced a major accomplishment or received a special gift or recognition. Describe the event below and how it made you feel at the time.

_____

_____

_____

Share your story with people you know and ask them to share their own. Rejoice together.

The Miracle of Comfort
Blessing from Pain

Comfort is God's "medication" for all forms of hurt that we experience as human beings. At times, we need to offer comfort to a person hurt by our own actions or words. Expression of genuine sorrow for someone we have hurt is a necessary part of the confession process. At other times, we are in position to minister comfort to one another for hurts that we had no part in causing. Could it be that each of us carries pain within us that has been there for years without ever having been comforted? If so, we cannot be fully free of its influence until we have experienced God's balm for that pain—comfort. Regardless of the nature or source of the pain, God's resource of comfort can lead to healing and freedom to love and be loved.

Matthew 5:4 says, "Blessed are they that mourn for they shall be comforted." That verse assures us that those who mourn will be comforted and blessed as a result. This means that when I hurt and grieve the hurt, and someone offers godly comfort, positive feelings begin to replace the painful ones. That is nothing short of miraculous. But the process of mourning and comforting can be defeated in two ways—either by refusing to acknowledge and grieve the pain or by failing to be afforded comfort by another.

Meredith came in for her first counseling appointment obviously nervous and apprehensive. She began to relax, however, when she realized that there would be no pressure or interrogation in our dialogue. Though in her early forties, Meredith confided that she had never shared with anyone what she was here to say. As a young adult, she and her boyfriend had been sexually active and she had become pregnant. Wanting to avoid disappointing her staunchly evangelistic parents, Meredith secretly had an abortion. Many years and two marriages later, Meredith had come in to unload the grief and guilt that she felt for many, many years. When asked if she had ever mourned the loss of the child or the lack of approval from her parents, Meredith said that she had cried for days at a time. Then, the next question left Meredith speechless. "Who was there to comfort you in your pain?" Her answer was predictable. "No one," she said. Meredith had indeed grieved her losses, but she had not been able to receive comfort from other people. Though God can, and does, provide supernatural comfort to us in many ways, He has charged us with responsibility to pass along His comfort to one another (II Corinthians 1:3-4). That day, Meredith received healing from God through seeking His forgiveness and His comfort, as her counselor expressed genuine sorrow for the tragic and painful journey she had traversed alone.

What does comfort look like? It involves one person focusing all attention on the painful story of another, expressing compassion with loving words or appropriate touch. In Meredith's case, comfort might have been expressed this way, *"Meredith, you've been carrying a heavy burden all these years. I'm really sad that no one came alongside to be with you in this. I see the sadness in your eyes for your lost child, and understand that you have deeply regretted your decision to abort. As I think about your hurt, I want you to know that I care and do not condemn you. I am moved with compassion by the sadness you expressed for the child that you chose to abort. I also hurt for you because of the years of estrangement from your parents whom you love and greatly admire. "*

Listed below are a number of sources of emotional pain that could have occurred in your lifetime. Begin this journey by reviewing the list and answering the questions that follow.

- Being the product of an unwanted pregnancy
- Receiving very little nurturance during infancy
- Losing a parent or parents through death or divorce
- Experiencing the chaos and terror of emotional or verbal abuse
- Experiencing the trauma, shame, and terror of physical or sexual abuse
- Experiencing the loneliness of neglect or preoccupied parents
- Losing friends due to moves from one area to another
- Feeling ridiculed for conditions over which you had no control, such as dyslexia
- Being manipulated or controlled by older siblings or domineering parents
- Feeling intense performance pressure from yourself or others
- Witnessing discord, strife, or even physical conflict between parents
- Being excluded or rejected by friends, cliques, or dating partners
- Feeling seriously inadequate in academic, athletic, or appearance domains

◆ Receiving condemning labels from friends or relatives such as lazy, selfish, or stupid
◆ Experiencing or causing an unwanted pregnancy due to premarital sex

Are any of these (or other) sources of pain applicable to you? Put a check next to the ones that apply. Now, write down some of the feelings that you are experiencing right now as you think about what you checked. (For example, *sad, disappointed, angry, hurt, inadequate, inferior, unloved, anxious, etc.*) _____

_____

_____

Can you remember what you felt when the items you identified were occurring? Write down here the feelings that you probably experienced back then. (For example, *rejected, ridiculed, sad, abandoned, insecure, afraid, threatened, pressured, unimportant, ashamed, inadequate, uncomfortable, bad, dirty, panicky, intensely angry, lonely, etc.*) _____

_____

_____

Referring to the list of *Ten Key Intimacy Needs* on page 38, what do you think you wanted and needed most when you were a child? (For example, *attention, security, support, respect, etc.*)

_____

_____

Pray now that God will give you comfort for all the pain that you recall having experienced in your childhood and your adult life. But pray also that He would put someone in your life who knows how to give comfort appropriately and genuinely. God may have already provided for your need through your group or journey-mates. There may be a married couple who together provide support to you and a safe place to share about your hurts and struggles. Some of you may choose to involve a pastoral or professional counselor for matters that seem to go beyond the expertise of your friends or group. But regardless of

_____ **Emotional Responding**

whom God provides as the "one who comes alongside," His provision for unhealed hurt is clearly comfort. It is good to not be alone as you travel this journey.

Personal Application
Mourn With Those Who Mourn

The second half of Romans 12:15 calls us to actively grieve or mourn with people who are in pain. Mourning is particularly appropriate when people have suffered losses, such as the death of a loved one, or loss of a job, a dream, or even one's dignity. All too often, people are left to grieve such losses alone. Typically, people who are grieving sense a degree of relief when others mourn with them. Mourning with someone might include verbal expressions, such as, *I feel deeply saddened for you because of the pain you are in right now."* Mourning with others may also include weeping for those who have experienced the loss. Who has wept for you? Who in your lifetime has joined into your pain rather than tried to "fix" it or minimize it?

Think of a time in childhood when you experienced a major loss, disappointment, or time of great hurt or embarrassment. Describe the event below and how it made you feel at the time.

_____
_____
_____
_____
_____
_____
_____
_____

Share your story with people you know and ask them to share their own. Use the skills you have just studied to respond emotionally according to the need of the moment. Mourn together.

Encountering God in His Word

"Feeling Sorrow for the Savior"
John 14:1-11 (focal passage: John 14:9)

Could it be that in order to fully empathize with our fellow man, we must first be able to feel genuine compassion for our Savior? Read Philippians 3:7-10, noting especially, verse 10, "I want to know Christ and the power of his resurrection and the fellowship of sharing in his sufferings, becoming like him in his death..." Paraphrase this verse here, using your own words:

_____

_____

_____

What does it mean to share in Christ's sufferings? Is there a way that we can actually *experience* this verse? I (David) struggled with this passage for nearly a year, trying to understand how to enter the fellowship of Christ's sufferings. It seemed almost mystical. Was it merely a poetic phrase, or an underlying truth that could transform one's life? One Sunday, I was speaking in a church about the death of John the Baptist. I described how Jesus, when told by the disciples of John's death, withdrew to a place where He could be alone with the Father, grieve the deep loss, and receive the Father's comfort. As I was driving home after church, I began to cry, and the tears continued despite attending to the traffic. I wondered, *"Whom am I crying for? Whom am I hurting for?"* The answer dawned suddenly, that my tears and my compassion were for Jesus! I was feeling genuine empathy and fellowship with the suffering of Christ!

◆ What do you think was most emotionally painful to Jesus during His ministry with the disciples? _____

_____

Now, read John 14:1-8, where Jesus is comforting his disciples in anticipation of His departure from their presence. His comments include, *"I am the way and the truth and the life. No* one comes to the Father except through me. If you really knew me, you would know my Father as well. From now on, you do know him and have seen him." After Jesus' profound and moving statements, imagine Philip looking at Jesus blankly and saying, "Lord, show us the Father and that will be enough for us."

◆ Given Jesus' reply, "Don't you know me, Philip, even after I have been among you such a long time?" write down what you think Jesus felt at that time. _____
_____
_____

> *Jesus wants an intimate relationship with us, but we must seek Him and believe Him at His Word.*

Group Dialogue

If you do not have a designated group leader, choose some-one in the group who will serve to facilitate the discussion. Begin by briefly reviewing the discussion guidelines.

Discussion Guidelines

- ◆ Allow everyone an opportunity to share thoughts and feelings
- ◆ Avoid long story telling
- ◆ Be quick to listen with empathy

- ◆ Be slow to give advice
- ◆ Speak the truth in love
- ◆ Say what you mean and mean what you say
- ◆ Protect the confidentiality of every person

Discussion Suggestions for Chapter Three

1. Have each person draw a large circle on a piece of paper. On the **inside** of the circle, list several events that you experienced during the past week. Next to each event, write down what you were feeling at the time. (For example, excited, stressed out, proud, put down, etc.) Now, on the **outside** of the circle, write brief descriptions of what other people might have observed about you during those events. (For example, were you smiling, worried, frowning, unemotional, etc.) Often, the emotions we feel inside are quite different than what we present to the world on the outside. Share about any inconsistencies between the feelings you recorded on the inside of the circle and the behaviors you listed on the outside of the circle. Discuss how such inconsistencies could cause problems in relationships.

2. Take turns sharing about a time that stands out in your memory when someone responded well to you when you were hurting or afraid.

3. Refer to the list of emotions on page 60 where you circled those that were commonplace for you during your childhood. Then, take turns sharing the emotions that you circled, mentioning specific times that you remember feeling these emotions as a child. As each person shares, pay close attention to the words, tone of voice, and body language. Experience Romans 12:15 by rejoicing when someone shares something positive, and mourning with them when something hurtful is shared. These times of sharing may be difficult for some, so be sure to give lots of eye contact, appropriate reassuring touches, and verbal support through emotional words that convey, "I care." Express concern for any sad or painful feelings that are disclosed. This exercise lets you practice both identifying feelings and responding emotionally.

4. Close your time together by praying for increased sensitivity and skill for understanding and responding to one another's emotional needs.

Journey-mate Encounters

◆ Set aside one to two hours for the meeting to give ample time for each person to share.

◆ Select a meeting location that minimizes distractions or interruptions.

◆ Read the chapter and complete all the written exercises *before* meeting to discuss them.

◆ Purpose to start on time and complete each exercise, staying focused on the material.

Suggestions for Journey-mate Encounter #3

1. Turn to page 69 and share with each other what emotions are typically filling your emotional cups. Practice helpful emotional responding as you listen intently to what your journey-mates are experiencing. Rejoice and mourn together as appropriate.

2. Discuss the symptoms you experience most often that rob you of some of your joy.

3. Discuss the tendencies you may each have to respond in unproductive ways and give permission to each other to gently hold you accountable if you use that way again. Ask your journey-mate(s) to verify that you are "hitting the mark" emotionally, and that understanding and caring concern are being conveyed.

4. Share with each other what filled your emotional cup as a child. Continue to practice good emotional responding.

5. Talk about how easy or difficult it is for each of you to receive comfort from others and why it is that way.

6. Pray for each other that your concern and understanding of each other's struggles will encourage you to enter more into the fellowship of Christ's sufferings, empathizing with His feelings as well.

Hiding the Word in Your Heart
Romans 12:15

Write the verse here: _____

_____

_____

_____

_____

_____

_____

_____

_____

_____

Repeat the verse from memory each day for several weeks. Using the space below, you may want to journal ways that God has allowed you to experience the verse as you have hidden it away in your heart. _____

_____

_____

_____

_____

_____

_____

_____

_____

_____

_____

_____

_____

Check the box at the right when you have committed the verse to memory. Continue to repeat the verse daily for at least three weeks.

Chapter Four

———— ◆ ————

FEARLESS FRIENDSHIPS
Faith Expressing Itself in Love

*"For God did not give us a spirit of timidity, but
a spirit of power, of love, and of self-discipline."*
II Timothy 1:7

Brad and Frank had worked together for years. They had
spent a good deal of time together going to sporting events and
even hunting together at times. But Brad was growing weary of
the relationship. Frank often presumed upon Brad to go places,
dropping by unexpectedly and staying for hours when Brad was
trying to complete work assignments. Brad usually said nothing,
hoping Frank would just become more considerate over time. It
had always been difficult for Brad to confront people about their
behavior. He was afraid it would make them angry or that he
would seem to be selfish or demanding—traits Brad did not want
others to associate with him. It finally occurred to Brad that his
friendship with Frank was not really genuine because there were
problems that never got discussed and feelings that often got
ignored. After reading Ephesians 4:15 one morning, Brad decided it was time to "speak the truth in love." He decided that he
would let Frank know that he wanted to maintain their friendship, but that there were some issues that needed to be
addressed.

Over the years, the fabric of our society has so deteriorated
that we have lost our "community compass" that could guide us
in the development of healthy relationships. There is little

agreement about the values and principles that constitute healthiness in relationships. There is even less awareness of what such principles look like in operation. Therefore, let's spend some time giving definition to the characteristics of healthy and unhealthy relationships and then apply them to our friendships, families, work environments, and communities so that, in Christ, we can love, rather than fear, one another.

Characteristics of Unhealthy Relationships

Listed below are several characteristics of unhealthy relationships, followed by healthier alternatives. This list incorporates characteristics defined by Hemfelt, Minirth, and Meier in their book, Love Is a Choice.

◆ **Involvement is compulsive or demanded.**
Unhealthiness is present when participation in relationships is forced or compulsive rather than chosen and free. It is appropriate for people to desire a connection to other persons. However, intense pursuit, craving, or possessiveness suggest the presence of unresolved personal issues and do not serve to "build up one another." Instead, they "feed" the participants in unhealthy ways. *In healthy relationships, involvement is invited, and each person freely chooses whether or not to engage.*

◆ **One or both persons' identities are threatened.** It is destructive when people label others as unacceptable or unlovable simply because they are different. *Godly relationships value and respect differences rather than disparage, condemn or stifle them. Each person preserves and honors the unique identity and God-ordained giftedness of the other.*

◆ **Reality is distorted or denied.** Damage results when tradition, culture, or selfish ambition are used to inaccurately "define" reality. Perception of reality is often distorted, particularly in young people, when God's revealed truth is not upheld. *Integrity and objectivity make relation-*

ships strong. Healthy friendships address problems, rather than ignore or deny their existence. Friends face disagreements with truth and love (Eph. 4:15), rather than avoid them.

◆ **Emotions are hidden or used to control and manipulate.** Melodramatic outbursts and masking negative feelings both produce imbalance and insecurity. Often, such behavior is a means of "taking" to get needs met, rather than revealing needs and allowing opportunity for the other person to respond. *Consistency of mood and behavior, and balanced, contagious giving to one another reflects healthiness.*

◆ **Possessive jealousy tries to take what truly must be given.** Insecurity and jealousy can be manifested in various interactions such as clinging or trying to "hold onto them." Often, such behavior "smothers" others and drives them away. Patterns of this type may escalate and often leads to abuse among spouses and cohabiting partners. *In healthy relationships, fear and insecurity are revealed vulnerably and addressed by reassurance that is given, not taken.*

◆ **Limited support networks add pressure.** Unhealthy dependency develops when a person looks to only one or two people to meet all of his or her relational needs. In other words, "all the eggs are in one basket." Anxiety will show up in the emotional cup because there is no "backup." *The presence of several relationships, at work, church, etc., which involve both giving and receiving reflects healthiness.*

◆ **Dependency replaces interdependency.** A plant that is not growing is unhealthy. Adults who are incapable of making decisions or who constantly defer to the judgment of others reflect immaturity rather than wisdom. Unhealthy relationships may have one person who acts parental while the other stays childlike. *Jesus created an environment that helped His disciples grow. He gave them respect, support and guidance, and then trusted them to be responsible, offering support if needed.*

◆ **Refusal to change or consider alternatives limits growth.** In unhealthy relationships, people continue to interact in ways that have proven ineffective in the past. Rather than learn and grow together, they stay stuck. *People in healthy relationships consider the lessons of the past in order to adapt and move forward. Each person exercises personal responsibility to grow as new insights are acquired about valid needs within the relationship.*

◆ **A focus on control stifles openness and freedom.** Vulnerable communication and deep knowing cease when one or more individuals try to control the others through domination or manipulation. *Jesus modelled the proper use of authority and power by washing the feet of His disciples. He was in control, but chose to give, leaving them free to respond to his servant leadership. Contagious giving leaves little room, or need, for controlling a friendship.*

Look over this list of relational characteristics and ask yourself which ones you may have experienced personally. Write those below and describe the effect they had on the relationships you were in at the time. _____

_____

_____

_____

_____

_____

_____

_____

_____

_____

_____

_____

_____

Christians, being imperfect people, are not immune to unhealthy relationships. We have all experienced these frustrations to some degree in virtually any relationship. Let's take a look now at how we can develop or adjust relationships to experience greater satisfaction and significance.

Building Healthy Relationships

Love the Lord with all your heart and with all your soul and with all your mind and with all your strength...(and) Love your neighbor as yourself. (Mark 12:30-31)

Healthy relationships are ones that demonstrate Great Commandment love regularly. These relationships have at the core of their existence, a love for God that involves each person's entire being. They share a commitment and connection to the Creator of life! In addition, each person loves the other person as much as he loves himself. As you imagine relationships built upon these two commands, you can see why Jesus said that all Scripture hinges upon them. Relationships that live out Great Commandment love are fearless. Those that don't live it out tend to be driven by fear and attempt to control or avoid pain. The diagram that follows summarizes some characteristics of healthy and unhealthy relationships where faith or fear, respectively, is the foundation.

Healthy Vs. Unhealthy Relationships

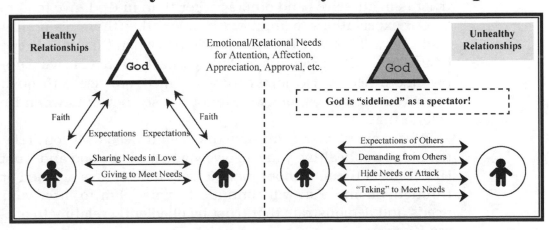

In healthy relationships, we look to God as the source of help, allowing Him to involve others in meeting our needs as He chooses. Rather than try to control or manipulate their responses to our needs, we "entrust" their maturation to God, leaving Him unhindered to accomplish His work in their lives. Healthy relationships share needs truthfully and vulnerably, rather than deny or angrily display them. A third component of healthiness is a dynamic of mutual giving to meet needs in contrast to selfish taking that is so prevalent in dysfunctional relationships. Now, let's begin a journey, learning how to incorporate Great Commandment love in relationships.

1. Place Trust in the Right Person—God (Phil. 4:19)

As you recognize that you have many needs that can only be met through relationships, you will naturally begin to look for someone you can trust to meet them. Unhealthy relationships pin the hopes and expectations for meeting all those needs on the other person. If the needs go unmet, we experience additional hurt, anger, and fear. Then, we may further compound our dilemma by trying to get what we want by nagging, demanding, criticizing, manipulating or controlling. Our choice to take matters into our own hands reveals that our trust is in ourselves and others rather than in God. We tend to tie our expectations to imperfect people rather than to a perfect God who will not give His children stones when they seek bread (Matt. 7:9). God promises in Philippians 4:19 that He will supply all our needs. He often chooses to meet our needs through other human beings, but we cannot foresee how and when He will do that.

Whom are you counting on to meet your needs? If your relationships are healthy, you will give your needs to God and trust Him to meet them, without making demands of how or when or through whom. You will continue to trust Him to meet your needs and demonstrate that trust by obediently relating to others His way.

The Focus for Your Expectations

Think of an intimacy need, such as approval, attention, or respect, which often goes unmet in your life and describe a specific example of how a significant person in your life has failed to meet this need. _____

_____

_____

_____

_____

(For example, *I was hurt when I moved to another city and my boss didn't even bother to send a card to express appreciation for my years of service.*)

Now, write down how you reacted to the need going unmet. What did you think, feel, and do?

_____

_____

_____

_____

_____

(For example, *I withdrew and got lost in a project; I retaliated by making very critical remarks to him; I began to talk behind her back to my other friends at church.)*

How did your manner of reacting reveal the person (or Person) upon whom you were depending to meet your need? _

_____

_____

_____

_____

_____

_____

_____

_____

(For example, The presence of anger rather than sadness implies that I had not released my hurt to God; my preoccupation with work when I felt disapproved suggests that I depend upon myself more than I realized; writing to my dad to let him know that I would appreciate more contact with him means that I am counting on God to touch my father's heart in due time.)

When expectations are placed in God, we continue to use His ways of relating even when our needs are going unmet in our relationships. We are better able to confront relational problems in a loving manner, or to grieve our hurts appropriately with other friends. When you expect God to meet your needs in His way and time, you can focus on how He would want you to *respond* in your relationships. You trust Him to supply your need according to His intimate knowledge of your condition. Faith, the substance of things hoped for and the evidence of things not seen, frees you to relate honestly, genuinely, and lovingly in your relationships. As you count on the Lord, the Father of compassion and the God of all comfort will sustain you.

Write out a prayer of commitment to God to trust Him to meet your relational needs in His way and in His time. It might sound something like this: *"Dear Heavenly Father, I seem to find myself needing more _____ (affection, support, etc.) from my friends, family, and co-workers. You created me with these needs and therefore, they are important. I know You are faithful and have planned an abundant life for me, so I will trust you to provide for my needs as you see fit. I commit to apply your principles for communicating my needs with love and honesty. Thank you for loving me, Lord. Amen."*

_____

_____

_____

_____

_____

_____

_____

2. Communicate Your Relational Needs Appropriately (Eph. 4:15)

Many of us send unclear messages or confusing signals to our friends when we are hurting or in need. For example, we may "say" that we are frustrated by slamming doors. We may show that we are anxious by laughing as we talk about a serious loss. We may withdraw when we feel lonely. Our friends may learn to interpret this behavior accurately, but there is more opportunity for confusion than understanding.

While we should ultimately direct our expectations toward God, a crucial first step in trusting Him is to express our needs to others clearly and openly. We have a responsibility to speak honestly and appropriately about our condition. Of course, self-disclosure of our neediness makes us vulnerable to disappointment, hurt, or even rejection. So, by communicating our needs in a loving and respectful manner, we must face our fears of being let down and reinforce our trust in God's faithfulness. God *will* be faithful to meet your needs, either through others or directly through His provision and comfort. In addition, vulnerable disclosure with friends, relatives, or associates expresses a degree of trust in them as well.

Rather than disclose the wounds we experience in our relationships, many of us respond in one of two alternative ways: hiding or hurling. We "hide" when we deny our pain instead of admitting it. We "hurl" when we lash out with anger, criticism, or sarcasm at the very people with whom we need to be close. Rather than hurling our anger at others when we are wounded or hiding the underlying pain, the Bible instructs us in Ephesians 4:15 to "speak the truth in love." If we rebuke an offending friend harshly or with vengeance, we may be speaking the truth but it is unlikely that our words are spoken in love. On the other hand, if we mask our disappointment from a hurt or loss, we are in effect, sending a false message. Restoration and intimacy are virtually impossible when we substitute hiding or hurling for honesty and respect.

Sharing Needs Vulnerably

A degree of trust is necessary for vulnerable disclosure to develop in relationships. Fear leads us to cover up our true thoughts and feelings. Think of situations that have discouraged you from being more transparent. As you reflect on these times, complete the following sentences:

"Sometimes I'm not open or vulnerable with my needs or feelings because I fear . . ." _____

_____

(For example, . . . *that my friends will laugh at me for being too sensitive; . . .that my relatives will be disappointed in my lack of achievement.)*

"I could be more vulnerable with others by sharing . . ."

_____

_____

(For example, . . . *how their actions leave me feeling excluded; . . . that I feel insecure in my job.)*

In spite of our fears, it is important to express our wants and desires honestly. Here are some examples of ways to disclose your needs more effectively.

Intimacy needs	How my friends or associates can meet the needs
to receive approval	*It means a lot to me when you say you are pleased that I am one of your trusted friends.*
to receive respect	*I really get motivated to try new ventures when you invite me to express my opinions in the staff meetings.*

to receive attention   *I feel really loved and cared for when you make time in your busy schedule to call to see how my new job is going.*

Use the spaces below to list your priority needs and how your friends can best meet them. In a way that is free from accusation or blame, state what you would like them to do.

Intimacy needs
(approval, respect, etc.)

How my friends or associates can meet the needs

1. _____   _____

2. _____   _____

3. _____   _____

Personal Application
Speaking the Truth in Love

Which are you more likely to employ when there are problems in a relationship, hiding or hurling? _____

What would we see you doing that would represent the answer you wrote above? _____
_____
_____

(For example, *I would busy myself in activities that would hide my true feelings and avoid meaningful conversation; I would become sarcastic and make critical remarks to my friend; I would become irritable around my children.*)

Think of a way that a close friend or adult relative has offended or hurt you recently. Describe that incident here: __
_____
_____
_____

Now, describe the way you reacted at the time: _____
_____
_____
_____
_____

Finally, write out a way you might "speak the truth in love" to seek healing and restoration in the relational problem: ___
_____
_____
_____
_____
_____
_____
_____
_____

(For example, *Rick, I am sure you meant well when you told me that I needed to pray more in order to feel less discouraged in my work. More than advice, however, I need understanding and compassion from you. My work is very difficult for me right now, and I feel most encouraged when people who know me express understanding and concern. Your friendship means a lot to me and that is why I wanted to share this with you.*)

3. Develop Contagious Giving in Your Relationships (Matt. 10:8)

Contagious giving is the third element in fearless friendships. Since we are created with needs that can only be met by another person or God, every human relationship can be said to include two needy people. The manner in which the two people seek to have their needs met will determine whether the relationship is healthy or not. In healthy friendships, the focus with regard to relational needs, is *giving to*, rather than *taking from*, one another.

Contagious Giving. In healthy relationships, a dynamic of mutual giving is active. Both people make conscious efforts to understand and proactively meet the relational needs of the other. Mutual giving of this type sends a powerful message to our friends and relatives that we love them in the unconditional, sacrificial manner that reflects the very nature of God. The Lord even said that others will know that we are His disciples by the manner in which we love one another (John 13:35). God's perfect love *gives* first. Selfishness, on the other hand, *takes* first.

You can give contagiously by:
◆ intentionally spending time listening to your friend to get to know him better
◆ inviting your friend to give you constructive feedback about any of your behaviors that are problematic for her
◆ surprising your relatives with unexpected phone calls, cards, or even visits
◆ reviewing all that you know about your journey-mates and asking God to impress upon you some changes that He would be wanting to bring about in you in order to bless them—then, pray with them about the changes you are asking God to build into your character

Infectious Taking. Selfish taking is also "catching," but it is not profitable. In unhealthy friendships, the satisfaction of intimacy needs is consciously or unconsciously sought through self-centered methods. We are not always consciously aware of our efforts because we learned how to do this at such a young age. Since none of us were raised by perfect parents, we are bound to have experienced unmet needs in childhood. For example, how about the first time we became hungry as infants. Our parents probably didn't figure it out until *after* we resorted to our natural need-claiming device—screaming at the top of our lungs.

As we grew older, we developed more sophisticated means for getting our needs met. We fine-tuned the "demanding" approach by learning to throw major temper tantrums, or developed the more genteel approach of "pleasing" until we got what we wanted. Some of us discovered that there was power in withdrawing our affection from those upon whom we depended, noticing that they came running when we pouted. Whatever the method, these are all ways that humans learn to take matters into their own hands to reduce the likelihood (and the fear) of needs going unmet. The three principles for fearless friendships described above provide a focus for growth in any relationship. Encourage one another to grow in these ways.

Facing Our Fear of Intimacy

Daniel was the youngest of four children and sensed early on that he had to "perform" in order to secure approval from his father. When Daniel was fourteen, he came home one evening to find his father's clothes strewn all over the porch, the result of an argument with Daniel's mom. Though neither parent had physically attacked the other, Daniel knew that their relationship was in serious trouble. His fears became reality, when one year later, his parents split up. As before, there was no guidance or comfort extended by either parent, and he began to seek help elsewhere. He sought comfort in drugs and alcohol. But even these proved inadequate when, only a short time later, two of his closest friends committed suicide. Again, he faced these losses alone, without comfort or healing. Daniel was beginning to learn, at a very young age, that getting close to people exposed him to a lot of emotional pain. He began to stop investing in relationships and became a loner instead.

Then, Daniel met Lisa. She was really cute and showed a lot of interest in him. He let his "walls" down and spent a lot of time with her during the next eighteen months. He felt secure in his relationship with Lisa and began to feel confident that his decision to invest again was a good one. Then, tragically, Lisa suffered severe brain damage in an accident and was not aware of Daniel's significance to her anymore. His world was once again in turmoil. The loss of his relationship with Lisa was excruciating. He seemed destined for further withdrawal and isolation.

But, there was a difference this time. He went to live with his grandparents who helped Daniel grieve the loss and provide comfort to him. They hurt with him and for him. He had never experienced someone bearing a portion of his pain before. This time, he did not feel alone in his pain. Through this experience, he began to invest in relationships again even though they brought pain at times. He learned that the rewards of the relationship could be enjoyed and the painful times could be endured and healed. His fear of intimacy began to subside. Daniel's grandparents had exercised perfect love that eventually "cast out" his fear as promised in I John 4:18. Daniel no longer needed to emotionally distance himself from others.

Yesterday's pain prompts today's fear about tomorrow. When hurtful experiences in relationships go unresolved, painful feelings are added to your emotional cup, and fear can grow like an emotional malignancy. The more such feelings are ignored or "stuffed," the more pain accumulates and the greater the likelihood that fear will inhibit subsequent efforts to be emotionally close with others. Thus, painful experiences from past relationships may be robbing you of godly intimacy in the present. But, this *robbery* may have gone unnoticed because the *thief* slipped into your mind so long ago, he became a part of you. The thief is fear, and fear of rejection, abandonment, neglect, control, guilt, shame, or abuse may be stealing the joy and peace available to you now.

Fear is produced as our minds alert us that we may experience similar hurts in subsequent relationships. Your mental "radar" alerts you to changes or threats in your environment, such as a car suddenly swerving into your path. This early warning system uses past experience to predict impending danger and helps you to respond automatically and immediately. But, in trust-based relationships, intimacy is forfeited when we rely only upon an automated protective system. In such cases, intimacy gets sacrificed on the altar of self-preservation.

Wouldn't it be tragic if our own actions and reactions undermined opportunities for free and intimate fellowship with others? Could it be that you are sabotaging your own desire to have healthy, satisfying, godly relationships? The challenge, then, is to learn how to relate to God and to others so that His perfect love can be employed to displace our fear. Otherwise, you can remain bound up instead of being free to express and receive God's love.

Like Daniel, you may have become a slave to such fear without knowing it. In a stern passage warning about false teachers whose depravity was controlling their teaching, the Apostle Peter said that, "a man is a slave to whatever has mastered him," (II Peter 2:19). For many of us, the "slave master" in our relationships is fear. Let's take a moment to examine your relationship history to see if you have experienced some emotional enslavement.

Personal Application
Evidence of
Emotional Enslavement

How would you know if your relationships are controlled or mastered by fear? One way is to survey some typical symptoms of fear-driven relationships. Look over the following list and put a check next to any of the items that seem characteristic for you.

_____ Failing to recognize or acknowledge your feelings of anger, hurt, or fear

_____ Sensing a chronic presence of anger, shame, emptiness, sadness, or guilt

_____ Endlessly asking, "Why?" someone does what he/she does

_____ Allowing a return to a clearly dysfunctional pattern of relating

_____ Taking responsibility for the actions or irresponsibility of another

_____ "Rescuing" others from consequences and pain of their irresponsibility

_____ Controlling, parenting, lecturing, or nagging other adults

_____ Seeking approval by trying to please others or *make* them happy

____ Depending only upon romantic relationships for emotional support

____ Suppressing feelings to avoid the reactions of another person

____ Losing your own sense of identity while devoting yourself to another

____ Failing to say "no" to conduct that violates your own conscience

____ Experiencing intense pain, fear, or hurt when being neglected

____ Feeling a sense of helplessness or powerlessness in relationships

____ Overconforming to the preferences of others

____ Telling others what *they* think or feel

____ Performing inordinate amounts of people-pleasing behaviors

Describe the feelings you have right now as you contemplate your survey of these symptoms. _____

_____

_____

How might the tendencies that you checked be rooted in your childhood experiences? _____

_____

_____

_____

With a close friend or fellowship group, share the characteristics you identified in yourself, inviting feedback about times and ways they may have witnessed these characteristics in you.

Responses to Fear

Fear is crippling to intimacy, whether we respond to it by avoiding or controlling. We do not have to be defeated by fear as adults, however. Let's take a closer look at ineffective ways for coping with our fear of intimacy. Two common types of fear associated with relationships are: (1) *fear of closeness* that might limit our freedom or dignity; and, (2) *fear of abandonment* that we might be left alone and insecure. Such fears will usually manifest themselves in one of the following responses— *trying to control* relationships or *avoiding* intimacy altogether.

1. Trying to Control Intimacy

David and Janice met while enrolled in the same graduate school. The majority of their classmates were married or had families to return to each night. As single adults, David and Janice returned to empty apartments, and before long, began to see each other for friendship and support. Though as different as two people can be, they enjoyed the fellowship and encouraged each other in their studies.

As their involvement intensified, the tension between them did also. Each was dissatisfied about the apparent inability of the other to meet emotional needs. David often complained that Janice gave him little respect, and she countered that he never had time for her. She disliked his cavalier attitude about commitment, and he was unhappy about her hesitancy to express affection. They became harmfully dependent on one another, inadvertently "taking" what they wanted by making demands or manipulating with guilt.

At one point, Janice gave in to David's pressure for her to engage in sexual activity with him, even though that was inconsistent with her values. At other times, Janice would use the promise of affection to manipulate David to neglect his studies in order to spend more time with her. The relationship became more and more "stuck" until a third party entered the picture and a "rescue" was effected.

Three characteristics of an unhealthy relationship were reflected in the story of Janice and David—"taking" to get needs met, problems setting and maintaining boundaries or convictions, and an unhealthy dependency. In direct or indirect ways, both David and Janice tried to control the status of the relationship rather than deal honestly and freely with each other. A healthier dynamic would have seen them inviting involvement, but not trying to manipulate or control it.

Reflect on your own past relationships and answer the following questions.

In what ways have I selfishly "taken" in my relationships?

_____
_____
_____
_____

(For example, *I let my roommates do my share of the work, I jealously insist that our group do everything together, I put guilt trips on my girlfriend if she doesn't show me enough attention.*)

In what ways do I have trouble setting boundaries in personal, work, or family relationships?

_____
_____
_____
_____

(For example, *I enable irresponsibility in my office mates by covering their mistakes, I let others talk me out of my standards and disciplines, etc.*)

What am I afraid will happen/not happen if I stand my ground and maintain my boundaries?

_____
_____
_____
_____

(For example, *the other person would leave the relationship or become critical or distant.*)

In what ways have some of my past relationships been "stuck" or unhealthy? _____

_____

_____

_____

(For example, *one person was always nagging and complaining while another was avoidant.*)

How have painful events in past relationships affected my ability to experience emotional intimacy in the present? _____

_____

_____

_____

(For example, *I constantly tried to gain approval from my father by achieving, and now I am so caught up in my career that I frustrate my closest companions who desire time with me.*)

2. Trying to Avoid Intimacy

Now, let's look at an example where painful experiences in the past led to fear that prompted an individual to be guarded in later relationships. This story also reveals how God can use other people to heal the hurts and dispel the fears caused by previous relationships.

Cheryl and Mary had been college roommates for the past two years. One morning they were awakened by the telephone ringing. Mary answered and before long, it became apparent to Cheryl that Mary's mother had suffered a severe heart attack and had been taken to the hospital. Cheryl came to Mary's side to comfort her as she continued to talk to her father. As Cheryl put her arm around Mary's shoulder, she felt Mary pull back, as if her comfort was unwelcome. Later, as they drove together to visit Mary's mother in the hospital, they talked about Mary's reaction. "I guess it goes back to my childhood. If I was upset about something and went to my father, he would usually tell me to go talk to my mom about it. But back then, she and I were not real close. At that time, she was not very nurturing. I knew that if I went to her, I would be criticized or shamed instead of consoled or encouraged. So, I learned to just tough things out on my own. So when you offered comfort this morning, I had trouble receiving it. I automatically stiffened as if a warning flag had been raised in the back of my mind."

In order to endure hurt and emotional abandonment in her childhood, Mary had employed self-reliance and a rock-hard determination to survive on her own. But that self-reliant manner almost cost her the comfort of a friend. Like Mary, you may be automatically erecting barriers to relational intimacy. To begin to change that tendency, recognize the presence of threatening feelings, examine the thoughts associated with the feelings, and make conscious choices about how to respond. Otherwise, your interaction with others will be driven by the underlying fear, insecurity, or anxiety. Use the following exercise to begin to address unhealed hurts from the past. If you have a friend, journey-mate, or small group available, share these hurts with them, allowing God's perfect love to help cast out your fear of intimacy that grew out of those hurts.

Think of two or three specific hurtful experiences from relationships with relatives or very close friends which were never resolved. Describe them here. _____
_____
_____
_____
_____
_____
_____
_____
_____
_____

(For example, *a broken engagement, betrayal of confidentiality, marital infidelity, repeatedly shown little respect for your time or possessions, given little attention or approval, etc.*)

What did you do in response to these painful experiences?

_____
_____
_____
_____
_____
_____
_____
_____
_____

(For example, I withdrew, became more tentative about getting close to others, attacked my friend/relative's character, escaped into work or pleasure, etc.)

What did your friend/relative do in response to the experiences? _____

_____
_____
_____
_____

How and from whom did you receive comfort and support?

_____
_____
_____
_____

Creating distance between yourself and others may protect you from potential pain, but it will also isolate you from the potential joy of healthy intimacy. The same walls you build to keep others out will also box you in. A pattern of distancing behavior can lead to "sabotaged" relationships, callous hearts, and little, if any, meaningful intimacy. Distancing in relationships is not always as obvious as staying at home by yourself. You can distance by keeping relationships superficial, not sharing much of yourself. Or, you can be critical or negative around others, in essence, pushing them away from you. Regardless of how it is done, distancing limits the opportunities you have to experience the joy of healthy relationships.

Daniel had kept others at "arm's length" to protect himself from additional rejection and abandonment. He "sabotaged" some existing relationships in order to control the pain of being abandoned. Freedom from such pain and reconciliation of damaged relationships are possible. Both require healing of the original hurts and developing new ways of relating in the present.

As children, we had little control over our relationships. But, as adults, we have the power to initiate or terminate a relationship. As we have seen, some relationships that are not healthy need to be changed or ended. Choosing to work on change may mean facing the fear and possibly some of the pain from our past. Knowing and being known by another is deeply rewarding, but can be frightening in an imperfect world full of imperfect people. That is why we need a perfect God with perfect love who understands us and our needs perfectly.

Displacing Fear Among Friends

Jesus said that He had come that we might have life, and have it abundantly (John 10:10). But in that same verse, He warned that the Evil One would try to steal, kill, and destroy what He wanted to give us. Why would God set us free from our sin and restore a relationship with Him? Could it be that He frees us from sin so that we might be free to love Him and the others that He places in our sphere of influence?

In our work of caregiving, counseling, and mentoring, it is not unusual to see fear develop even as people begin to experience increased intimacy in their relationships. As people learn to become more understanding of one another and more vulnerable with their feelings, they also become more aware of their exposure to relational pain. Satan seems to capitalize on this vulnerability, undermining the progress by paralyzing the positive changes that are being made.

Drew, my (Bruce's) 15-year old son, was returning to school this year with some considerable apprehension normal for his age. He feared rejection by his peers and typically would avoid gatherings that had any potential for embarrassment. At the start of the school year, some parents invited all of his class-mates over for a get-acquainted party. As the evening approached, Drew began to come up with all types of excuses for not going. Even as we headed to the party in the car, he com-plained that he shouldn't be made to attend. Though I wanted to encourage him to go, I decided it had to be his decision if he was to genuinely face his fear. So, I calmly turned the car around and headed home, assuring him that the decision was not being forced on him. As we turned onto our street, Drew declared that he had decided he would go after all. He was not enthusiastic, but he was deciding to face his fear, hoping that it would work out alright. God was faithful exceedingly abun-dantly. Not only did he have a good time, he was voted "most gentlemanly" among his peers by the girls in the class. In this case, God's perfect love meant for me to not try to control Drew's fear, but to listen attentively to his complaints and encourage him to face his fear without coercion.

The Scripture says that fear must be *displaced by perfect love* (I John 4:18). Fear cannot be eradicated by acting like it isn't there. It cannot be eliminated through bravado—wearing a macho mask hoping that the fear will be fooled into subsid-ing. No, fear must be acknowledged as present and respected as a serious problem for anyone who feels it. Then, faithful care must be offered and trusted so that the fear can be dis-pelled. Let's look at a few principles for learning to dispel one another's fears as we experience I John 4:18 together.

1. Perfect love lives in the present.

Abundant life is always experienced in the present. When God has blessed you in the past, you experienced the blessing in the present moment. As children of God, we will be blessed one day with the glorious richness of heaven. But, when we actually experience heaven, we will be doing so in the present. The *hope* of heaven is a blessing we are experiencing now—in the present moment.

Satan will often try to rob us of our present-day blessings by tricking us into living in the past or in the future. Just as we must empty our emotional cups of anger, resentment, and guilt from the past through confession and forgiveness, we must keep them keep them free of fear, anxiety, and worry by living in the present as we practice God's perfect love for Him and one another. This means I will focus more on what's going on inside of me at any moment (thoughts, feelings, and attitudes) and respond to it in ways that God endorses as consistent with His Great Commandment love. Thus, I will minimize my efforts to control or avoid the future and live for the moment.

2. Perfect love gives first.

Do nothing out of selfish ambition or vain conceit, but in humility consider others better than yourselves. Each of you should look not only to your own interests, but also to the interests of others. (Phil. 2:3-4)

In relationships with others, it is beneficial to live out Philippians 2:3-4. When we wait on the other person to begin to initiate needs-meeting, we increase the likelihood that fear will take root and block the development of godly relationships. On the other hand, when we trust that God will bless us as He deems fit, we are free to demonstrate His love for others in a way that is unconditional. Then, intimacy is developed, both people are blessed, and God gets the glory. Now, that's a good deal!

3. Perfect love reflects mutual submission as God's sanctifying work is completed in us.

God is at work in each of His children to bring about the changes He desires (Phil. 1:6). He has made it clear that we are to be submissive and respectful to our brothers and sisters in Christ (Eph. 5:21; Rom. 12:10). One of the most powerful ways that we can be used of God to dispel some of the fear in each other is through praying that God will reveal ways that He would have each of us change *in order to dispel some of the fear that exists in our friend.* We call this "perfect love praying." Here is an example of how this would work.

While growing up, Darrell was often sent disapproving looks by his mother. Since he was a very sensitive kid who needed lots of acceptance, he felt a lot of pressure whenever he saw those frowns. He didn't work best under that type of pressure, either. So Darrell often found that the harder he tried to please his mother, the more he seemed to perform poorly, prompt more disapproving glances, increase the pressure he felt, recommit to try even harder to please, etc., etc., etc. When Jim first heard about Darrell's background, he felt terrible because he realized that he had added to his friend's feeelings of disapproval and condemnation. For example, if Jim found Darrell's clothes lying around the apartment they shared, he would "stew" rather than address the issue constructively. Tension developed that never got discussed, being "swept under the rug," instead. One day, Jim took the initiative to apologize to Darrell for his insensitivity. Then, in his presence, Jim prayed that God would help him change his tendency to send negative messages without confronting issues with Darrell in a non-threatening, problem-solving manner. Darrell was struck by Jim's transparency, initiative, and caring concern for him.

Perfect Love Praying

Write out below an issue that you think contributes to fear or insecurity in the life of a friend or relative. Ask God to impress upon you any aspects of your attitudes or behaviors that might have contributed to your friend's stress. (For example, *I leave my roommate anxious about her finances when I threaten to move out over relatively minor disagreements.*) Write down the changes that God would want you to begin making and plan a time to meet with your friend to share your intentions. Pray with him or her that God would, in fact, bring about these changes as you remain humble before Him.

Friend's/relative's issue of fear or insecurity: _____

_____

_____

Behavior/attitudes of mine that contribute to that fear or insecurity: _____

_____

_____

_____

As I reflect on some of my important relationships, I think that God might want me to become more and/or less _____ in order to remove some of the fear or insecurity felt by some of my friends, relatives, or associates.

More: _____   Less: _____

More: _____   Less: _____

More: _____   Less: _____

(For example, *God might want me to become more patient and less irritable when people ask me for help at the office so they wouldn't quit seeking my support when they really need it.*)

Whether we are consciously aware of it or not, our behavior in relationships is often driven by fear. As fear begins to command the minds of individuals, the risk of emotional pain begins to overshadow the potential rewards of intimacy. Underneath every fear is a lie, and people begin to believe the lie that the costs of a relationship outweigh the benefits. Once this lie is believed and acted upon, the relationship loses momentum and may eventually be terminated unless there is some type of intervention. If we become more aware of the lies at the heart of our fears, we are more likely to bring fearful thoughts "captive to Christ" (II Cor. 10:5), renew our minds (Rom. 12:2), and replace old relational patterns with new ones that God endorses (Eph. 4:22-25). The next chapter will help you eliminate other obstacles to healthy, God-honoring relationships.

The Perfect Love of Christ"
John 18:12-27 (focal passage: John 18:15-18, 25-27)

I (Bruce) remember a time when I was faced with fear and guilt at the same time. A friend and I were exploring a creek that ran just outside my home town when we came upon some large, partially-submerged glass jugs used to trap minnows. With youthful enthusiasm, we attacked those jugs with every rock we could find. Within minutes they were "history." But just then, we heard a jeep approaching. Sure enough, it was the fellow who set the traps. Duane and I ran as fast as we could through the prairie grass until we were safely out of the area. We had escaped unrecognized, but I knew what we had done was wrong. Much worse, I knew that I did not want my father to know that I had violated his trust by destroying someone else's property. I returned to my father's feed store out of breath, sweating, afraid, and more than anything, ashamed. Though normally an honest, responsible child, I never did confess that wrongful act to my dad. I think I was afraid he would never look at me the same again.

Simon Peter is a disciple we would not typically associate with fear. Most see boldness and aggressiveness reflected in his character. But, on the night before Christ was crucified, Peter went from sword-swinging aggressor to lying fugitive. As He hid in the shadows of the courtyard picking up pieces of the conversations about Jesus who had just been arrested, Peter must have felt a multitude of emotions. Perhaps he felt fear for his life, shame for hiding his identity, and grief for failing to stand up for his Lord. I can imagine He wondered if Jesus would look upon Him differently, too. Can you understand his dilemma? Have you ever been there?

◆ Read the passage and describe in your own words what you think Peter was experiencing on the inside._____

_____

_____

_____

_____

_____

_____

_____

◆ Now, look at Mark 16:7 where special note is made for the women at the tomb to tell Peter that the Lord is risen. Read John 21:15-23, where Jesus reinstates His relationship with Simon Peter. Could it be that Jesus knew of the inner pain that Peter must have felt for having denied the Lord? Respond here with your own thoughts about a Lord who loves us even when we have let Him down. _____

_____

_____

_____

_____

_____

_____

_____

_____

> *Nothing can separate us from the love of God. The knowledge of His presence alleviates our fear.*

Group Dialogue

If you do not have a designated group leader, choose some-one in the group who will serve to facilitate the discussion. Begin by briefly reviewing the discussion guidelines.

Discussion Guidelines

- Allow everyone an opportu-nity to share thoughts and feelings
- Avoid long story telling
- Be quick to listen with empathy

- Be slow to give advice
- Speak the truth in love
- Say what you mean and mean what you say
- Protect the confidentiality of every person

Discussion Suggestions for Chapter Four

1. Using the listing at the beginning of the chapter, take turns sharing one unhealthy or healthy characteristic that you have experienced in your adult relationships.

2. Take turns sharing one need you listed on page 97 that often goes unmet and how you wish others would minister to that need.

3. Share some reasons that it is difficult to share your needs honestly and vulnerably with others.

4. Discuss the symptoms of emotional enslavement listed on pages 106-107. Let volunteers identify specific symptoms they have experienced and how they feel as they reflect on these.

5. Share whether or not you tend to manifest your fear of intimacy by controlling or avoiding. Describe how you tend to "hide" or "hurl" rather than speak the truth in love.

6. Go around the group sharing ways that you have experienced emotional intimacy within your *Discovering Intimacy* group. Affirm people for ways they have already met the priority needs each person recorded on page 37. Share specific ways the group can continue to meet each person's relational needs.

7. Ask a volunteer to pray for all group members, especially for increased faith to trust God to meet their relational needs in His way and in His time.

Journey-mate Encounters

◆ Set aside one to two hours for the meeting to give ample time for each person to share.

◆ Select a meeting location that minimizes distractions or interruptions.

◆ Read the chapter and complete all the written exercises *before* meeting to discuss them.

◆ Purpose to start on time and complete each exercise, staying focused on the material.

Suggestions for Journey-mate Encounter #4

1. Share some of the fears that you have felt in close personal relationships. Share the ways these fears were most often manifested. Tell your journey-mate(s) what he or she could say or do to help to displace those fears in present-day relationships.

2. Talk with each other about how you may struggle at times to leave the *outcomes* of your relationship struggles up to God.

3. Take turns praying "perfect love prayers" for each other, referring to your answers to the questions on page 117. There you would have recorded some changes that you have discerned God wanting to bring about in you in order to better meet your journey-mate's needs and dispel fear that he or she may have. Discuss your feelings after each of you has prayed.

Dear God, knowing what I now know about my friend's fears or insecurities, help me to become more _____ and/or less _____ in order to be used to help dispel a portion of the fear that he/she lives with at times.

Hiding the Word in Your Heart
II Timothy 1:7

Write the verse here: _____

_____

_____

_____

_____

_____

_____

_____

_____

_____

Repeat the verse from memory each day for several weeks. Using the space below, you may want to journal ways that God has allowed you to experience the verse as you have hidden it away in your heart. _____

_____

_____

_____

_____

_____

_____

_____

_____

_____

_____

_____

_____

_____

_____

_____

Check the box at the right when you have committed the verse to memory. Continue to repeat the verse daily for at least three weeks.

Chapter Five

—— ◆ ——

REMOVING ROADBLOCKS
Transforming Unhealthy Relational Patterns

"Do not conform any longer to the patterns of this world, but be transformed by the renewing of your mind." Romans 12:2

Eric and Gwen had been dating for more than a year now. They were both sports enthusiasts who enjoyed many activities together. But Eric's fiery temper, equipped with a very short fuse, often interrupted their fun. Sometimes he would berate himself, spewing critical, derogatory words at himself for missing a single shot while playing basketball. Even when Eric held his anger in, Gwen would become nervous as she sensed its presence. It was as if there was an emotional umbilical cord connecting them. Without thinking or hesitating, she would go out of her way to try to lift Eric's spirits, praising him for his many positive attributes. To her dismay, Eric ignored such comments. His self-condemnation would continue. But no matter what it took, Gwen was bound and determined to keep these conflicts under control. Often, that meant ignoring her own discouragement about their relationship so that she could stay focused on Eric's unhappiness. No matter what she did to please and praise Eric, it was not enough. Out of frustration, Gwen had decided to end the relationship several times but kept hanging on for some unknown reason. Now, she was scared about their future. She certainly did not feel free.

The anecdote about Gwen and Eric depicts a pattern of unhealthy interaction. Their ways of responding to one another include control, manipulation, and avoidance, evidently fed by distorted thinking. These unproductive behaviors are symptoms of underlying, unresolved hurt, pain, and fear that is filling their emotional cups. What may not be so obvious is that these symptoms are present-day reflections of relational pain that existed long before Gwen and Eric knew each other. In order for their relationship to become more healthy, they will need to see themselves from God's perspective, be willing to face some of their underlying pain and fear, and allow God to help them change so that they are able to love one another better.

Let's examine the link between unmet relational needs from the past and the relational patterns of the present. The goal of this examination is to put each of us in better position to make the changes necessary to experience deeper relationships and to love one another better.

The Potential and Pain of Intimacy Needs

An important step toward resolving our relational struggles in the present is to understand our experiences of the past. As our intimacy needs were met in childhood, we felt loved and cared for, and experienced an overflow of love and gratitude that enabled us to freely give love to others. That is God's relational design working as it is supposed to work. But in the hands of sin-riddled humanity, His design and plan were often discarded or ignored. Whenever our relational needs went unmet, pain resulted. We began to rely on self-reliance, self-condemnation, and self-centeredness to try to get our needs met—imperfect responses to environments that failed us.

Most relational struggles from our childhood get "replayed" in some manner in our adult relationships. Often, however, we are not even aware of this phenomenon. Unhealed hurt and unresolved fear will continue to surface in our adult relationships unless we understand and address them God's way. Unless the Lord has finished your sanctification process, you have some relational "stuff" to work on as an adult that has its origins in your childhood developmental experiences. The question each of us should be asking is, "*How much* of this "stuff" is active in me at any given point in time, and am I responding to it well?" Regardless of how it got in us, as adults we are responsible for what we do with our "stuff" today.

Now, let's take a look at the potential and pain of intimacy needs in childhood—a contrast between being blessed through the consistent meeting of our needs or being hurt by having these needs go unmet time after time. We'll see a definite connection between our needs, our way of thinking, our feelings, our behavior, and our expectations. We'll see how each of these is shaped.

Allen enjoyed painting pictures the first time he was handed a brush at vacation Bible school. His father had been gone many of Allen's pre-school years serving on a submarine in the Atlantic. Once, when Allen was six, his dad was home on leave and Allen was painting in the kitchen. He painted a rainbow using every color he could find. As soon as he finished, he excitedly carried his masterpiece into the living room where his father was reading the newspaper. "Look, Dad. See what I did." His father never looked up from the paper, muttering only, "I'm busy Son, go show your mother." Dejected, Allen returned to the kitchen and quietly put his paints back in their box and put the paper rainbow in the waste basket.

What underlying intimacy *need* do you think Allen was expressing in this scenario? (see page 38) Write it here: _____
_____

What do you suppose Allen was *thinking* as he saw the lack of interest by his father? _____
_____

What might Allen be *feeling* at this point? (see page 59) _____
_____

How might he *behave* after this experience? _____
_____

If this type of interaction occurred repeatedly during Allen's childhood, what do you think he might come to *expect* in relationships with others close to him? _____

_____

As children, we are like sponges as we develop an understanding of ourselves and others. We soak up whatever is occurring to and around us, interpreting it from a child's perspective. We are born with needs that require positive human responses. We don't outgrow our need for food or sleep, nor do we outgrow our need for attention or affection. If those relational needs go unmet most of the time, we will conclude negative things about ourselves, experience hurtful emotions, turn to coping behaviors that will be largely unproductive, and develop deeply-rooted unhealthy perspectives about ourselves and others with whom we are related. Barring some form of effective intervention, we will probably enter adulthood with these distorted perceptions of self and others largely intact, replaying and reinforcing these patterns and perceptions over and over again. The way this conditioning process works is shown below using the example of Allen.

Allen's need for attention/approval goes unmet (e.g., Dad *ignores drawing)*

      ↘

    His thinking is affected (e.g., *I'm not very important)*

      ↘

      His feelings are evoked (e.g., *hurt, rejection, unimportant)*

        ↘

        His behavior is influenced (e.g., *quits trying)*

          ↘

          A pattern is reinforced (e.g., *complacency)*

Imagine this cycle being repeated hundreds, or even thousands of times in childhood. Imagine the impact of this cycle on a child's self-concept and expectations of others in relationships.

Repeated frequently, this process can lead to deeply rooted:

◆ **Core beliefs** *(about one's self)*

◆ **Expectations for relationships** *(about others)*

The Bible says in Proverbs 23:7, "For as he thinks within himself, so he is" (NASB). If your childhood conditioning left you with some distorted perceptions and unreasonable expectations of yourself or others, now may be the time to make them more accurate and objective. No matter how deeply rooted and distorted the pictures, change is always possible for an almighty God. "Do not conform any longer to the patterns of this world, but be transformed by the renewing of your mind," (Rom. 12:2). The patterns can be reversed and the joy of relational intimacy secured.

Allen is now working in Toledo as a commercial artist. He's been dating Barbara, a medical student, for a little over a year. Though serious about each other, they have decided to wait until Barbara gets out of school to marry. Lately, she has been especially busy with her school and helping her widowed mother. It's been several weeks since they have gone out together. Allen drops by to see if Barbara wants to get some ice cream together. She begs off, pleading that he understand. Allen acknowledges his disappointment and, without pouting, turns to go back home. Barbara reaches out, touches his arm, and looks him in the eye. She lovingly states, "Allen, I appreciate your patience and understanding. But, it is not right for me to put you in second place so much of the time. I care about you and can see that you have been feeling neglected. I feel sorrow for the hurt you have experienced. Though I can't change my plans for tonight, I will clear my schedule this Friday if you would be available to do something then."

What will Allen think due to Barbara's response? (For example, *"She cares about me and considers me an important part of her life. She really wants to spend time with me."*) _____

_____

What might Allen be feeling now? (For example, *loved, cared for, significant.*) _____

_____

How might Allen's behavior be influenced by this interaction? (For example, *he might go home and focus energetically on some tasks rather than dejectedly killing time watching TV.*) _____

_____

_____

_____

How might Barbara's response and follow-through impact Allen's self-concept and future relationship with her? (For example, *he will regard her busyness as a characteristic of hers, rather than a reflection of himself, and he will remain open to disclose his feelings without demanding performance from her.*)

_____

_____

_____

_____

The underlying motivation for what we think, feel, and do is rooted in our inherent need for intimacy with God and others. Therefore, the way that others respond to our relational needs molds and shapes our self-concept and our expectations about relationships. An overall pattern of having our needs met encourages healthy thinking, positive feelings, and productive behaviors and lifestyles. When relational needs go unmet for extended periods of time, distorted thinking, painful emotions, destructive behaviors and lifestyles are likely to result. The chart on the next page summarizes the impact of relationships that actively work to meet needs and those that don't.

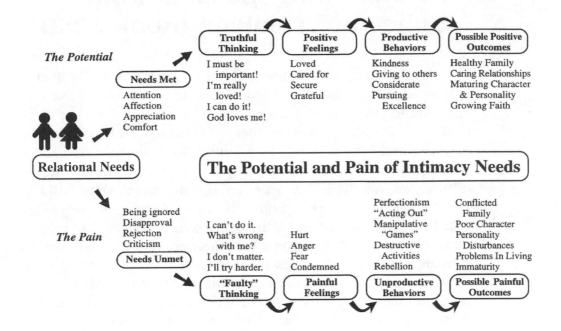

The Potential

Needs Met
Attention
Affection
Appreciation
Comfort

Relational Needs

The Pain

Being ignored
Disapproval
Rejection
Criticism

Needs Unmet

Truthful Thinking
I must be important!
I'm really loved!
I can do it!
God loves me!

Positive Feelings
Loved
Cared for
Secure
Grateful

Productive Behaviors
Kindness
Giving to others
Considerate
Pursuing Excellence

Possible Positive Outcomes
Healthy Family
Caring Relationships
Maturing Character & Personality
Growing Faith

The Potential and Pain of Intimacy Needs

I can't do it.
What's wrong with me?
I don't matter.
I'll try harder.

Hurt
Anger
Fear
Condemned

Perfectionism
"Acting Out"
Manipulative "Games"
Destructive Activities
Rebellion

Conflicted Family
Poor Character
Personality Disturbances
Problems In Living
Immaturity

"Faulty" Thinking

Painful Feelings

Unproductive Behaviors

Possible Painful Outcomes

Implications for Childhood

Personality development is intense during the first six years of life as a child experiences the complex maze of physical, social, emotional, intellectual, and spiritual needs that are normal for human beings created in the image of God.

Unmet needs are inevitable as imperfect children grow up in imperfect families in an imperfect world. We have all been "under-nourished" in some areas of need. **Healthy** families address the hurt of unmet needs as they inevitably occur; **dysfunctional** families deny the hurts, ignore the needs, and/or shame the child for being needy!

Children don't comprehend their needs, so it is essential for parents to understand these needs, validate their importance, and focus on giving to meet each child's needs.

Implications for Adult Relationships

Unmet childhood needs "follow" us into adulthood. Without realizing it, we often enter adult relationships expecting to receive the acceptance we missed, the affection we longed for, or the attention we desired but did not get in childhood.

Great hurt is experienced when needs that went unmet in childhood remain unmet in our adult relation-ships. Sadly, many receive the opposite of what is needed—rejection when they longed for acceptance, coldness rather than affection, or neglect instead of attention.

Great love is felt when needs that went unmet in childhood are fulfilled in our adult relationships. Spiritually healthy adults work to understand the relational needs of others and consistently give to meet such needs.

Implications for Parenting

Unmet needs underlie a great deal of a child's acting out behavior. For example, lack of attention might evoke anger and missing out on approval and acceptance might prompt withdrawal. Successful parents address inappropriate behaviors as well as explore unmet needs. In the parent, this requires awareness of one's own needs, openness about feelings and a healthy self-image.

Need frustration is seen as a factor that contributes to living difficulties (labeled "pathology" by many). Unmet needs contribute to lack of identity, low self-worth, insecurity, discouragement, self-defeating attitudes and behaviors, loneliness, and abusive or addictive patterns harmful to oneself and others.

Renewing the Mind from Unhealthy Thinking (Rom. 12:2)

As children, we all developed a belief system about our-selves, about others, and about life. Our beliefs were based on the interactional messages we received in our families and from society.   People conveyed these messages through words, actions, and by example. In a sense, we tape-recorded these messages and stored them in our belief system. Now, as adults, we live them out, whether the messages were valid or not in the first place. Some of those messages were very painful, involving faulty values, impossible goals, unrealistic expectations, denial of one's significance, or even violation of our dignity. Most families have no intention of hurting their children, but in spite of their good intentions and motives, their methods may have missed the mark. Here are some common messages young people hear that wound the soul:

> *You're stupid. . . . Don't cry or I'll really give you some-thing to cry about. . . . Act your age. . . . Never quit under any circumstances. . . . Be serious. . . . You'll never amount to anything. . . . Win at any cost. . . . If you're going to cry, go to your room. . . . Don't get too close to anyone. . . . Don't trust anyone. . . . No matter what you do, it's not good enough. . . . Shut your mouth*

When children hear messages like these repeatedly, nega-tive perceptions get internalized. Their identities get formed with these statements in mind. These deeply rooted beliefs can carry over into adulthood. Instead of accusation and error, truth should be repeated and reinforced in the context of a car-ing relationship. Statements like these, particularly when they are conveyed in critical or derogatory tones, are not consistent with scripture. No one is justified in making them. Ephesians 4:29 states:

Do not let any unwholesome talk come out of your mouths, but only what is helpful for building others up according to their needs, that it may benefit those who listen.

Childhood labels such as "lazy," "stupid," or "ugly," can become self-fulfilling prophecies, serving as scripts which people may continue to "perform" as adults. What can we do to eradicate such messages from our minds? How can we help others who struggle with mental pictures of themselves that devalue those whom Christ paid such a high price to save? For unless these deeply rooted distortions are countermanded by truth that is reinforced in meaningful relationships, they will continue to steal joy in the present.

Personal Application
Correcting Distorted Images

As you think back on your childhood, write down any hurtful names, labels, or messages you heard from certain peers, authority figures, or caretakers that may have given you a distorted or negative image of yourself. Below each one, write a more accurate and loving comment.

_____
_____
_____
_____
_____

There are several steps we can take to replace unhealthy thinking patterns with God's truth.

1. Identify Unhealthy Thinking or Self-Talk.
Inappropriate messages often become strongholds that Satan uses to negate the worth bestowed on us through Christ. Proverbs 23:7 states, *"For as he thinks within himself, so he is"* *(NASB)*. The first step for counteracting faulty thinking is to

monitor what you are saying to yourself. Begin to track your self-talk by maintaining a journal of your thoughts, feelings, and attitudes. This can become a part of your daily time of prayer and Bible reading, as you let the Word of Christ reveal ways that your thoughts are inconsistent with God's truth about you.

2. Dispute Faulty Thinking. God did not leave us without instruction for dealing with damaging accusations and distortions of truth that have become ingrained in our minds. The apostle Paul wrote, *"We demolish arguments and every pretension that sets itself up against the knowledge of God, and we take captive every thought to make it obedient to Christ" (II Cor. 10:5).* The second step for renewal is to examine the thoughts and messages that are being played on the tape recorder of our minds in the light of God's Word. The truth of God must be declared when inconsistencies are found between what He says and what our thoughts say. Declare the truth even when your feelings don't match up immediately. *"Whatever is true . . . think about such things." (Phil. 4:8)*

3. Practice New Responses in Relationships. The truth that sets us free (John 8:32) is made real as we live it out in our relationships. We need to *experience* God's truth in our relationships rather than merely give intellectual assent to it. We realize the blessings of God as we put what He says into practice. James 1:25 states, *"But the man who looks intently into the perfect law that gives freedom, and continues to do this, not forgetting what he has heard, but doing it—he will be blessed in what he does."* Our renewed thinking must be manifested in our behavior in order for the transformation to be complete. Our old programming, reinforced hundreds of times in childhood, is extinguished as the truth is practiced over and over in the present.

Faulty Thinking Patterns

Unhealthy thinking *patterns* can result from experiencing years of distorted messages about life, others, and who you are. Six faulty thinking patterns that could affect anyone are listed here.

Personalizing—regarding life events as personal attacks or rejections. A "personalizer" thinks that everything that happens is about himself. Assuming that most life events are personal attacks or rejections creates unnecessary stress for ourselves and others. For example, if a woman cuts in front of you on the freeway, it doesn't automatically mean she is intentionally trying to ruin your day. It is much more likely that she is late and doesn't have the same driving standards that you do. You may have to react quickly to avoid injury, but you can do so without the stress of feeling personally attacked. What other people do says much more about them than you.

Magnifying—exaggerating life events until everything seems like a catastrophe. This thinking pattern reflects the old cliché, "making mountains out of molehills." Relatively small problems seem to be monumental events. We are not designed to cope with a life that feels like a crisis all the time. Nor are relationships likely to survive the constant bombardment of a "magnifying" partner. "Magnifiers" often use words like always, never, every, worst, terrible, and awful. Their exaggerated thinking may produce anger, self-condemnation, or unending self-pity. These thinking patterns may have developed in home environments where small errors were blown out of proportion, parents overreacted with emotion, or became preoccupied with fear, anxiety, depression, or helplessness.

Generalizing—relying on past experiences to predict the future indiscriminately. Persons who have developed this thinking pattern think that "history always repeats itself." This is a deterministic view that doesn't discriminate sufficiently. Generalizing can feed a cynical, pessimistic outlook. Thus, "generalizers" carry lots of doubt, fear, and insecurity. There is a tendency to label others, overreact to discouragement, and "write people off." "Generalizers" may cease to exercise their freedom of choice and empowerment. To counteract this tendency, it helps to focus on living in the present and examining life situations objectively.

Emotional Reasoning—confusing feelings with facts. This thinking pattern reflects a statement, "If I feel something, it must be true." For example, though she had no real evidence to support it, Sharon felt unloved and betrayed by Todd. She concluded that he was seeing other women. In spite of Todd's efforts to demonstrate his love by doing a lot for Sharon, she would declare, "You don't love me, because if you did I would *feel* loved." Sharon may have grown up around one or more fearful parents, or even witnessed betrayal in the home in which she grew up. The healthier pattern is to use thinking to discern reality objectively, and then to experience the feelings that are consistent with that reality.

Polarizing—viewing life as being all or nothing, good or bad, black or white. Individuals who think this way are often very uncomfortable with ambiguity or complexity. They try to define every issue simplistically. "Polarizers" tend to be judgmental and exacting, often with unrealistic standards. Due to this perfectionistic bent, there may be no such thing in their minds as "adequate." Homes that are either extremely controlling or extremely unstructured might contribute to the development of this tendency. To grow out of "polarizing" patterns, begin to consciously define the middle ground of an issue and identify multiple options for each problem.

Minimizing—denying or discounting feelings associated with significant life events or issues. Persons who minimize say, "It really doesn't matter." By so doing, they are, in effect, declaring that *they* don't matter. Phrases that are consistent with minimizing include "That's just the way life is," "I'm fine" (when the situation suggests otherwise), or, "Everyone has problems, don't they?" "Minimizers" often have trouble labeling or experiencing emotions other than anger. They often come out of homes where personal needs were neglected or overlooked, or where difficulties were typically faced with a "stiff upper lip." In such families, feelings were regarded as signs of weakness. In some cases, persons who minimize as adults grew up around family members who *exaggerated* their feelings, leaving a distaste for *all* emotional expression. To overcome this tendency, identify emotions that are appropriate for a situation, and give yourself permission to actually feel them before they disappear. Label the feelings that are present.

Appendix D is an *Unhealthy Thinking Questionnaire* that can be used to assess your own thinking patterns and tendencies as well as those of a friend or journey-mate. After completing the questionnaire, you might discuss your answers together in order to better know each other and to replace any unhealthy thinking patterns with valid ones.

Personal Application

Freedom from Unhealthy Thinking

Of the six faulty thinking patterns defined above, the one that I think fits me the most is _____ and it prompts me to act in the following manner:

_____

_____

_____

_____

For example, *I have a tendency to minimize which prompts me to brush off the seriousness of problems that are facing me or my friends. Consequently, my friends don't share much with me any more about what is going on in their lives.*

List below any of the six faulty thinking patterns that you might have seen displayed by members of your family of origin, either as children or adults. Next, describe how that family member(s) acted as a result of the thinking pattern, and how other people responded to him/her.

Thinking Pattern: _____

Family Member: _____

Behavior Prompted by this Thinking:_____
_____

Responses of Others to this Behavior:_____
_____

Thinking Pattern: _____

Family Member: _____

Behavior Prompted by this Thinking:_____
_____

Responses of Others to this Behavior:_____
_____

The solution to faulty thinking is to declare the truth in the context of a caring relationship. God's truth presented in love can set the captive free (John 8:32). It can renew the mind of individuals who have been "programmed" with unhealthy thinking patterns by the ways of the world (Rom. 12:2).

Replacing Unhealthy Attitudes and Behaviors

Not only can our thinking be affected over time, so can our individual attitudes and behaviors. Inappropriate behaviors in relationships often reflect selfish, self-reliant, or self-condemning attitudes. Ultimately, these behaviors are self-serving. Let's examine a few of these approaches as they appear in adult relationships. As you read through these examples, look for one or more that parallel your own responses when others fail to meet your emotional needs.

Controlling: *Jerry realized early in life that his loud voice and determined manner gave him command of many situations others avoided. When he got married the first time, he took a well-refined dominance into that relationship. He would simply let his intensity and voice level raise until his wife yielded to his* demand. Eventually, she bailed out of the relationship, out-gunned from the start.

Manipulating: Mack was cunning. He could always figure out how to get people to do something they didn't want to do, and to do so without realizing that Mack was the beneficiary. Typically, Mack might invite a roommate to go out for a pizza together and then casually ask him to cart him around afterwards to run errands he needed done. His polite manner masked the fact that he was using the relationship to accomplish his own interests without regard for the needs and concerns of the other person.

Avoiding: Donna wanted peace at all costs. Conflict frightened her so much that she would walk on the opposite side of the campus to avoid a possible encounter with a student who liked to challenge her Christian beliefs. When she went home on breaks, she would park her car in the street rather than risk a negative look from her dad if he found her car blocking his.

Appeasing: Jennifer was the hero of her family. She never complained or acted in rebellion. Jen endeavored to do whatever was expected of her. She had a well-developed "radar" that could pick up her boyfriend's dissatisfaction before it was ever voiced. Sometimes, she felt confined and compromised when pleasing him meant violating her own conscience.

Complaining: When Bert was young, he only got attention when he was seriously ill. His grandfather, in particular, would go out of his way to buy Bert comic books and visit with him when he had the flu or mumps. Bert loved those times of closeness with his "Pa." Without realizing it, he began to develop a tendency to describe minor complaints to his friends in his singles group at church. In a good-natured way, they responded with attention and comfort. The needs meeting only seemed to extend one direction, however, for Bert never reciprocated.

Withdrawing: Kerri's childhood was a painful one. Her parents divorced when she was seven, and she rarely saw her dad *after that. He had been close to her, taking her to the park, and reading to her often. In fact, they spent more time together than her parents did with each other. But when her father moved away, the emptiness in her heart wouldn't go away. Though she was not aware of doing so at the time, she kept distant from most people and let very few get close to her. When she fell in love for the first time, she ended the relationship over a minor disagreement. She was determined to never go through the pain of losing someone close to her again, so she learned to "manage" the risks inherent in all relationships—ending them on her terms if they began to show any signs of wear and tear.*

All of these approaches are efforts to get what we want in relationships. They all rely on our own power, strength, wisdom, and cunning. We are either trusting in ourselves or in the other person in the relationship. That is why these approaches produce temporary success at best. Scripture states that all of us have turned to our own ways rather than trusting God for His, and that these ways are ultimately futile (Isa. 53:6; Prov. 16:9). Consequently, these methods of securing intimacy and avoiding pain require constant maintenance and produce only elusive counterfeits. In the end, we settle for relationships that fall far short of abundance in Christ.

If our relationships are to grow and eliminate fear, we must replace selfish taking with mutual giving that is borne out of genuine concern for one another. Philippians 2:3-4 states, *"Do nothing out of selfish ambition or vain conceit, but in humility consider others better than yourselves. Each of you should look not only to your own interests, but also to the interests of others."*

Considering the Interests of Others

Of the unhealthy attitudes and behaviors defined previously (controlling, manipulating, avoiding, appeasing, complaining, and withdrawing) write down the one that you have most often relied upon to get what you want in relationships.

_____

For example, *I have tended to be a "pleaser," so appeasing would be the primary one for me.*

Describe the last time you recall using this approach. ____
_____
_____
_____

For example, *My younger sister complained about the rest of the siblings failing to offer to help take care of our parents at Christmas time. Though I was physically ill from a major illness, I said nothing to her and took an extra day of vacation to help out. As I think about that, I realize that I was unwilling to face her.*

What was the response of the other people involved when you acted this way? _____
_____
_____

For example, *My sister said nothing about the help I offered, even to thank me for coming early.*

How could you begin to proactively meet the intimacy needs of your friends and relatives? Think of a close friend or relative and, based upon your knowledge of the individual, write down his/her top three intimacy needs (you may want to refer to page 38).

1._____ 2. _____ 3. _____

Then, given all that you know about this person's childhood, other life experiences, personality and fears, ask God to reveal ways that He might want you to change in order to more effectively meet the needs of this person. Record your thoughts from this time of prayer here:

_____

_____

_____

Now, for each need listed above, think of a specific way that you can proactively meet it.

1. _____

2. _____

3. _____

Begin this week to implement some of your ideas and trust God to bless your efforts in His time.

Recognizing Unhealthy Relational Patterns

In relationships, people develop patterns of responding that they repeat over and over again. Your interaction patterns reflect the "stuff" that both of you carry from your relational programming. One person's "stuff" tends to feed the other's in ways that are counterproductive. The result is a predictable pattern of interactions that tends to remain unchanged. Yet, few people realize that their underlying needs and programming are driving their interactions with others.

It is as though every person carries a mental blueprint into every relationship. The blueprint guides them in knowing how to interact and respond. But, who was the architect who designed it? The responses outlined in God's blueprints for relationships reflect Great Commandment love. When you follow His instructions, you are doing everything you can to lay the right foundation and using the best materials. But, if you disregard God's guidance and rely only upon what *seems* right, you will continue the patterns of the world and reap what you sow. You are accountable for your choices as you build relationships using God's plans, but you are not responsible for the choices or actions of the other persons. That is between them and God.

How would you know if you are relying on your ways or God's? First, examine the repetitive patterns of interaction in your meaningful relationships. Then, work to "put off the old and put on the new" (See Eph. 4:22-25 below). Here's an example of a common unhealthy relational pattern.

Carolyn and Sarah had been friends for many years, but were having more and more conflict in their relationship. Sarah was very sociable and liked to go out. Housekeeping was not one of her major priorities. Carolyn, on the other hand, was compulsive about neatness and resented the fact that Sarah took her cleaning up for granted and rarely helped out. Here is how the conflict frequently got "played out."

Sarah → *Walks into the kitchen after returning home from a movie.*
Frowns silently as she finishes cleaning the kitchen. ← **Carolyn**
Sarah → *Asks Carolyn what is bothering her.*
Asks Sarah angrily why she can't do her share. ← **Carolyn**
Sarah → *Makes excuses for not helping and promises to try harder.*
Accuses Sarah of having no regard for her. ← **Carolyn**
Sarah → *Tells Carolyn she's being unreasonable—impossible to please.*
Leaves the kitchen upset and goes to her room. ← **Carolyn**
Sarah → *Sits down at the table and shakes her head in frustration.*

•
•
•

Time Passes

•
•
•

Life resumes as if nothing happened . . . that is, until the next incident.

The pattern that Carolyn and Sarah fell into was not effectively addressing the needs or the hurts that each had. They were not increasing the depth of their knowledge of one another, nor were they being vulnerable as they faced conflict. Their pattern will be no more effective a year from now. They will only become more frustrated if they keep perfecting a dysfunctional approach. Instead, they need to work on new ways of relating. The first step is to acknowledge the futility of the present method and take personal responsibility for changing their parts of it.

Here are some typical patterns that might help you to identify some of your own tendencies:

Complainer/Procrastinator. In this pattern, one person, the Complainer, requests help from the other. The Procrastinator agrees to the requests, promises help, but rarely follows through. Eventually, the requesting becomes nagging and emotional cups begin to fill with resentment and shame. Even if the Procrastinator performs the tasks, the underlying needs get ignored.

Deny/Interrogate (The Nothing's Wrong Game). One person communicates through voice tone, facial expression, body language, or actions such as slamming doors that a problem exists. The other person tries to pry the truth out of the reluctant friend, often feeling manipulated in the process. This pattern serves to draw attention to unmet needs without being truly vulnerable.

Attack/Defend (The Blame Game). When friends or relatives play the Blame Game, they seem to justify their own behaviors by comparing it favorable to the other's, or by completely diverting attention from their own shortcomings. For example, one friend might tell the other, "I wouldn't lose my temper and yell at you if you wouldn't walk away during the middle of an argument!" A tendency to avoid personal responsibility as an adult may have a variety of roots in childhood.

Performer/Yes, But (The Help Me, Don't Help Me Game). In this pattern, the Yes, But individual shares a need or desire, then sabotages helpful "solutions" proposed by the Performer. A single father, for example, mentions how much he misses fishing trips, but refuses to let his brother keep his kids, convinced that the brother would resent it. A Yes, But person may have become convinced that her needs will never be met lovingly, whereas, Performers may fall unwittingly into this pattern in order to secure approval, acceptance, etc.

Outdone/Sweet Martyr (The One-Up Game). Another counterfeit method employed to secure unmet needs for attention, comfort, etc., looks like this: one person shares a problem or concern and the other responds by describing one of his own that seems more serious. Rather than focus on the need raised by the Outdone partner, the self-absorbed Sweet Martyr directs attention to herself. Selfish taking, rather than mutual giving, is common in such relationships. Outdone partners may tire of the effort, minimize their own needs, or look elsewhere.

Frustrated/Never Enough. This game is in operation when the Never Enough person makes requests (really veiled demands), but refuses to be satisfied when the Frustrated partner carries them out. The Never Enough player simply shifts the "target" to something else, keeping the Frustrated player searching for ways to please or secure approval. Intimacy needs must be given, not taken by manipulating or demanding.

Replacing Unhealthy Patterns
(Eph. 4:22-25)

Principles for breaking free from unhealthy relational patterns are found throughout the Bible:

You were taught, with regard to your former way of life, to put off your old self, which is being corrupted by its deceitful desires; to be made new in the attitude of your minds; and to put on the new self, created to be like God in true righteousness and holi-

ness. Therefore, each of you must put off falsehood and speak truthfully to his neighbor . . . (Eph. 4:22-25)

We encourage friends, relatives, dating partners, or work associates to exercise personal responsibility by working on their own side of the relational equation. All can focus on changes in themselves that would glorify God. Here are some practical steps for moving from any of the unproductive patterns listed above to dynamics that reflect Great Commandment love.

1. Increase your awareness of patterns of interaction that are typical in your relationships. Gain a more objective perspective of your own contribution to relational "stuckness" by writing down the behavior that another person would see if they videotaped a typical conflict in your relationship.

2. Identify the underlying intimacy needs of you and your partner in the relationship. Discern the unmet needs that are driving the behavior in the unproductive pattern so that you can begin to replace the unproductive behavior with biblically-based ways of relating.

3. Do not compromise your integrity or your witness— speak the truth in love (Eph. 4:15). Communicate openly and lovingly with your friend about the underlying needs you suspect to be at issue in your relationship. Be as concerned for your friend's needs as you are about your own.

4. Begin to carry out needed changes in yourself even if your friend is not yet doing so. Experience Romans 12:18, doing all that is within your power to relate better to others. As you do so, you will be exercising faith that God will work in the hearts and minds of the others involved.

Replacing Unproductive Patterns

It is unlikely that anyone has lived to be an adult without becoming involved in relationships that had unhealthy dynamics. Write the name of the unhealthy relational pattern from pages 144-145 that most closely resembles one that you have experienced in a relationship of your own.

_____

Now, describe how that unhealthy pattern was or is "played out" in your relationship. Do this by listing in order, the different actions of each person that a bystander would have seen or heard. (You can refer to the interaction that occurred between Sarah and Carolyn above for an example).

YOU   **ANOTHER**

_____   _____
_____   _____
_____   _____
_____   _____
_____   _____
_____   _____
_____   _____
_____   _____
_____   _____
_____   _____
_____   _____

What underlying needs do you think were motivating some of the unhealthy behavior patterns of you or your friend/relative/co-worker? (For example, needs for attention, respect, etc.) _____

_____
_____
_____

What do you think God would encourage you to begin doing differently in order to bring about positive change in the relationship? _____

_____

_____

_____

_____

_____

_____

Though we come to understand how God would have us interact in our relationships, we can remain locked in unproductive patterns of interaction. The story of Gwen and Eric at the beginning of this chapter is an example of such "stuckness." Whenever Eric would get upset, he would try to hold his emotions in, but his anger would be obvious. Gwen would try to "fix" the problem by going out of her way to please Eric. Though the intensity of his feelings might diminish for a time, the deeper concerns of his heart were not being addressed or resolved. Neither were Gwen's.

Fear often contributes to stagnation in relationships. We become so familiar with the patterns that any variation triggers anxiety. Change is threatening to many of us, and we tend to resist change that we cannot totally control. Jesus cautioned us about staying in our comfort zone when He has shown us a better way. In John 12:35, He says, *"...walk in the light that the darkness may not overtake you..."* Note that all we have to do to be overtaken by darkness is to stand still. Instead, we must move forward, proactively walking in the light, applying these principles in our relationships on a daily basis. Work to understand your unproductive relational patterns, and if possible, discuss them with your friends, enlisting their support to work together toward positive change.

Encountering God in His Word

"Trusting in the Lord"
Proverbs 3:3-6

Let love and faithfulness never leave you; bind them around your neck, write them on the tablet of your heart. Then you will win favor and a good name in the sight of God and man. Trust in the Lord with all your heart and lean not on your own understanding; in all your ways acknowledge him, and he will make your paths straight.

God has warned us that our lives on earth will be loaded with trials and difficulties (John 16:33). Our Heavenly Father cares about us and promises to be with us even during those times (Heb. 13:5). But, like most of us, you may doubt that God will come through for you or that He is really working in your best interests. This may be especially true when you have struggled with something for a long time without much relief. Our relationships are important arenas for such tests of faith. We are frequently tempted to rely upon our own devices and schemes to get our needs met. Yet, the God of the universe loves us even when we were in rebellion against Him. He just cannot honor or bless our counterfeit solutions to His real blessing. Will we continue to follow His ways when we cannot see the outcome of our obedience until later? What has your journey of faith looked like with regard to your relationships?

◆ Describe a time in a relationship when you "took matters into your own hands" rather than follow God's guidance, only to see later that it was a mistake to do so. _____

_____

_____

_____

_____

_____

_____

_____

_____

◆ Read the passage over several times, contemplating what it means to "lean not on your own understanding" when it comes to relationships. Write your thoughts here. _____

_____

_____

_____

◆ With regard to your friendships and other close relationships, what do you think God might want to see happening in your life that would be evidence that He had "made your paths straight" (or, "directed your paths" in another translation)? _____

_____

_____

_____

Christ knows the pain of rejection and the joy of reconciliation. He can be trusted with your heart.

Group Dialogue

If you do not have a designated group leader, choose someone in the group who will serve to facilitate the discussion. Begin by briefly reviewing the discussion guidelines.

Discussion Guidelines

- Allow everyone an opportunity to share thoughts and feelings
- Avoid long story telling
- Be quick to listen with empathy
- Be slow to give advice
- Speak the truth in love
- Say what you mean and mean what you say
- Protect the confidentiality of every person

Discussion Suggestions for Chapter Five

1. Take turns sharing one positive or negative characteristic from the list at the beginning of the chapter that you have experienced in your adult relationships.

2. Have each person write down names or "messages" received during childhood from peers, authority figures, or parents that were hurtful or bothersome to you. Then, go around the group sharing the names. As each person shares, allow a moment for someone to offer affirming "names" that seem more accurate for them today.

3. Share with other group members one unhealthy thinking pattern that you witnessed in your family as you grew up. Mention the effect it seemed to have on you then, and now.

4. Discuss the unhealthy attitudes and behaviors from pages 138-140 in terms of how some of these have been a problem for you personally.

5. Identify one of the unhealthy relational patterns from page 144-145 that you have experienced personally, and share what you feel inside when you are involved in such a pattern.

6. Ask a volunteer to pray for all group members, especially for courage to let God bring about changes in their thinking, behaving, and inner character.

Journey-mate Encounters

◆ Set aside one to two hours for the meeting to give ample time for each person to share.

◆ Select a meeting location that minimizes distractions or interruptions.

◆ Read the chapter and complete all the written exercises *before* meeting to discuss them.

◆ Purpose to start on time and complete each exercise, staying focused on the material.

Suggestions for Journey-mate Encounter #5

1. Share with you journey-mate one of the intimacy needs from the list on page 38 that was met well for you during childhood. Then, identify one that was not met frequently or that you wish had been met more often.

2. Share with each other the unhealthy labels or names that you were each given in childhood by siblings, class mates, parents, or others. Express comfort for painful messages sent to your journey-mates during childhood that may still be "present" today.

3. Complete the Unhealthy Thinking Questionnaire in Appendix D and share the results with your journey-mate. Discuss your ideas about how some of your thinking patterns developed.

4. Identify to your journey-mates one unhealthy attitude or behavior from the lists on pages 138-140 that you are likely to exhibit in a relationship. Encourage one another to grow in these areas without being judgmental.

5. Review the list of unhealthy relational patterns on pages 144-145 and discuss any that you have experienced. Share

your thoughts with each other about your own relationship. Do you think any of these patterns are occurring? Listen thoughtfully and express concern or compassion for your friend if they are. Take turns inviting your journey-mate to tell you how you could respond better for his or her sake.

6. Pray together expressing gratitude to God for His patient support as we continue to grow and change in order to experience more of his abundant love in our relationship with Him and others.

Hiding the Word in Your Heart
Romans 12:2

Write the verse here: _____

_____

_____

_____

_____

_____

_____

_____

_____

Repeat the verse from memory each day for several weeks. Using the space below, you may want to journal ways that God has allowed you to experience the verse as you have hidden it away in your heart. _____

_____

_____

_____

_____

_____

_____

_____

_____

_____

_____

_____

_____

_____

Check the box at the right when you have committed the verse to memory. Continue to repeat the verse daily for at least three weeks.

Chapter Six

—— ◆ ——

THE FAMILY CRUCIBLE
Your Programming for Intimacy and
Relationships

*"...stop thinking like children...in your
thinking be adults." I Corinthians 14:20*

*When prompted by a concerned friend, Jim pondered what his
childhood was like. Though he was given everything he needed
materially, Jim was also given something he would like to leave
behind—a loud, critical voice that pointed out even the slightest
flaw in his performance. The voice seemed to be saying, "No
matter what you do, it is never good enough!" Jim knows where
the voice originated, for he remembers his father's constant pressure, endless demands, unattainable expectations, harsh punishment, and embarrassing put-downs as though it were only
yesterday. But the voice continues. Only now, the voice is his
own. Jim has taken over the job of whipping himself into
shape—using pressure and condemnation as his leverage to
secure the desired ends. Not surprisingly, many of Jim's adult
relationships have been characterized by demanding and critical
interaction. "Dad's voice became my conscience. But, I'm start-
ing to realize that I can turn that voice off if I want to, and
respond differently to people who speak to me critically."*

It's time to get personal. Perhaps uncomfortably personal.
It's time for you to examine your own childhood and the environment in which you grew up that has colored who and what
you are today. "But, what do my childhood experiences have to

do with my relationships and vitality today?" you ask. "What's done is done, right? Let bygones be bygones. Anyway, I don't believe people should blame their mistakes as adults on their parents. They should take responsibility for their own actions."

Well, not so fast there. Without doubt, adults are accountable for their actions (Rom. 14:12). But when you grew up and left your childhood home, you didn't go away empty-handed. In addition to your material possessions, you packed your spiritual, emotional, and psychological bags with all the "stuff" your family gave you—good and bad. From the time you were born, the way that your caretakers and others interacted with you had tremendous influence on who you are today and how you relate to others. During your childhood, you had hundreds and thousands of interactions with your parents, siblings, and other important people. Those interactions and the messages they implied served to mold and shape your perceptions of who you are, what to expect from people who know you, and generally speaking, what to expect in life.

Marla's home environment didn't have the rigid, militaristic atmosphere that Jim faced. "Our home was a madhouse, everybody doing his own thing, keeping his own hours, setting his own rules. My parents didn't believe in rules or maybe they were just too lazy to enforce them. They didn't try to run my life—they ignored me. I practically had to stand on my head to make them notice me. Sometimes I just wished they would take enough interest in what I was doing to say 'You can't do that.' or 'You can't go there.' or 'You've got to be home by ten.' I had to muddle along and set my own rules by trial and error, and I constantly had to compete with my brothers and sisters for bits and pieces of my parents' attention. The child giving the best performance won out, and it usually wasn't me. I think that might be why I became a singer. I couldn't stop performing, trying to get somebody's attention!"

What about you? Did you grow up in a demanding home like Jim's, or a neglectful one like Marla's? Or was it one that had many positive aspects, yet left you wishing there had been even *more* attention, affection, comfort, or approval?

Relational Programming

In my (Bruce's) work as a professional counselor, I have noticed that many of the problems people experience in their adult relationships are essentially "replays" of struggles they had in childhood with parents or siblings. For example, if they fought to secure approval as children, it is not surprising to see them doing the same thing as adults. Or, if the opinions of a young man were never considered as a teenager, he may be easily angered when his girlfriend frequently interrupts him during a conversation. It is as though you were programmed for certain struggles.

The "baggage" you carry into your adult relationships may include a priority for certain needs to be met, a paradigm or way of regarding yourself and others, an emotional predisposition, and a predictable way of responding to emotional pain. Most of us enter adulthood unaware of these patterns of thinking, reacting, and behaving.

When Mike was seven, his mother bought him a piano and announced, "Mikey, dear, all my life I dreamed of playing the piano. Now you'll have the chance I never had. I'm going to see that you become an accomplished pianist!" It didn't matter to Mike's mom that he hated practicing and would rather have spent time drawing or making model airplanes. Hour after hour he hammered out the scales on those ivories, seething inside because he couldn't follow his own dreams. Twenty years later, Mike found himself overreacting with rage and frustration to minor events. When his friends urged him to play a sonata for his dinner guests, he could feel that familiar knot in his stomach, like he felt when his mother made him perform for her church friends. "Stop pushing me!" he exploded at his friends. Another time, when he was shopping and a friend suggested a particular tie for him, he accused her of trying to run his life. One day, another friend suggested they take a toll road instead of the interstate, and Mike erupted angrily, "Don't tell me how to drive!"

With whom do you really think Mike is angry? Why?

_____

Margaret is a forty-year old woman whose track record with men has never been good. In both her marriages, she longed in vain for affection and attention from her husbands. Trying her best to please them, she ended up brokenhearted when affairs ended both marriages—one with another woman, and the other to his ministry. With tearful eyes, Margaret shared a memory from her childhood. "Night after night I would sit by the window of my second story bedroom watching for my dad to come home. I knew he was out drinking, and it made me feel sick and panicky inside. I couldn't bear to crawl into bed until I was sure Dad was home too. So, I would prop my pillow on the window sill and lay my head down and wait. More often than not, that's where I'd wake up in the morning. When I was older, he would often promise to pick me up after school. I'd wait and wait, then finally walk home alone to find him passed out on the couch. Dad's broken promises continued to haunt me years after he died. When one of my husbands would be gone from home, or if we were having a dispute, I would get that same sick feeling of abandonment in the pit of my stomach. Even though these men were not like my father otherwise, I still felt like that needy little girl waiting by the window sill for daddy to come home.

Did Margaret's dad jinx her relationships? What do you think Margaret is really dealing with here? _____

_____

Nick faced his share of the inevitable pains and disappointments of childhood and adolescence. He came in fourth in the intercity track meet, his team lost the "big game" his senior year, and he broke up with his best girl after two years of steady dating. Nick's parents typically responded to such setbacks with a load of advice for him. After each disappointment, they would deliver their usual pep talk, filled with little homilies and clichés. For example, "It's not so bad, honey. At least you got to the finals." "Don't worry, your team will do better next time." "Look at the bright side. You did better than the others." "Give it a lit-

tle time." "Tomorrow's another day." "Wait and see. You'll find a girl twice as nice." Now, Nick is an adult and his relationships with his friends have hit a few bumps in the road. It seems that every time a friend comes to him for support or comfort, he or she ends up feeling unheard or misunderstood. He's proud of all the helpful advice he gives to his friends, but they claim he's insensitive and unsympathetic.

What do you think is really going on here with Nick? _____

_____

These vignettes are all examples of the ways that emotional baggage gets packed into our hearts and minds and later unpacked in our relationships. It is essential that we understand the patterns and predispositions we carry so that we can consciously work toward more productive ones. There was a sense in which Mike, Margaret, and Nick had not yet completed the process of leaving home. Though miles from home, and separated by death in one case, it was as though an invisible emotional umbilical cord still linked them to their families of origin.

Personal Application
Unpacking Your Relational Baggage

Let's begin to examine what kind of "baggage" you might carry into your adult relationships by completing these sentences:

Perception of self. I see myself as a person who is: (For example, *honest, loyal, lazy, incompetent, strong, weak, intelligent, clumsy, unlovable, assertive, timid, etc.*)_____

_____

_____

_____

_____

Priority of needs. My three priority intimacy needs (from page 37) are _____ , _____ , and_____. As best I recall, these needs were _____(met/not met) consistently during my childhood.

Expectations of others. When I become involved in close relationships, deep down, I expect the other persons to eventually _____.
(For example, *stay loyal, lose interest in me, find me boring, like me, etc.*)

Emotional Predisposition. My general mood is typically _____.
(For example, *upbeat, positive, discouraged, complaining, critical, dependent, self-reliant, etc.*)

Response to Emotion. When problems occur or emotions get tense or conflicted in a relationship, I tend to react or respond by _____.
(For example, *withdrawing, taking control, insisting that we talk it out, being defensive, trying to mediate to make everyone 'happy' again, getting busy, lashing out in anger, etc.*)

Leaving Home Emotionally

One of the developmental tasks for all adults, single or married, is to differentiate emotionally from the family of origin in order to form healthy intimate relationships of their own. We must grow so that we can function freely in our adult lives. Such leaving does not mean we cease to love or care for our parents. It means recognizing and facing the pain of unmet relational needs from the past in order to receive healing and be free to experience intimacy in the present. It also means being able to share thoughts and feelings truthfully and respectfully without fear of reprisal.

Failure to do this leaving keeps us enslaved to the hidden predispositions and programming we acquired during childhood. Such conditioning hinders and limits our adult relationships, and may keep us locked into the same unhealthy relational patterns we experienced in childhood. The Bible says you are a slave to whatever masters you (II Pet. 2:19). The relational programming we experienced can master and control us like an invisible cage. Whenever that programming is inconsistent with God's ways for relating intimately, it is time to do some *reprogramming*, or "renewing of your mind," (Rom. 12:2). The result will be a freedom in Christ that allows you to more fully experience God's abundant life in your relationships today.

Here's a lighthearted assessment of our need to leave home emotionally.

Top Ten Indicators of a Need to Leave Home Emotionally

10. You occasionally refer to dates by your mother's/father's first name.

9. You feel compelled to visit your mother every other weekend just in case some light bulbs need changing.

8. You have never celebrated a major holiday (Christmas, Thanksgiving, Easter, July Fourth, Presidents' Day, National Secretaries' Day) apart from Mom and Dad.

7. You still carry Dad's EXXON card—and you still use it!

6. Your mom still calls to tell you to wear a jacket outside when it's so cold.

5. After establishing a career in another state, your elderly mother offers to pay you $2000 per month to resign and move back home to take care of her.

4. You're still not sure what your favorite color is—you always pick what Mom or Dad like.

3. Though all your roommates hate your meat loaf recipe, you still cook it once a week because, "It's Mom's recipe, and Dad liked it."

2. You're buying a house where Dad is carrying the note—and you haven't made a payment in five years.

1. After fifteen years of living away from home, your mother still drives 100 miles twice a week to give you an allergy shot saying, "I'm the only one who can stick him so it doesn't hurt."

Now, let's take a more serious look at the specific ways that your relational programming, whether helpful or harmful, influences your present relationships, and how you can build upon it. We'll begin by helping you assess where you are today and then look at your childhood to offer added insight.

Personal Application
Leaving Home

One way to assess how much "leaving" you have done is to take the following survey. Put a check mark next to each statement that is actually true about you today.

❑ I feel free to choose the career I want to pursue.
❑ I do not feel controlled emotionally by material assistance my parents/others might offer.
❑ I feel free to spend vacations and holidays with, or apart from, my family of origin.
❑ I am free of guilt trips levied by others in an attempt to manipulate my behavior.
❑ I feel free to ask my parents/others for input, but retain freedom to make a decision alone.
❑ I am free to form and express my own thoughts and opinions regardless of social pressure.

- ❑ I no longer depend solely upon my parents'/others approval for my self-worth.
- ❑ I can experience and relate respectfully to all persons as peers.
- ❑ I am free to establish standards and traditions for my lifestyle which may or may not be similar to those of my family of origin.
- ❑ I can take full responsibility for the actions I have taken as an adult.
- ❑ I can voluntarily initiate or receive intimacy and maintain boundaries at the same time.

Each check reflects a degree of emotional freedom to act and relate with respect and honor for one's parents, yet without being enmeshed with or disengaged from them emotionally.

Shaking the Family Tree

For most of us, our relational programming was acquired primarily in our family of origin—the parents and siblings with whom we lived during our childhood. And an increasing number of families include step-parents and extended family members who serve as the primary caretakers for the children at least part of the time. Whether simple or convoluted, the family tree yields some helpful (if not always pleasant) "fruit" in our search for intimacy with God and others.

While a graduate student in seminary, I (Bruce) had the privilege of teaching a class called, "Relationships in Ministry." One of the objectives of that class was to help the students gain a more accurate view of themselves and their families of origin. We knew that this would better equip them for adult attachments in their roles as ministers, counselors, and teachers. One assignment during the course called for each student to give a written description of the relationship that existed between every two people in the family. (For example, father-son, father-mother, mother-son, father-daughter, son-daughter, etc.) It was not uncommon to hear comments from the students about the difficulty of this assignment because they had never before contemplated their families from an objective perspective. Many gained some profound insight which was both sobering and freeing.

You, too, may find it difficult or uncomfortable to examine your family of origin experiences. You may even strongly object to the idea. Some think the process is simply *unnecessary*, maintaining an attitude that, "what's done is done, and people should just move on." Please realize that when we look at our past, we are seeking truth that will enable us to live Christlike lives in the present. Jesus said that we are to know the truth and the truth will set us free (John 14:6). Of course, that implies that we will *respond* to the truth in the manner He did. Therefore, we look at the past in order to understand how it influences us in the present. The fact that all of us have blind spots makes it wise to seek more understanding.

In addition, you may sense that you are *dishonoring* your parents by identifying and discussing ways they failed to meet your needs. How can we honor our parents well if what we are really honoring is a distorted, incomplete picture—one that may have been idealized over the years. That would actually be dishonest and hypocritical. It is actually more honoring to see people as they are (warts and all) and *then* to love and respond to them as Jesus would. For example, consider His response to the adulterous woman about to be stoned by the Pharisees. He knew all about her, but responded to her honestly and lovingly. Jesus didn't condemn or reject her, nor did He condone her past behavior that had missed the mark.

Some regard this process of examining the past to be *wallowing* in pain rather than rising above it, and thus find it humiliating. We propose that you look face-to-face at the pain you still carry inside from the past *in order to move beyond it*. Experience the biblical process of mourning the losses and receiving comfort in order to be healed and blessed. Experience the biblical process of confession and forgiveness in order to be free from guilt, shame, bitterness or resentment. The process of looking back at the past in order to experience abundant life in the present is a biblical one that God can use to heal, restore, and liberate.

Intimacy Needs In Childhood

The purpose of this exercise is to assess the degree to which your intimacy needs were met or not met by your caretakers in childhood. Unmet needs in childhood could still be influencing your relationships as an adult unless those needs are understood and the losses faced.

Listed below are the ten Intimacy Needs that were introduced in Chapter Two. You may wish to turn to page 38 to review their definitions before proceeding. Assess your childhood experience by completing the following steps.

1. As you look through each of the Intimacy Needs on the list, ask yourself, "How did my mother meet this need?" If you can recall specific ways in which she met this need, put a half-circle in the space next to that Intimacy Need. For example, for "attention," you might recall times when your mother would read stories to you as a child or attended your games or concerts.

2. Next, ask yourself the same question about your father, "How did my father meet this need?" If you can recall specific times and ways your father met this need, put a half-circle in the space next to the need. For example, for "comfort," you might recall how your father once put his arm around your shoulder and told you how sad he was that your best friend moved to another city.

3. If only one of your parents or caretakers met a need, you will have one half-circle in the space provided. If both parents met the need, you will have a full circle formed by the two half-circles.

4. After you have assessed each of the ten needs, go back and place an X in any space that is blank, indicating that those needs were not met consistently by either parent.

NOTE: If your childhood involved caretakers other than your biological parents due to death or divorce, complete the exercise first by reflecting upon how your needs were met by your biological parents. Then, look at each of the intimacy needs again and assess how well the step-parent(s) or other caretakers met your needs. The fact that one of your biological parents was not there to meet these needs represents a significant loss that may still need to be grieved.

Intimacy Needs
Met ( ) or Unmet ✕ by Caretakers

Acceptance - *receiving another person willingly and unconditionally* _____

Affection - *expressing care and closeness through appropriate touch* _____

Appreciation - *expressing thanks, praise, or commendation* _____

Approval (Blessing) - *building up or affirming another* _____

Attention - *taking thought of another; entering another's world* _____

Comfort - *responding to a hurting person with words, feeling, and touch* _____

Encouragement - *urging another to persist and persevere toward a goal* _____

Respect - *valuing and regarding another highly; treating another as important* _____

Security (Peace) - *harmony in relationships; freedom from fear or harm* _____

Support - *coming alongside and gently helping with a problem or struggle* _____

After completing the assessment of how well your intimacy needs were met during childhood, answer the questions on the following page.

How would you summarize what you *missed or needed more of* from your **mother**? _____
_____
_____

from your **father**? _____
_____
_____

from **other caregivers** (step-mother, step-father, grandparents, etc.)? _____
_____
_____

Are the things you missed or needed more from these caretakers still important to you? How? Be specific. _____
_____
_____

What are some of the needs that were met well by your caretakers? _____
_____
_____

How are the needs met in childhood still important to you? ____
_____
_____

What feelings have been evoked within you as you have completed this exercise? List them here. _____
_____
_____

How do you feel about the number of circles or half-circles you marked above? How about the number of 's you marked? ____
_____
_____

How do the met and unmet needs of your childhood seem important in your adult relationships? Be specific. _____
_____
_____
_____

How do the needs you recorded as unmet in childhood compare to the priority needs you identified for yourself in the exercise on page 37? _____

_____

It is normal for us to want to have the needs met in our childhood continue to be met in our adult relationships. We will also want our adult friends to meet the needs that went unmet in childhood. For example, if the family atmosphere you experienced in childhood was chaotic and filled with conflict, you may insist upon giving in to the preferences of your room-mates rather than risk an argument. You may, of course, expect them to do the same. The problem is, that in an effort to ensure that our needs are met, we may use methods that are counterproductive or even destructive to ourselves or our friends.

Personal Application
Constructing Your Family Genogram

The exercise you completed above helps assess the specific needs that are most important to you and how these may have been related to your childhood experiences. This genogram exercise will offer another method for discovery. It will help you better understand the dynamics of the relationships in your immediate and extended family environments and how these impacted your own development and relational programming.

A genogram is a pictorial representation of your family tree and the relationships between its members. In the past, this tool has been used primarily by counselors to help individuals and families better understand the origins and dynamics of their relational problems. In order to draw a genogram for your own family of origin, you will need to identify the members of the family and later, describe the quality of the relationships that existed among the people in the family who were most significant to you.

First, however, let's define some important terms we will be using to describe certain types of relationships.

◆ *Close* will be used to describe a relationship with a lot of heart-to-heart communication and sharing, and where the adults in the relationship are seeking to meet intimacy needs of the others.

◆ *Superficial* relationships may include conversation and even joint activity, but without deep knowing or the awareness or meeting of intimacy needs by the adults. Each person is still alone.

◆ *Distant* relationships would exhibit little sharing like this and might seem disengaged with very little communication or vulnerable disclosure.

◆ *Estranged* relationships are ones that have been cut off, broken, or severed, possibly due to divorce, abandonment, or unresolved conflicts.

◆ *Conflicted* relationships could represent those with arguing or fighting that is out in the open or more hidden conflict where tension seems to always be present.

◆ *Enmeshed* relationships offer little individuality or separation of emotions. These relationships often involve a child being relied upon to meet some of a parent's emotional needs, as in the case of a mother whose looks inadvertently to her young son for the acceptance and attention she had needed from her ex-husband.

Now, let's look at a sample genogram for Allen, whom you met earlier in Chapter Five.

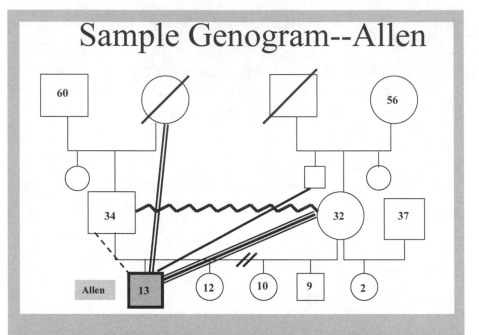

Sample Genogram--Allen

Using the "key" at the right, you can see from this genogram that Allen grew up in a family with four children, with one more added later when Allen's mother remarried after she and his father divorced. The ages and the quality of relationships of the people on the diagram reflect the time Allen was growing up, specifically the time he was an adolescent. You can see that the relationship that he saw modeled by his biological parents was very conflicted, though the conflict was not violent. He was distant from his father and enmeshed with his mother. He became somewhat of a caretaker for his younger siblings. One of the bright spots for him was his paternal grandmother who took a special interest in him and encouraged his artistic talent and skills. Detailed definitions of the genogram symbols are provided in Appendix F, entitled, *Genogram Symbols and Construction.*

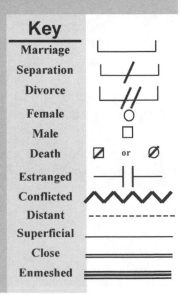

Key	
Marriage	
Separation	
Divorce	
Female	
Male	
Death	
Estranged	
Conflicted	
Distant	
Superficial	
Close	
Enmeshed	

Family of Origin Genogram for: _____

1. Using the area on the following page, begin to construct your family of origin genogram by drawing symbols (boxes for males and circles for females) for the caregivers who played important roles in your life. Though you may not choose to include every person in the family tree, be sure to include all of the adults who were responsible, at least in part, for raising you or for nurturing you. (For example, biological parents, guardians, step-parents, adoptive parents, etc.) Draw the genogram to reflect the way things were when you were growing up. We suggest it represent the time you were 12 years old (unless events in your teen years need to be depicted).

2. Draw lines connecting these caregivers to reflect whether or not they were married and add the appropriate symbols if they had divorced or separated.

3. Above these symbols, add any persons in the previous generation who have had significant impact on you either positively or negatively. (For example, your grandparents, aunts, uncles, etc.)

4. Next, draw symbols to represent yourself and any brothers or sisters that you had (include half-siblings or step-siblings). You may want to show each person's age relation to your own at the time.

5. To complete your genogram, think about the relationships that existed between family members, and indicate the type of relationship by drawing the appropriate connecting symbol shown in the key below (close, superficial, distant, enmeshed, conflicted). Again, you do not have to describe the relationships between *every* two people on the genogram, but be sure to include the relationship between your mother and father and any others that were significant to you.

Family of Origin Genogram for: _____

Key	
Marriage	⎿_____⏌
Separation	⎿__/__⏌
Divorce	⎿__//__⏌
Female	○
Male	□
Death	◪ or ⊘
Estranged	—┤├—
Conflicted	∿∿∿∿
Distant	- - - - - -
Superficial	————
Close	════
Enmeshed	≡≡≡≡

Now, having constructed your own genogram, respond thoughtfully to the following questions.

When you were growing up, *who* frequently met the following needs for you in a demonstrable way, and *how* did he or she do it?

attention? _____
(For example, *who left his or her world, entered yours, and did things you enjoyed.*)

approval? _____
(For example, *who expressed affirmation and commendation to you verbally.*)

affection? _____
(For example, *who conveyed care and closeness with words and appropriate touch.*)

comfort? _____
(For example, *who expressed empathy and compassion for you when you were hurt.*)

What thoughts and feelings do you have about the answers you gave? _____
_____
_____
_____
_____
_____

What emotions do you think might have been filling your emotional cup as a child based upon the perspective offered from the genogram exercise? _____
_____
_____
_____
_____

Future Packing Tips

Having journeyed back to that part of our lives that shaped and molded many of our expectations about ourselves and those close to us, it might be good to ponder how to best apply this for our present-day friendships and our current interactions with our family members. Remember Marla? Listen to her comments after examining her own genogram. *"I was surprised by what I experienced. I knew I had some hostile feelings toward my parents for not giving me attention when I was little,"* she confessed, *"but, I didn't realize those feelings extended to my brothers and sisters as well. I always wondered why we weren't closer. Now I see that part of the problem was me. I was holding them at a distance to punish them for getting the attention I had longed for, and I didn't want to risk further hurt by sharing my pain with them. Now I know how to begin mending some fences in my family."*

God surely rejoices any time His children are involved in healing and restoring relationships. Yet, on our own, we cannot accomplish everything that God might be seeking to accomplish. He only asks that we do the part that depends on us and commit the rest to prayer (Rom. 12:18).

Comforting Pain from Childhood

In the process of completing this chapter, you may have recognized a measure of emotional pain resulting from your childhood. What will you do with it now? Centuries ago, Christ addressed what it takes to be happy when He delivered His oft-quoted Sermon on the Mount. In what sounds today like a paradox, Jesus said, *"Blessed are they that mourn, for they shall be comforted"* (Matt. 5:4). How can mourning be connected to happiness? Knowing that we would experience pain on earth, Jesus made it clear that we would need comfort from others. He also gave us the sequential order for His "prescription." First, we must grieve or mourn the hurt. Then, we must receive comfort from others.

If there has been unhealed pain inside you for so long, you may be wondering why you haven't recognized or addressed it before. It is very likely that you haven't faced this pain before because there was no comforting, supportive environment in which to confide your hurts. Instead, you may have held your thoughts and feelings within, effectively forfeiting any potential for comfort to be received. Take a moment now to reflect on the opportunities you have had in the past to either reveal pain or experience comfort for the pain or losses from your childhood. How did you and the others around you respond to your hurtful childhood experiences? _____

_____

_____

_____

_____

_____

_____

_____

_____

_____

It is never too late to experience God's truth about healing hurts expressed in Matthew 5:4.

Personal Application
Journaling

Find a quiet, safe place. Make sure you have plenty of uninterrupted time to complete this exercise. Find a loose-leaf notebook, note pad, or blank book to begin recording your own thoughts and feelings about your childhood experiences. Don't concern yourself with grammar, punctuation, or articulation. Your goal will be to express yourself as honestly and transparently as you can. The *process* of recording your thoughts is more important than the *product*, the pages you actually produce.

Now begin to write your journal, documenting your feelings about your experience as a child. Write down what you think and feel about the unmet needs you have identified. Identify each source of pain and what you feel about it. Record what you did in response to your pain, and how others responded to you then, as well. An example of a journal entry might sound like the following: *I missed out on attention from my mom when I was young. She worked nights and was asleep when I left for school each day. I would come home from school and she would give me a list of chores to do as she walked out the door to go to work. She didn't even talk to me or ask me about my day. I felt so unimportant, as though I was the maid, the hired help.*

Personal Application
Therapeutic Letter Writing

After you have spent all the time you need on your personal journal, we encourage you to begin another exercise to heal further the pain that resulted from unmet intimacy needs in your past. In this exercise, you will write letters to each of your parents (even if one or both were absent or unavailable some or all of the time) and to any other significant caretakers or relatives. However, *these letters are not to be mailed.* Take your time to draft these letters using the questions that follow as suggested outlines. Keep writing until you have said everything that you need to say, giving the letters the significance and intensity they deserve. Write the letters as though you are actually conversing with the individuals to whom they are addressed, even if they died years ago. Here is a list of "prompts" for your letters:

Dear Dad/Mom/Step-father/Grandma/Former Spouse, etc.,

> I've been thinking about what it was like living with you and how I felt then about some of the things that I experienced.
> Some of my earliest memories of our time together are...and these events left me feeling...

I appreciated...
I loved the times we...
It hurt me a so much when...
Now, I find myself often feeling...
It would mean so much to me now if...
Even today, I wish I could hear you say...

Sincerely,

Your son/daughter/granddaughter/former spouse,
etc.

After you have finished writing your therapeutic letters, we recommend that you schedule a meeting with a journey-mate or your small group that has been working through *Discovering Intimacy*. Schedule plenty of time so that you can take turns reading aloud your letters to each other and practicing good emotional responding for the person sharing the hurts he or she has experienced.

As a listener, focus primarily on comforting and encouraging the person expressing pain from the past. If anger is disclosed, acknowledge it and listen for underlying hurt or fear that accompanies it, giving comfort for the pain that was experienced. Remember to avoid giving advice, minimizing the hurt, changing the subject prematurely, or focusing on anger evoked in the listener. The "job" of the listener is to walk alongside the one sharing in a safe and attentive manner, something that almost certainly did not take place in this matter before. Refer to the "*Developing Intimacy Skills . . . Emotional Responding*" chart on page 77 for examples.

You may wish to communicate ahead of time any specific ways that you would want your journey-mate or group members to comfort you. For example, would you want the others to express sorrow verbally or sit next to you and put a hand on your shoulder?

If you are part of a small group, you may want to schedule this exercise over a number of meetings or plan a weekend retreat for this purpose.

"Valuing the Least of These"
Mark 10:13-16

This is the passage that tells about parents bringing their children to Jesus, asking Him to bless them. Read the verses deliberately and let your mind picture the dusty villages and roadsides where these encounters probably took place. All kinds of people were approaching Jesus seeking one thing or another. Now, here come these parents with their kids. The disciples intervene, probably thinking they were doing Jesus a favor, protecting Him from the noisy crowds. But Jesus startles them again by His ways. He gives priority to the "least of these" and affirms their innocence and teachable nature as something adults should emulate. He then expresses affection and gives them His undivided attention, hoisting the children in His arms, and blessing them.

◆ If you had been one of the children, what feelings would the Lord's actions have evoked in your young, naive heart? __

_____

_____

_____

_____

_____

_____

◆ If you had been one of the parents, what would have gone through your mind as you see the difference between the behavior of the disciples and that of the Master? _____

_____

_____

_____

_____

_____

_____

_____

◆ Ask the Holy Spirit to give you discernment about the heart of the Savior and write down here what you see about His nature that the Pharisees and even the disciples had trouble recognizing at this point in their journey with Him. _____

_____

_____

_____

_____

_____

◆ Record the response of your heart to a God who takes time to fellowship with children on their level, meets needs that parents often fail to meet, and lifts up those who are often overlooked and downtrodden. _____

_____

_____

_____

_____

_____

An incredible truth is that God has special concern for the oppressed and the unwanted. When children's needs go unmet, the Father of compassion and God of all comfort cares.

Group Dialogue

If you do not have a designated group leader, choose some-one in the group who will serve to facilitate the discussion. Begin by briefly reviewing the discussion guidelines.

Discussion Guidelines

◆ Allow everyone an opportu-nity to share thoughts and feelings
◆ Avoid long story telling
◆ Be quick to listen with empathy

◆ Be slow to give advice
◆ Speak the truth in love
◆ Say what you mean and mean what you say
◆ Protect the confidentiality of every person

Discussion Suggestions for Chapter Six

1. Ask the group how their families of origin regarded and responded to the intimacy needs of the children. Ask them to briefly describe what each parent would have *said or done* to meet such needs as attention, affection, approval, or comfort. If discussion seems limited, ask the group mem-bers to comment about how their parents would have responded to the scenario of six-year-old Allen running in to show his drawing to the parent (Chapter 5, pages 127-128).

2. Invite group members to share similarities or differences between their unmet needs from childhood and the three priority needs each one identified previously on page 37. Discuss why you think the similarities or differences exist.

3. Ask each group member to turn to the emotional cup dia-gram they completed on page 69 and share what was filling his or her emotional cup *as a child*, or what each one want-

ed and needed most as a child. Share words of comfort and compassion for one another in the group as members ponder some of the pain that may yet need to be grieved. For example, *"John, I feel sad for you that you tried so hard to secure approval from your father by excelling in school but to no avail."* Be prepared also to rejoice with those group members who recall positive, encouraging memories.

4. Go around the group, sharing how each one reacted as a child when needs went unmet. (For example, *withdrew, pouted, threw a tantrum, tried harder to please the parents, etc.*)

5. Share brief examples of relational struggles experienced in childhood that have "replayed" in adult relationships. For example, *"My boss has little sympathy for the pressure I am under to perform at work. As I recall, there was little comfort offered anyone in my family either."*

6. Ask a volunteer to close the group time by praying especially that each one might feel grateful for the positive contributions of the parents and healing for areas that were painful.

◆ Set aside one to two hours for the meeting to give ample time for each person to share.

◆ Select a meeting location that minimizes distractions or interruptions.

◆ Read the chapter and complete all the written exercises *before* meeting to discuss them.

◆ Purpose to start on time and complete each exercise, staying focused on the material.

Suggestions for Journey-mate Encounter #6

1. Begin by sharing with your journey-mate(s) the kinds of feelings that were evoked when you completed the needs assessment from your childhood and the genogram exercise. Be alert to the feelings that may be attached to each other's disclosures and respond with compassion and genuine concern for one another. Discuss also the needs that were met well during childhood and rejoice with one another about those.

2. Share any new insights that the exercises in this chapter help you to see.

3. Take turns reading your therapeutic letters to each other, offering comfort and compassion as appropriate.

4. Draw a diagram representing the immediate family in which you grew up. Put your own initials in the center of the page and arrange those of the other family members around yours in a way that reveals how "close" they were to the other members of the family. For, example, if your father always seemed to "side" with your oldest sister and went out of his way to praise her, you might put their initials close together. Now, use symbols to depict what kinds of "mes-

sages" were commonly sent between the different members of the family. For example, arrows might represent criticism; brick walls might represent neglect; stones, condemnation; ladders, support; hearts, expressed comfort. Share your diagrams with each other, and discuss the feelings that were evoked as you drew them.

5. Purpose to do something creative during the coming week to meet one of the significant needs of each of your journey-mate(s) that went unmet in childhood. Ask God to help you find an opportunity to give one of these "random acts of kindness."

6. Pray for one another that your intimacy with God will continue to grow as the barriers of unresolved hurt and pain continue to be torn down.

Hiding the Word in Your Heart
I Corinthians 14:20

Write the verse here: _____
_____
_____
_____
_____
_____
_____
_____
_____

Repeat the verse from memory each day for several weeks. Using the space below, you may want to journal ways that God has allowed you to experience the verse as you have hidden it away in your heart. _____
_____
_____
_____
_____
_____
_____
_____
_____
_____
_____
_____
_____
_____
_____
_____
_____

Check the box at the right when you have committed the verse to memory. Continue to repeat the verse daily for at least three weeks.

Chapter Seven

———— ◆ ————

RECONCILIATION
Healing Relational Conflicts and Wounds

"Therefore confess your sins to each other and pray for each other so that you may be healed."
James 5:16a

For nearly two years, I (Bruce) had worked with a colleague of mine to form a joint ministry venture. Then, as we neared a decisive point, I began to lose confidence in our partnership and in the venture itself. At the last minute, I confronted my friend with my "irrevocable" decision to withdraw from the partnership. My withdrawal effectively scuttled the project, affecting the plans of three churches and many individuals. My action caused my friend much embarrassment and turmoil. Though many of my concerns were substantive, the abruptness of my withdrawal compounded the matter. My friend was put in a bad light and given no real opportunity at that point to rectify the situation. He felt deep betrayal and hurt. We exchanged some tense words that served only to increase the distance between us.

As time passed, we would occasionally run into each other. Our interactions were polite, but neither of us made an effort to address the hurt that had developed. I told myself that he should take the next step, since I had already admitted my error in acting so abruptly. A year passed without any resolution of the distance in our relationship. An opportunity developed requiring a move to another city. While making preparations to move, I knew in my heart that it would be wrong to leave the area without seeking reconciliation. I wrote a letter of confession, stating specifically what I had done that was wrong and identifying the *pain that I thought my actions had caused him to feel. The letter also included a genuine expression of sadness that I felt for him, and a humble request for his forgiveness. Having taken, rather than avoided, this necessary step toward reconciliation, I experienced God's peace within me. That peace was related to the Father's promise of forgiveness (I John 1:9). But a gracious reply from my friend expressing his forgiveness and offering encouragement in my new work made my joy complete.*

Conflict occurs because people's objectives are not fully compatible. Though the appearance of conflict may differ from one relationship to another, none are entirely free from it. Conflict will occur as long as there are imperfect people living in an imperfect world. Therefore, the question is not *if* we will experience relational conflict on earth, it is *when* will we experience it, and *how* we will respond when we do.

We are encouraged frequently in Scripture to resolve our conflicts and restore unity in our friendships. For example, Jesus placed a very high priority upon reconciling with those who have something against us (Matt. 5:23-24). Each of us is responsible for doing everything within our power to live at peace with one another, maintaining harmony in our relationships (Rom. 12:18).

God's love is powerful. It does not ignore relational discord, point fingers to justify remaining stuck, or store up bitterness and resentment by keeping track of the wrongs. Instead, His love works in the present to move toward reconciliation, the reestablishment of friendship and the resolving of differences (I Cor. 13:4-7). God demonstrated this initiative to reconcile by sending Jesus to die for our sins that we might have our relationships with Him restored. God did not wait until we were taking initiative ourselves. He took the first step of reconciliation *while we were yet sinners* (Rom. 5:8). Clearly, the Lord is in the business of restoring relationships and wants us to be involved in that work.

Think about some of your relationships for a few moments. Are there any that have some unfinished business? Do you have a friend who might be holding something against you? Have you been the victim of a relative's wrongdoing that has never been addressed? If so, write a brief description of the offenses and how they are affecting you now. (Some examples: *I bad-mouthed my pastor behind his back because I disagreed with his direction and now I feel guilty and ashamed for having done so; I still resent my former roommate for breaking a lease and causing me to forfeit my rent deposit; Since I moved to Virginia three years ago, my mother hasn't called or written to see how I am doing. It reminds me of the old adage, 'Out of sight, out of mind').*

Ways I have hurt others: _____
_____
_____
_____
_____
_____
_____
_____

Ways I have been hurt: _____
_____
_____
_____
_____
_____
_____
_____

Ask God to give you the courage and concern for your friend, relative, or work associate, so that you might take initiative to reconcile your relationship. Write out here what you want to pray to God: _____
_____
_____
_____
_____
_____

In our work helping people reconcile conflicted relationships, several perspectives have proven to be helpful. First, hurt occurs in relationships from two types of offenses—those that are intentional and malicious and those that are inadvertent, though painful. The first type has to do with the offender's *motive*, whereas the second is an error in his or her *method*. It is important to distinguish between the two as we seek to restore the relationship. The reconciliation process is more difficult when wrong motives are *assumed* apart from valid evidence.

Relational breakdowns are shared struggles. They are rarely caused by only one person. It is true that one person's behavior can be more destructive than the other's. However, it is wise to examine both sides of the relational equation for needed changes.

When people experience conflicts in their relationships, they often continue to invest energy and effort in unproductive, repetitive patterns of interaction. For example, two friends had developed a conflict pattern where one was openly critical while the other kept distancing. As time went on, they would continue to get "better" at criticizing and distancing. They would keep doing the same thing that was unproductive in the first place. Sadly, their refinements only served to keep the relationship stuck rather than moving it toward a more healthy and satisfying dynamic. Relationships do not get better unless a noticeable change occurs.

Finally, it is our firm belief that no relational conflict is unresolvable. Many relationships have experienced great pain and destructive behavior. These people will need much understanding, support, and encouragement as they work to heal wounds and restore trust. However, we who call upon the name of the Lord, have a resource that is unlimited—the love and grace of our redeeming God.

The Restoration Process

When conflict persists in a relationship, negative feelings such as anger, bitterness, resentment, hurt, guilt and shame are filling the emotional cups of each individual. Eventually, these emotions will spill over in unproductive symptoms like irritability, rage, depression, or withdrawal. At that point, we may be tempted to retaliate or simply end the relationship and look for greener grass. There is a solution to any relational problem. Often, people give up their efforts to reconcile before both apply God's methods. Remember, He is in the business of restoration. He has not left us without instruction in such matters. There is hope as long as there is a willingness to trust God at the point of His word that applies to relational conflict. All friendships experience conflict. Healthy ones heal and resolve these inevitable hurts rather than ignore them or retaliate.

If we can empty the painful emotions that have built up in our relationships, many of our symptoms, such as sarcasm, disrespect, criticism, and temper outbursts, will go away. How does this emptying of painful emotions happen? It happens as we experience God's process of confession and forgiveness in our relationships. James 5:16 states, *"...confess your sins to each other and pray for each other that you may be healed,"* and Ephesians 4:32 says, *"Be kind and compassionate to one another, forgiving each other, just as in Christ God forgave you."* We can empty guilt through confession and we can empty anger, bitterness, and resentment through forgiveness. First, let's examine a major deterrent to restoration—a focus on blaming or changing the other person in the conflict—and a biblical principle for overcoming this deterrent.

The Log and Splinter Principle

When Adam and Eve committed the first sin in the Garden of Eden, did you notice how they responded to their error? You'll find answers in Genesis 3:8-24. First, they tried to hide from their Creator. Of course, they found out that it is impossible to hide from God. Next, Adam avoided God's direct question by pointing a finger at Eve, *"the woman You put here with me. . .,"* saying she was the cause of it all. Then, Eve did the same thing, putting the focus on the serpent. Most of us have done the same thing. We have focused blame on others and/or tried to get those persons to change. It is more difficult to objectively assess our own part of the conflicts, and to remain open and teachable when the examination reveals shortcomings. The following diagram depicts the choice that we have every time we are in conflict with another person—a choice to focus first and foremost on the *fallenness* (actions, words, attitudes) of others, or to focus first on the ways that our own fallenness has hurt others or contributed to their *aloneness*.

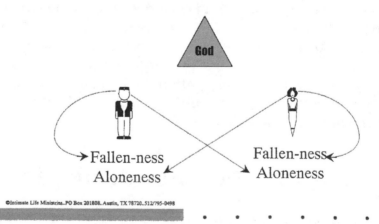

Where is Your Focus...

...your log or another's splinter?

(Matthew 7:3-5, Romans 14:12, I Corinthians 12:25)

God

Fallen-ness   Fallen-ness
Aloneness   Aloneness

©Intimate Life Ministries..PO Box 201808..Austin, TX 78720..512/795-0498

God revealed a radical approach for reconciliation and conflict resolution in the parable of the log and splinter. Jesus made the following comments while presenting the Sermon on the Mount.

> *"Why do you look at the speck of sawdust in your brother's eye and pay no attention to the plank in your own eye? How can you say to your brother, 'Let me take the speck out of your eye,' when all the time, there is a plank in your own eye? You hypocrite, first take the plank out of your own eye, and then you will see clearly to remove the speck from your brother's eye." (Matt. 7:1-5)*

This passage, instructs me to shift my focus from how the actions of others are hurting me (a focus on their fallenness) to examine how my actions might be hurting others (a focus on my own fallenness and their aloneness). I cannot justify my resistance to reconcile and change by pointing a finger at someone else. Instead, I must admit that I am free and responsible to begin addressing changes that God would have *me* to make (Rom. 14:12; I Cor. 12:25). People stay stuck in conflict when they continue to try to change the other person or rely on blaming, controlling, or manipulating rather than follow God's principle of the log and splinter.

Be aware that living out the log and splinter principle does not mean denying that you are being hurt in a relationship. It does not mean that you are to permit or enable abusive behavior or deception to continue without seeking safety or security from harm. It simply means that we are to take responsibility for our actions and repent of any wrongdoing, letting God move us with compassion for the harm that our inappropriate actions may have caused others. It means letting God be unhindered as He does a work of conviction and/or discipline in others as needed. If both people in a relationship apply the log and splinter principle, the conflict can be resolved.

Do you find it easier to identify ways your friends have hurt you or to identify ways you have hurt them? Could it be that you were trained to focus on one or the other growing up? You may have grown up in an environment where you got blamed or criticized frequently. If so, you may have responded by blaming and criticizing *others* or by concluding that the conflicts were *all* your fault. It would have been better if you had been shown how to listen carefully to each person's concerns and relate to the pain in each person's emotional cup. Then, you would have been more free to seek a resolution to the conflict rather than to blame, attack and defend, or stuff and wait.

Describe the model for conflict resolution that was demonstrated to you in childhood:

_____

_____

Simply put, God has not put us in charge of the changing of other adults. He is in charge of that. We have responsibility to work on the changes and the part of the healing process assigned to us. As we do that humbly and faithfully, the Lord may use our actions to encourage or convict our friends to change. God is better at changing hearts than we are. Galatians 5:6b is a guide for our response to conflict, *"The only thing that counts is faith expressing itself in love."* A significant way to do that is to contritely confess to our friends how we have been hurtful to them.

The Healing Power of Confession

Do you still carry some unhealed hurt, anger, or guilt from a current or previous relationship? If so, God's process for confession and forgiveness can help you experience genuine healing. Confession, done God's way, empties our emotional cup of guilt and shame. Forgiveness drains anger, resentment, and bitterness from within us. So, what does confession look like? A godly confession identifies specific offenses, understands the emotional impact of the offenses on the other person, expresses heartfelt sorrow for the pain that was caused, regards these offenses the way God does, and asks humbly for forgiveness. Let's examine these components of confession.

1. Identify specific offenses.

In relationships, hurt is experienced one specific event at a time. Vague, general apologies serve only to minimize the pain inflicted by the events. We seem to be trying to secure release from responsibility rather than facing the pain of our actions. Specific confessions of wrongful behavior reassure the wounded person that you know what you did and take responsibility for your actions. Though genuine confession does relieve stress in the offender, its primary goal is to offer healing to the one who was hurt. Therefore, identify specific behaviors, attitudes, or events that you know were wrong.

2. Understand the pain that was inflicted.

Try to view the hurt that your friend or relative experienced from his or her perspective. Resist any tendency to avoid responsibility, minimize the harm done, blame the other person, or make excuses for your actions. Your behavior may have been unintentional, but still very hurtful. The other person may not have revealed his hurt, and you may not have been aware of his pain. Nevertheless, your friend is hurting, and you are in a position to minister to him according to the need of the moment. You will need to minister *compassion* if the pain your friend is experiencing is due to behavior of yours that was appropriate in God's eyes. But if your behavior was inappropriate, you will need to include *confession* along with compassion.

To understand the pain experienced by the other person, try to imagine what he or she must have felt as a result of your actions. (For example, *hurt, upset, afraid, neglected, put down, unloved, or rejected.*) It will be very helpful for you to verbalize your understanding of the pain and let your friend clarify your understanding if necessary.

3. Develop genuine sorrow for the other person.

You have just tried to imagine what the *other* person felt due to your actions. Your friend is in pain. The question now becomes, "Do you care, and if so, why?" If you have acted in a way that was unloving or unkind, you will probably feel guilty or ashamed. These feelings are useful because they alert you to the *need* for change. However, they are not the feelings that the Bible says will *produce* the needed change in you. The scripture says that it is *godly sorrow* that leads to repentance, turning from one way to another (II Cor. 7:10). Godly sorrow is produced when our focus is on the wounded person, and we genuinely long for his or her healing. As you consider the pain that you added to the other person's emotional cup, ask yourself what you are feeling *for* him or her. Godly sorrow *for* the other person is evidence of genuine confession. It motivates us to change from sinful behavior to that which honors God and blesses others. Genuine sorrow for the other person conveys something that apology alone cannot.

4. View the offense the way God does.

How does God regard what we did (or didn't do) that contributed to another person's pain? Confession means to agree with God. To do so, we must examine our thoughts, attitudes, and behavior using His microscope. God's standards go far beyond following rules, especially in relationships. Jesus summed up the entire Law with two commandments: to love the Lord with all your heart, soul, mind, and strength, and to love your neighbor as yourself (Mark 12:30-31). When we fall short of this standard, God does not "rescue" us by justifying our sin or minimizing its impact on others. He calls it wrong, but offers forgiveness and cleansing when we repent (I John 1:9). Notice, for example, that Jesus did not condone the behavior of the adulterous woman who was about to be stoned by the Pharisees. Nor did He condemn her or leave her without hope. Instead, He intervened in a way that gave her opportunity to repent and left her free to go, but with clear instruction to turn from her sinful behavior (John 8:1-11). Therefore, when we confess our shortcomings in relationships, we need to call them wrong as God does. It will not help to try to minimize, justify, rationalize or make excuses for inappropriate behavior.

God also knows the full impact of our wrongful actions. Difficult as it may be, pray for eyes to see the pain that He can see. Not only is the other person in the relationship hurt, so is God! How can that be, you ask? Consider that our sinful behavior in relationships is part of the reason God had to send His only Son to die on the cross in order to give us hope for salvation. For as Isaiah 53:5 states, Jesus was "pierced for our transgressions...crushed for our iniquities." With gratitude and humility, we need to acknowledge the hurt we have caused God and others and seek their forgiveness.

5. Ask God and the other person to forgive you.

No matter what you have done, God has promised to forgive you when you confess and turn from your sin. You confess by communicating to God in prayer, admitting that what you did was wrong and asking Him to forgive you. God will do that because He keeps His promises (I John 1:9). Receive this unmerited favor from God today if you have not already done so.

But, what about your debt to the person wounded by your actions or inactions. In addition to identifying ways that you have hurt another person, confessing to the individual that your behavior was wrong, understanding the pain that your behavior caused, and expressing genuine sorrow for the pain you caused, it is now time to ask for forgiveness from the person you wronged. This is a humble and open invitation for that individual to respond.

Just as we don't *deserve* God's forgiveness, we don't deserve that of our colleagues. They must choose whether or not to let go of their grievances against us. It is a matter of their wills. That's what makes such a request difficult. We have no control over their choices and they may not always be ready to forgive us the way God is. Both confession *and* forgiveness are required for relationships to be fully healed and restored. The offender is responsible for repenting and seeking forgiveness. The response of forgiveness will be a work of God in the wounded person. It is a matter between that person and God. We can pray for His healing work to be completed through the process of forgiveness.

Confession or Compassion?

Joyce taught sixth grade at a Christian school in Texas. One of her students had a severe learning disability that required modification of teaching plans, extra tutoring, and special encouragement. One day, Joyce learned that the child's mother had written a critical letter calling her incompetent and claiming that she didn't care about the special needs of the child. The mother sent the letter directly to the principal without first presenting her concerns to Joyce. Obviously, the woman was concerned for her daughter. There was a lot of pain in her emotional cup. But in her pain, she had made inaccurate assumptions and acted upon them by attacking Joyce's credibility and character. When they met, Joyce avoided being drawn into an argument or defense of her competency and concern for children. Neither did she agree with the woman's false accusations. Instead, Joyce offered compassion to the mother about the difficulty the child was having in a school that had limited resources for special needs children.

Sometimes, a friend has an expectation for us that is completely unrealistic. Some accuse us of impure motives or harboring unkind thoughts that are not there. Should you confess to something just because the other person is upset or angry? What if you have examined your heart and your actions and concluded that you are not guilty of wrongdoing? What if the hurt being felt by your friend is based upon inaccurate data or assumption? How should you respond?

In cases like Joyce's above, it would confuse matters for us to confess or apologize for something that is not valid or true. Arguing or defending will do nothing to empty the cup of either person. However, we can respond to our accusers with concern and compassion, even in the face of their anger. Proverbs 15:1 says that a soft answer turns away wrath, but grievous words stir up anger. When we show empathy for another's pain, even when it is based on inaccuracy or misunderstanding, we get more of God's grace and comfort into circulation. He can work wonders with that.

Personal Application
Healing Hurts I Have Caused Others

The first step in healing relational wounds is *accepting* responsibility for your part of the conflict and taking initiative for your part of the reconciliation process. This means that you confess hurtful attitudes and actions against the other person in the relationship. Think now of a relative or an important friend with whom you have some unresolved issues. As you recall that relationship, allow God to bring to your mind specific ways that you hurt that person. Consider behaviors that were selfish, critical, insensitive, disrespectful, verbally abusive, unsupportive, ungrateful, unfaithful, rejecting, or unforgiving, as well as specific hurtful events, arguments, fights, or other actions that may need to be confessed. Make a list of these offenses using the space below. Include one-time events or ongoing patterns of behavior that were hurtful to the other person.

I hurt my friend/relative/colleague and our relationship by: (For example, *I consistently let my own hobbies and activities take precedence over spending time with my friend; I was not honest about my feelings toward my boyfriend, leading him along; I pressured my former wife sexually before we married; I was insensitive and disrespectful to my pastor, talking about him in negative ways behind his back.*) Write your list in the space provided at the top of the next page.

_____

_____

_____

_____

_____

_____

_____

Now, let's take one of these offenses and work through the process of confession as described above.

1. Identify specific offenses. Choose one of the ways that you hurt someone from the list you made previously and rewrite it here. (For example, *I pressured one of my girlfriends to be sexual outside of marriage.*)

One of the ways that I have hurt someone in a relationship is: _____

_____

_____

2. Understand the pain that was inflicted. Try to view the emotional pain that your actions would have caused your friend from his or her viewpoint. (For example, you might say, *I can imagine that you felt compromised, guilty, and ashamed. Though you may have enjoyed the physical pleasure, your spirit would have been in conflict with God's, so I can imagine you also felt anxious and troubled.*) Refuse to minimize, avoid responsibility, blame your friend for your actions, or make excuses.

As I consider what I did to you, I can imagine that you felt:

_____

_____

_____

3. Develop genuine sorrow for the other person. Ask God to give you compassion and godly sorrow for the one you hurt. Identify the feelings you have inside that are *for your friend.* (For example, you might be feeling some of the following for the person you hurt: *compassion, deep concern, sadness, hurt, or grief.*) You may also be experiencing other emotions such as guilt, shame, anger, or regret, but these are all feelings that are about, for, and/or directed toward yourself. Therefore, they are not the ones that your friend needs to hear about now.

As I reflect upon the pain that I caused you, I feel _____

for you, and I care about the pain that you have experienced due to my actions or inactions.

4. View the offense the way God does. Write out what you sense that God might say and feel about how you have hurt the other person. This part of your confession should include a clear statement in which you take full responsibility for your behavior. It should label your actions or inaction as wrong with no disclaimer. It should also acknowledge the pain that resulted for the person as well as for God, and that you need forgiveness from both. Continuing with the previous example, your statement might sound something like this: *God would say that I have been inconsiderate of my friend's need for respect. He would say that it was wrong for me to encourage her to be sexual outside marriage. That behavior on my part was hurtful in that it tempted my friend to disobey God. My wrongdoing is part of what required Jesus to suffer and die on the cross. It was a very costly sin. God would say that I could have met my friend's legitimate needs for affection and respect by acting differently. I need to seek His forgiveness and that of my friend.*

_____
_____
_____
_____
_____
_____
_____
_____
_____
_____

5. Ask God and the other person to forgive you. In the space below, express to the person you offended the confession that you have already made to God. Be sure to include your unconditional ownership of the behavior, your understanding of the emotional impact on your friend, and your feelings of sorrow or sadness for him or her. Add your request for your friend to forgive you. Using our example from above, it might sound like this: *Dear (name of your friend), I take full responsibility for my actions when I pressured you to be sexually active with me outside of marriage. It was wrong of me to do that, and I can imagine that it left you feeling disappointed, hurt, troubled, and even used. I deeply regret my actions and feel sad and deeply concerned for the impact they had on you. I have asked God to forgive me and ask you to forgive me as well, for my actions were harmful to you.*

_____

_____

_____

_____

_____

_____

_____

_____

_____

_____

_____

6. Pray for healing for your friend. Now, write out a prayer that you offer to God for your friend's healing. Here is an example: *Dear Heavenly Father, I am grateful that you are a loving and understanding God who promises to forgive us when we truly repent of our sin against you and our fellow human beings. I thank you for forgiving me in this matter. I now pray for my friend whom I hurt by pressuring her to be sexually involved with me. I pray that she will be healed of the emotional pain that she has experienced, and that her relationship with you will be fully* *restored. I thank You for the promise of comfort and the strength that comes from trusting in You. Amen.* _____

_____

_____

_____

_____

_____

_____

_____

_____

The Freedom of Forgiveness
(Eph. 4:32)

Rod and Heidi had married just before they graduated from college in Arkansas. With great excitement, they headed to seminary so that Rod could prepare for full-time family ministry. Heidi took a secretarial position in a law firm while Rod concentrated on his studies, served as a part-time youth minister in a local church, and worked evenings as a janitor on campus. As is true for most seminary couples, their finances ranged from tight to non-existent. They were both under tremendous stress and had no extended family nearby. As ministry leaders at church, they frequently functioned as care-givers, but never as care-receivers. There seemed to be no time for each other, much less spending time with friends.

As tension mounted in their relationship, both reacted by keeping their feelings suppressed and trying harder to juggle the responsibilities. They told themselves that they just had to press on for three more years. Then, Rod would graduate and take a full-time ministry position. However, that day never arrived because something happened that neither had expected. Heidi had an affair with one of the lawyers at her office. He was successful and handsome, and seemed to be able to put everything aside to visit at length with Heidi, empathizing with her struggles *and lightening her load by taking her to expensive restaurants for lunch and giving her money to "help out." He also endorsed her religious values, having become a Christian himself as a teenager. Heidi eventually developed more intimacy with this man than she had with Rod. Her feelings for him grew and, rather than work to reconcile the relationship with Rod, she left him and filed for divorce.*

Five years later, Rod was working as a construction supervisor, having dropped out of seminary. He felt robbed of an opportunity to pursue his calling as a family minister, since his own marriage had failed. Rod was still full of anger and resentment toward Heidi. He could not fathom how she was capable of such betrayal. Worst of all, he was deeply hurt that she had never expressed remorse about it. She had only given excuses and claimed that she had to "follow her heart." Betrayal and abandonment from the past still imprisoned Rod in the present.

Anger, resentment, and bitterness can extend the harmful effects of old relational wounds. In fact, research suggests that prolonged anger can contribute to the hardening of arteries, strokes, and other life-threatening maladies. In addition to physiological problems, these hostile emotions constrain the heart and soul, denying full expression of joy and celebration. We tend to hold onto anger because it is a *powerful* emotion that seems less threatening than facing *vulnerable* feelings such as loss, powerlessness, and sorrow. But holding onto anger in any of these forms will not free us from the pain of the past or bring about real change in an offender. God wants to restore our joy in the present. He has given us a way to escape the cage of bitterness, resentment and anger (I Cor. 10:13). He has given us the way of forgiveness.

Just as sincere, humble confession empties our emotional cups of guilt, forgiveness frees us from anger, resentment, and bitterness. But forgiveness is a process that involves more than intellectual assent. The more you have been hurt, the more you realize that true forgiveness requires a letting go from deep within that touches the emotional fiber of the soul. All too often, this process gets short-circuited by avoidance of the pain, distortion of the facts, or holding onto the debt owed to you.

Let's look at how Jesus modeled the process of forgiving those who do wrong to you. We will see that He didn't get caught in the anger trap, nor did He minimize the suffering that was caused by His offenders. Jesus understood what was going on from God's perspective and He freely chose to keep no "I.O.U." against His tormentors. Jesus faced the hurt, understood the truth, and then chose to forgive.

1. Face the hurt.

The night of His arrest and interrogation, and less than 24 hours before He would be crucified, Jesus goes with His disciples to Gethsemene. Taking Peter, James, and John along, He retreats into the garden to pray (Matt. 26: 36-46). Jesus did not discount the seriousness of the situation. He did not minimize the pain that He knew was coming. Nor did He try to put it out of His mind by staying busy. Instead, Jesus faced his dilemma directly.

We know that Jesus' struggle was intense, for the passage says He was deeply troubled in His soul, feeling "overwhelmed with sorrow to the point of death." In His divinity, the Lord could have marshalled angels to alter the course of events. But in His humanity, He experienced the same kind of emotions we face in our struggles. He allowed those feelings to be present, though they were unpleasant. He even disclosed his sorrow to those who were with Him, admitting vulnerability, rather than presenting a "stiff upper lip."

As you think seriously about your relationships, acknowledge the pain along with the joy. Do not deny or minimize the pain that you experience, whether it involves rejection, neglect, ridicule, criticism, manipulation, or abandonment. Do not dismiss it as unimportant or spiritualize it. If it would be painful to others, admit that you, too, are vulnerable. Jesus did.

2. Understand the truth.

Jesus knew the truth about the circumstances surrounding His dilemma and the people involved. He never condoned their behavior or minimized its impact. However, He looked beyond the *behavior* of the soldiers and His betrayer to see them as people whom He loved. He understood that these offenders were more than their behavior. They were flawed human beings with needs of their own, blinded to the truth of His identity. He saw at the time what we often can only see afterwards, that God was at work for eternal good even in the midst of a bad time. Even as He was being arrested, Jesus said, "...all this has all taken place that the writings of the prophets might be fulfilled" (Matt. 26:56).

It is good for us to examine the offenses accurately and objectively, using God's standards for determining if they were appropriate or not. We also need to clarify who was responsible for the behavior, for as adults, we are each responsible for our own actions, not those of others. If a friend makes comments that provoke our anger, she is responsible to God for her comments and you are accountable to God for how you respond, for example, lashing out aggressively, versus taking time out to calm down and return later to discuss the matter in love.

3. Choose to forgive the offender.

Jesus made a choice to forgive His offenders. He verbalized this request on the cross, saying: "Father, forgive them, for they do not know what they are doing (Luke 23:34)." Jesus didn't rely on His feelings in order to make this request of the Father. It was an act of His will, the cancelling of a debt, a choice reflecting the unsurpassed love of God.

Sometimes, we say we forgive someone, yet know in our hearts that we have not cancelled the debt as Jesus did with His very life. Our words may remain shallow until we have faced the pain of the loss from the offense. We can then begin to look beyond the wrongdoing to see the offender as someone worth loving anyway. Forgiveness is a radical, illogical response to behavior that deserves punishment. Yet, it is this act of faith and love that God often uses to bring about His purposes in us. Forgiveness sets us free to experience more joy, peace and contentment.

Special Considerations

The order of the steps in the process of forgiveness is essential. If we ignore the step of facing our hurt, we minimize our pain and forgive partially if at all. We can only forgive as deeply as we have felt the pain of the offense. If we view the offense and the offenders from a distorted perspective, our efforts to forgive may be misdirected or blocked completely. In order to be effective, the choice to forgive must come from the soul and reflect God's perspective of the person and the situation.

Pardon or Consequences. One obstacle that might inhibit us from forgiving is a fear that the offender will get away with a crime, either figuratively or literally. Does forgiving people mean that you are to disregard the offense or remove the consequences of their behavior? Not necessarily. God uses consequences to train us and bring about further maturity. He does that for your good (Heb. 12:10-11). But, check your motives before responding with consequences. If your goal is to take vengeance, then you are trying to take God's job from Him (Heb. 10:30). But, when your motive is the same as God's, there will be times when consequences will be necessary in order for the offender to grow.

Forgiveness vs. Trust. Does forgiving someone mean that you must trust them to not hurt you again? Not necessarily. Forgiveness and trust are two distinct choices. You can forgive an offense without choosing to make yourself vulnerable to it again. For example, you can forgive a friend for wrecking your car while driving recklessly without choosing to loan your car to him in the future. You may want to see that some character development has occurred first. Trust is an important aspect of a relationship and whenever it is broken effort is required to restore it. We earn trust much like we did as children—we demonstrate responsibility with what we have been given in order to be entrusted with more (Luke 16:10). God is a God of second chances, but wisdom is required to decide when and how much trust to bestow once it has been forfeited.

Unresponsive Offenders. What about forgiving offenders who are either dead or who minimize, deny, or avoid talking about what they did? Many of us were hurt in childhood by persons who used us or abused us for their own gratification. Since you were hurt, you will need comfort. If the offender is unavailable or unwilling to confess the sin and facilitate your healing, you will need comfort from others in whom you can confide. Our emotional cups are drained of hurt through comfort as described in Chapter Three. Therefore, begin to mourn the hurt or loss and allow others you trust to comfort you. Also, you can complete the forgiving process even though the offender is deceased. Forgiveness is a transaction that does not require the participation of the other person, though that is obviously better that way. The *Personal Application* exercise that appears later in this chapter will give you that opportunity.

Unhealed Hurt Hindering Forgiveness. Sometimes, forgiveness is limited to our head and doesn't involve our heart. This may happen when there is unhealed hurt related to the offense we have experienced. In order for hurt to be healed, comfort must be offered to a person who is grieving or mourning the hurt. If the pain of the hurt has not been understood and comforted by someone who cares, anger, fear, or other damaging emotions may continue to hinder the freedom that comes through forgiveness. The following story, taken from David Ferguson's book, *The Great Commandment Principle*, published by Tyndale House, illustrates this dilemma and the solution—comforting the hurt in order to remove barriers that would hinder forgiveness.

A pastor and his wife approached me during a break in one of our conferences. They wanted to talk about Rachel, a woman in their church they had been counseling for months. As a little girl, Rachel had been sexually abused by her father. Anger and resentment were eating her life away.

"David, we have tried everything we can think of to help her forgive her father, but she won't let go of her bitterness," the pastor lamented. "We reminded her that God has forgiven her for things she has done, so she must forgive also. We tell her that forgiving is for her own freedom and that it doesn't mean what happened to her was right in any way. We have gone through all that and more, but nothing works. She is as bitter as ever."

"As you have come to understand Rachel's pain from her past," I said, "what kind of feelings for her has it prompted in you?"

The couple's response was classic. "Feelings? Just as we said, we feel she needs to forgive her father."

"Yes, Rachel needs to forgive," I agreed. "But what do you feel for Rachel as you consider the painful trauma she experienced?"

I received blank stares, so I rephrased the question. "Can you imagine how God feels toward Rachel for all she went through? This innocent little girl was betrayed and violated by someone she trusted. She probably lay awake in terror countless nights, dreading her father's appearance at the door of her room. What do you think God must have felt toward Rachel every time this defenseless little girl was physically and emotionally wounded?"

The couple was silent for several moments. Then they began sharing their reflections. "God must have felt loving compassion for little Rachel. He probably hurt deeply for her. Her pain must have caused him great sorrow."

Then I said, "If God feels such loving compassion and sorrow for Rachel—and I believe he does—do you think it would be all right if you did?"

Silence again. The pastor seemed to be processing the concept through his theological training. He finally concluded that it was sound.

"The next time Rachel comes in," I continued, "instead of focusing on her need to forgive, try comforting her lovingly for what she has gone through. Say something like, 'As we think about the abuse you suffered, we just want you to know that we really hurt *for you. It saddens us that you went through all that.' Simply share your love and comfort and see what happens."*

The couple agreed. Several weeks later I received a note from them. It read, "It worked! We shared comfort with Rachel like you suggested, and something wonderful began to happen. She seemed so deeply affected by our sadness and love for her that she is now dealing with the issue of forgiving her father. It's a miracle!"

Did Rachel need to forgive her father? Yes. Were this pastor and his wife wrong to urge Rachel to forgive as she had been forgiven by God? Absolutely not. Forgiveness was essential to Rachel's spiritual health and growth. Then why had this couple's ministry to her been, at least in part, ineffective? Because it lacked the full impact of Great Commandment love. Rachel needed someone to challenge her to obey the Scriptures with regard to her father. But she also needed someone to minister to her God's heart of compassion for the pain she had suffered. She needed someone to hurt for her just as God hurt for her and to minister God's love and comfort. When this couple simply expressed sorrow for her, she was comforted. Once someone began to meet her deep need for compassion and comfort, Rachel was better able to deal with her need to forgive.

Responding to Hurts
I Have Experienced

Now you will have an opportunity to address some of the pain that you have experienced in relationships that may not yet be healed or resolved.

1. Face the hurt.

Begin this process by identifying some specific ways that you have been hurt by others in your adult relationships. This could include relationships with close friends, room-mates, work associates, dating partners, brothers or sisters, or even your parents.

Some of the ways I have been hurt by others are: (For example, *a man I was dating seriously hid from me for months that he had been seeing another woman, devastating me at the time; my brother who is an atheist has refused to speak to me since I became a Christian, leaving me feeling rejected and judged; I have been teased repeatedly by co-workers about my weight, causing me to feel ridiculed and ashamed.)*

_____
_____
_____
_____
_____
_____
_____
_____
_____

Now, write down some of the feelings you are experiencing as you ponder the ways you were hurt. _____
_____
_____

Referring to the *Ten Key Intimacy Needs* on page 38, identify some of the needs that went unmet related to the hurts you listed above, for example: *affection, attention, respect, comfort, support, approval, etc.* Some of my underlying needs that went unmet in these relationships were: _____

_____

_____

_____

_____

Write down your thoughts about what God feels for you given the hurt you experienced. (For example, *I think it grieved God that I was hurt that way; I know that God really was concerned even though He did not choose to intervene supernaturally to stop my friend from ridiculing me.*)

_____

_____

_____

_____

2. Understand the truth

Now that you have identified some ways that the behavior of others has hurt you, try to see the situation and the people involved from God's perspective. Though their actions may have been terribly wrong and hurtful, remember that they are still people for whom Christ chose to die. They, like we ourselves, received God's offer of forgiveness even before they were ready to accept it (Rom. 5:8). Realize that you were not *responsible* for their behavior, so what they did or didn't do reveals more about them than about you.

For each of the offenses you listed above, and for which you identified the painful impact it had upon you, write down something that it teaches you about the offender. (For example, *the fact that my atheist brother won't visit me anymore suggests something about his own fear or need for acceptance rather than*

about my own choice of values as long as I am not being judg-
mental or rude to him.) _____

_____
_____
_____
_____
_____
_____
_____
_____

Write down what you think God would say about the behavior of the person whose actions were hurtful to you. (For example, *God would say that your brother's rejection of Christ is wrong and likewise his rejection of you for believing in Christ. He would say that these actions need to be confessed.)* _____

_____
_____
_____
_____

Now write down what you think God would say about the *person* who did the offense. (For example, *You are of great worth because I sent my Son to die for you so that you could be forgiven of your sins; I do not want any to perish, including you; I will cleanse and restore you if you will just trust Me and repent.)* ____

_____
_____
_____
_____

3. Choose to forgive the offender.

You do not have to wait for the other person to seek forgiveness in order to give it. It is a conscious decision on your part to let go of the debt and the anger associated with it. Forgiveness brings healing to your life regardless of the change or lack of change in your offender.

Write down an expression of your forgiveness for the offender in the form of a letter, as if you were actually talking to him or her now. Refer to the behaviors that were hurtful to you and how they made you feel. Then read this statement of forgiveness aloud, as if you were talking to the offender. (For example, *Dear Brother, When you told me that you no longer wanted to speak to me because of my decision to follow Christ, I felt hurt, rejected, and angry. This rejection is especially painful because I have always wanted your acceptance and for years tried to "earn" it. But I choose to forgive you, my brother, for I have been forgiven much by God. I am releasing the anger that I had carried and free you from any obligation or expectation to change or make this up to me in the future. Though I know it is best to not depend upon you or others for acceptance, I look forward to a time that we can get to know one another better and talk freely again.*)

_____

_____

_____

_____

_____

_____

_____

_____

Now, describe what you have experienced as you completed this exercise. (For example, *I felt relieved, as though a burden had been lifted from my shoulders; I felt happier and free to reach out again to my brother who had been so critical of me.*) _

_____

_____

_____

_____

_____

_____

_____

_____

Though conflict is inevitable in human relationships, God can bring about reconciliation when caring is increased through faith in Him. Even if only one person in the relationship submits to the ways of God, He can bring about healing.

Encountering God in His Word

"Bruised for Our Iniquities"
Isaiah 53:1-12 (focal passage: Isaiah 53:4-6)

Read and ponder Isaiah 53 which speaks of Christ's suffering for us. Verse 5 says He was wounded for our transgressions; He was bruised for our iniquities. The first important truth of this verse is that God declares our worth through the gift of His Son. The second truth is that our sinful actions are what caused Him to have to die. As you seek to experience genuine confession and forgiveness for your sins, recognize the relevance of these two truths. As we approach God with a humble spirit, we acknowledge the wrongness of our actions. As we are grateful for His forgiveness, we recognize that He chooses to look upon us as His precious children, made worthy by His grace.

◆ Once again, think about some of the ways that you have "turned to your own ways" (Verse 6) in relationships. Write some of these ways in the space below. _____

_____

_____

_____

_____

_____

◆ Now, think about how God was actually leading you in another direction for your own benefit because of His great love for you. Write down your thoughts and feelings related to God's love and provision of guidance that we so often reject and despise.

_____

_____

_____

_____

_____

◆　　　Imagine what God must have felt as you turned from His loving guidance and relied instead upon what seemed right or justified in your eyes. Write to God about the feelings you think He has any time you, one of his precious children, act in ways He knows will eventually hurt you. Express your sorrow for Jesus who suffered physically for you, but also endured humiliation and the pain of being separated from the Father as He took on the sin of the world.

_____

_____

_____

_____

_____

_____

◆　　　Note the impact this time of meditation and self-examination has had on you. Are there any new thoughts that have come to mind? Write down any changes in attitude that may have taken place. _____

_____

_____

_____

_____

God gives to any who humbly seek and receive Him the power to become His child.

Group Dialogue

If you do not have a designated group leader, choose someone in the group who will serve to facilitate the discussion. Begin by briefly reviewing the discussion guidelines.

Discussion Guidelines

◆ Allow everyone an opportunity to share thoughts and feelings
◆ Avoid long story telling
◆ Be quick to listen with empathy

◆ Be slow to give advice
◆ Speak the truth in love
◆ Say what you mean and mean what you say
◆ Protect the confidentiality of every person

Discussion Suggestions for Chapter Seven

1. Read out loud the "log and splinter" passage from Matthew 7:1-5. Discuss which list you find more difficult to make—the ways you have hurt others or the ways others have hurt you.

2. Go around the group, sharing specifically how your parents or caretakers modeled the process of confession and forgiveness. For example, do any group members remember having a parent come to them humbly confessing a wrongdoing, such as yelling in anger because a chore had not been completed correctly? Discuss what difference it might have made if adults had modeled confession and forgiveness to you at a young age?

3. Discuss within the group what makes a confession genuine and effective. Contrast the characteristics you identify with some of the "confessions" you have seen in public settings or in your own personal experience.

4. Since godly sorrow brings repentance or change, name one area of change you are anticipating that God wants to bring about in your life.

5. Take turns sharing what you find most difficult about forgiving those who have done wrong to you.

6. Close by praying together for courage to practice confession and forgiveness daily.

◆ Set aside one to two hours for the meeting to give ample time for each person to share.

◆ Select a meeting location that minimizes distractions or interruptions.

◆ Read the chapter and complete all the written exercises *before* meeting to discuss them.

◆ Purpose to start on time and complete each exercise, staying focused on the material.

Suggestions for Journey-mate Encounter #7

1. While avoiding slander or gossip, share a struggle that you are having in an ongoing relationship. (For example, *I am feeling a lot of disrespect in my relationship with a colleague at work who carries on long, loud telephone conversations while I am trying to do detailed financial work.*) Ephesians 4:15 says that we are to "speak the truth in love," which would rule out hiding our concerns or lashing out with them in an angry or condemning manner. Discuss how you would want to be approached about the conflict if you were the other person.

2. Review your responses to the personal application section about confessing ways that you have hurt others. Discuss how difficult you found this exercise to be and what you felt as you completed that section. Also, invite your journey-mate(s) to hold you accountable for initiating reconciliation in a specific relationship.

3. One step in the confession process is to experience a sense of godly sorrow for the one hurt by your actions. Godly sorrow produces repentance (II Cor. 7:10), literally, a "turning

from" or change. Name one area of change God would want to see you make in your relational life.

4. Take turns sharing your responses to the personal application section about forgiveness of others who have hurt you. Discuss how difficult you found this exercise to be and what emotions you experienced as you completed that section.

5. Take turns sharing one issue from the list of ways you have been hurt for which you have not yet received comfort. The hurtful experience you share could be drawn from either your adult or your childhood relationships. Practice good emotional responding by listening attentively to each other's hurts and expressing genuine sorrow and compassion for pain that each experienced. If your journey-mate(s) is willing, share additional hurts and continue giving comfort as time permits.

6. Close your time by taking turns praying for continued healing and freedom from hurt and anger in all relationships. Pray for the courage to practice Ephesians 4:15 (speak the truth in love), James 5:16a (confess your sins to each other and pray for each other so that you may be healed), and Ephesians 4:29 (let no unwholesome word proceed from your mouth except that which is for the building up of one another according to the need of the moment).

Hiding the Word in Your Heart
James 5:16a

Write the verse here: _____
_____
_____
_____
_____
_____
_____
_____

Repeat the verse from memory each day for several weeks. Using the space below, you may want to journal ways that God has allowed you to experience the verse as you have hidden it away in your heart. _____
_____
_____
_____
_____
_____
_____
_____
_____
_____
_____
_____
_____
_____
_____

Check the box at the right when you have committed the verse to memory. Continue to repeat the verse daily for at least three weeks.

Chapter Eight

— ◆ —

SEXUALITY AND ROMANCE

*Affirming Sexuality and Avoiding
the Pain of Sexual Sin*

*"That you may be able to discern what is best
and may be pure and blameless." Phil 1:10*

Danielle and Roger met in the singles department of a large Midwestern church. After dating off and on for eight months, they became very serious about each other. They even began to talk about engagement. Both were determined to remain sexually pure out of obedience to God and respect for one another. One day, following an intense argument that left both upset, Roger approached Danielle to apologize. She accepted his apology and they embraced affectionately. However, on this day, they extended their hugging until both became sexually aroused. Eventually they progressed well beyond the boundaries observed since their dating began. Though the experience was pleasurable at the time, both felt guilty afterwards, knowing that their behavior had violated God's standards for single adults. The passions they had fueled through their behavior could only be satisfied by completion of the act. Thus, by moving in that direction, they had placed stumbling blocks in the way of each other's pursuit of purity and intimacy with God. Later, as he took the matter to God in prayer, Roger pondered how his actions had been hurtful to God, to Danielle, and to himself. Roger felt deep sorrow for the hurt he had caused. He met with Danielle to confess, seek her forgiveness, and pray for healing. Danielle also took responsibility for her part of what happened between them. They agreed to *seek out mature same-gender mentors with whom they could be accountable.*

The expression of physical affection has been a particular challenge for Christians in close personal relationships. Today, singles live in an environment where sexual involvement outside marriage is not only encouraged, but readily available. The pressure to conform is tremendous, given the endorsement of unrestrained sexual involvement so prevalent in the media today. Sadly, when it comes to expressions of sexuality, many Christians are behaving in ways that are inconsistent with the Word of the Lord who lives within every believer. Why is this so?

Many stumble because they buy into the deception that their happiness will be maximized through sexual involvement in dating relationships. They see sexual involvement as a viable way to remove their loneliness. Others are being deceived by the pleasure inherent in sexual sin. But such pleasure is short-lived (Heb. 11:25) and is soon followed by guilt, shame, or other negative symptoms. Furthermore, pleasure for the moment never justifies sin or offsets its consequences. That is why there can be no real and complete peace for Christians who are trusting in pleasure rather than God and His Word. Still others are buying the lie that there is no harm in sexual intimacy among consenting adults. The truth is, they will inevitably experience painful outcomes, either as victims, as offenders, or both, because a "not good" results when God creates something good and humans misuse or abuse it.

It is genuine intimacy, rather than sex, that you cannot *live* without. Inner joy and peace are available through spiritual and relational intimacy with God and others. Sexual experience outside God's parameters obstructs that intimacy with Him for both you and your partner. Therefore, sex outside of marriage cannot be God's provision for you. Remember that Jesus came that we might have life and have it abundantly (John 10:10). Satan, on the other hand, wants to steal our lives through dangerous and deceptive counterfeits. He would have us think that we cannot truly live without experiencing sex. Loving God with all our being and trusting that He has our best interests in mind is an act of faith that can be applied to the sexual aspect of our lives.

This chapter will help clarify how single adults can guard God's precious gift of sexuality through the exercise of Great Commandment love. Let's begin taking stock of what we were taught about our sexual nature and the examine how that compares to a biblical view of sexuality and how it should be expressed as a single adult.

Personal Application
Embracing My Sexuality

Describe how comfortable you are being created as a sexual being with sexual desires and capacities. _____
_____
_____

What beliefs and messages about sexuality were conveyed to you verbally or by implication during childhood? *(For example, "My parents never talked about sex, but always switched the TV to another channel when a love scene occurred in the program we were watching. I guess it seemed that sex was supposed to be bad if we couldn't watch it or talk about it.")* _
_____
_____
_____
_____
_____

How have these messages helped or hurt you? _____
_____
_____
_____
_____
_____

Seeing Sexuality From
An Eternal Perspective

Sexuality is a part of God's creative design of humankind. It was not an accident or a result of sin entering the world. Genesis 1:27, says, *"So God created man in his own image, in the image of God he created him; male and female he created them" (Gen. 1:27).* Gender differences were defined prior to the Fall of Mankind recorded in Genesis 3.

Our sexuality is truly a gift from God. Even the urges and feelings that are part of our sexuality, such as attraction and arousal, are part of God's incredible design that He called good. In His sovereign will, God has chosen to restrict the full expression of sexual intimacy to the marriage relationship. But, as with the tongue, our ability to speak, the sexual part of our being can be used for both good or evil, life or death. God calls us to place our sexuality under the lordship of Christ to maintain its purity and intended purpose. It is a precious asset that merits respect and honor. Sexuality is God's gift that calls for stewardship and responsibility, not misuse, abuse, or denigration. It needs to be experienced and expressed in ways that honor Him.

Biblical Truths
about Human Sexuality

✝ **Our sexuality is a gift from our Creator that He has called good.** Maleness and femaleness preceded the introduction of sin in the world. Therefore, it is something to be valued and cherished rather than denigrated, cheapened, or denied.

✝ **Sexuality includes much more than the physical aspect of a person.** It is multi-faceted, having intellectual, emotional, relational, and social aspects as well.

✝ **Sexuality is a gift for which each person is a steward.** We are responsible to manage this gift that the Creator has entrusted to us. Sexuality involves our whole being and therefore, what we do with it affects our whole being.

✝ **Sexuality is not forfeited by inactivity.** We remain sexual persons whether or not we are engaging in sexual activity. We are no less male or female, even if called to singleness for life.

✝ **As my creator, God knows the boundaries that are best for me sexually.** As He has with other areas of life, God has defined certain limits within Scripture for sexual experience and expression in our relationships. These Scriptures focus primarily on defining *who* can experience sexual intimacy together—a husband and wife.

✝ **Out of love, God has put limits on sexual expression for our good.** He loves us and cares for us as His own children. He is able to see the pain and heartache caused by irresponsible use of the gift of sexuality. His vision is 20:20, and far-reaching.

✝ **The God-given relational needs of single adults can be met without sinning.** Relational needs such as affection, acceptance, comfort, and approval are the same for singles as they are for married people. These needs can be met in non-sexual ways. They should be distinguished from sexual desires, thinking patterns and urges such as attraction, sexualization, and arousal.

✝ **Dealing with our sexuality is a life-long process.** Like our relational needs, our sexuality is a permanent aspect of our being. However, the nature of our sexual desires may change to some degree in different stages of our lives.

Compare these statements about God's design and plan for experiencing and expressing human sexuality to the cultural myths that follow later in the chapter. Then, assess where you are placing your trust. When we are exposed to God's truth, we are in position to apply it. But all we have to do to let darkness overtake us is to stand still rather than walk faithfully in the light we have been given (John 12:35-36). As we grow in the grace and understanding of the Lord, it is important to catch the larger vision of His plan for all needs—trusting Him for the provision.

Your Intimacy Inventory

At the beginning of this book, we pointed out that God made human beings three dimensional. They have a spirit, soul, and body, and can experience intimacy with others in every dimension. God seems to give greater emphasis to spiritual and relational intimacy than to physical intimacy without diminishing the value and beauty of sexual intimacy experienced within a marriage.

As you contemplate God's intended purpose for intimacy in relationships in the physical, emotional, and spiritual dimensions of our beings, take a few minutes to assess the depth and quality of your current experience. Turn to the Appendix A and complete the *Intimacy Inventory for Single Adults.* After you have finished, record your results on the Spiritual, Friendship, and Physical scales on the back of the inventory. The answer the following questions.

What thoughts and feelings do you have about the areas of intimacy in relationships that you feel most comfortable about and those that you think are most difficult for you? _____

_____

_____

_____

_____

_____

What seems to hinder you from being able to experience intimacy appropriately in each dimension while a single adult? __

_____

_____

_____

_____

_____

_____

_____

Trusting in God's
Provision and Priority

In our close personal relationships, God would first want us to experience the fellowship of oneness in Him through a common faith in Christ—a knowing that transcends our emotional and physical being. Next, he would have us know one another deeply on an emotional and intellectual level, able to share our deepest concerns and celebrate great triumphs together. Finally, in God-honoring ways, He would have friends express affection for one another. This can be done in ways that honor God, respecting Him and our close friends. Affection can be expressed without transgressing boundaries God reserved for the marriage relationship.

What do dating relationships look like when they reflect God's priorities for intimacy—spiritual, then soul, and eventually, physical intimacy? First, we might see a couple talking about their faith in God and their walk with Him. They might experience worship together and begin to pray frequently with one another, discussing the changes God seems to be bringing about in their lives. They would develop a respectful interest and concern for the spiritual growth and maturity of the other person without trying to control the process.

Intimacy of the soul would flow from the spiritual closeness as the two people begin to share their inner thoughts, feelings, dreams, and fears with one another. There would be greater freedom to talk about aspects of their lives that had originally triggered hurt, pain, shame, or anger. They would learn which relational needs are most significant to the other and deliberately set out to meet those needs. They would become great friends, "knit in the soul" yet retaining their objectivity.

The physical aspect of their relationship could manifest a degree of intimacy as well, though submission to God's boundaries would reflect a faith that He really does know what is best for each of them at any given point in time. These two individuals might express caring affection for one another by going for walks together or holding hands. They might give affectionate, non-arousing hugs to one another, particularly in the presence of others.

Society has inverted God's order and priority for intimacy. The importance of sexual intimacy is so magnified today that emotional and spiritual intimacy seem to have lost significance. On the cusp of the 21st century, our culture communicates the following priorities for intimacy—the physical (sexual) aspect is essential, emotional intimacy is optional, and spiritual oneness is a frill. Society has turned God's priority for intimacy upside down.

A number of trends we see in today's society may be tied to widespread emphasis on the physical dimension of intimacy. Affairs between men and women are becoming commonplace, in part because of their implied "normalcy" in films, television, and publishing. Children are being led to think and act sexually at younger ages. Many adults are experiencing problems with impotency, often because they have internalized unrealistic performance expectations for sex. The harmful impact of pornography is increasing, particularly with its availability on the Internet. These *symptoms* of aloneness and fallenness would diminish if society experienced more genuine intimacy with God, among friends, and within marriages and families.

Each of us faces a choice. Do we pursue God's provision for intimacy or the world's? Those choices reflect our priorities— saying 'yes' to some things and 'no' to others. It helps to know that God is with us when we choose His priorities. Kenneth Boa, in *That I May Know God*, states:

> *Whenever He asks us to avoid something, it is not because He is a cosmic killjoy, but because He knows that it is not in our best interests. And whenever He asks us to do something, it is always because it will lead to a greater good. . . . But the risk of obedience is that it will often make no sense to us at the time.*

The Danger and Deception of Cultural Counterfeits

We live in a dangerous era. A youth minister in Oklahoma once said, "Young people today are making bigger decisions with greater consequences at a younger age than ever before." A generation ago, the most dreaded consequence of inappropriate sexual behavior was the embarrassment of contracting a sexually transmitted disease. The diseases that were prevalent then could be cured with medication. But today, many of these diseases are resistant to treatment, producing life-long symptoms. Now, the ultimate danger for sexually active persons is AIDS, leading eventually to death.

There are other, potentially more harmful, consequences than physiological diseases, however. There is the pain of loss of the gift of virginity for a marriage partner. There is the guilt and shame that may linger in the heart years after a relationship ended. There is tremendous hurt and devastation to a family that has been broken apart by an affair. Insecurity and anxiety related to sexual performance in marriage may be the offspring of illicit sexual encounters. Damage can be inflicted on the perceived identity of individuals who experienced sexual trauma or abuse. Though God can heal wounds as serious as these, sexual sin can affect people for decades, even later generations.

Barry is thirty-three, gainfully employed, and living in his own condominium. Since a three- year live-in relationship in college, he has not seriously considered a proposal of marriage. Barry's parents divorced when he was sixteen, and quite frankly, he doesn't have a lot of confidence in the institution of marriage. Though morality was stressed during his childhood, Barry became sexually active in high school. Since then, most of his dating relationships have featured common interests, lots of fun-seeking, and lots of sex. Barry does not consider his behavior promiscuous. He regards sex as acceptable behavior among consenting adults. He does not get sexually involved with one woman while dating another. Barry takes precautions to minimize the risk of disease or pregnancy. Once, one of his girlfriends got pregnant and decided to get an abortion because they were not really committed to each other. Like most single adults his age, Barry assumes that marriage will be in his future. It is just a matter of time and finding the right person. Soon, that confidence will ebb as a different prospect invades his thinking.

Barry will begin to wonder if he will ever enjoy the security of a permanent, faithful, trust-based relationship. But for now, he is content to take what life offers.

Barry has decided that the cultural standard for relationships is the best available. We disagree. The deepest needs of Barry's soul will not be met by sexual encounters that fall outside the bounds of God's plan and provision. In His awesome and wonderful creativity, God made him a sexual being with legitimate desires and longings. However, Barry has been influenced by a culture that often distorts the meaning of these desires and offers counterfeit alternatives for satisfying them. God knows that Barry's greatest needs are for relationships and righteousness that go far beyond temporal pleasure. God's provision for Barry is intimacy that touches the spirit and soul, not just the physical body. However, genuine intimacy involving his spirit and soul may require more of Barry than he wants to give. How about you? How much will it require of you?

Imagine that God sends an angel to earth to conduct a thorough study of sexuality in our culture using all the information available in the press, radio, television, Internet, and other media sources. If the findings of the study were based upon the *quantity* of data rather than the *truth* of it, you might see the following myths reported back to heaven.

Cultural Myths
about Human Sexuality

- ◆ **Sexual involvement is the central aspect of a relationship.** Sex is the axis upon which many movies, TV sitcoms, and novels revolve. Genuine intimacy—deep, mutual knowing for the purpose of caring involvement—often is not represented in story lines at all.
- ◆ **Sexual experience is a measure of the significance of a relationship.** The bond between two people is often judged by the degree of sexual activity in the relationship.

- **Sex is the primary means for developing closeness in a relationship.** People of all ages are experiencing physical closeness without knowing the hearts of their partners. Sex is seen as a way to *become* close rather than a true *expression* of closeness reserved for marriage relationships.
- **Sex is depicted as mankind's primary need that *must* be satisfied.** Whether sex is regarded as a "right" or a biological necessity, this myth suggests that life cannot be meaningful or rewarding unless sexual drives are fulfilled.
- **Sexual involvement is appropriate on the first or second date.** It is now expected that couples experience sex early in their dating relationship.
- **Sexual intimacy is deemed a "cure all" for whatever is ailing in the relationship.** Couples may find that the pleasurable feelings of a sexual encounter mask the negative feelings produced by earlier conflicts. In reality, sex is only serving to mask or cover up serious problems and unmet needs that require other interventions.
- **Cohabitation is necessary to ensure the viability of a long-term relationship.** More and more dating couples are living together prior to marriage though divorce rates for these marriages are higher than for couples who don't cohabit first.
- **Sexual relations between consenting adults are okay regardless of marital status.** This opinion is frequently given when people are accused of sexual behavior that the Bible defines as immoral.
- **Sexual compatibility should be tested before two people marry.** The new "morality" encourages such evaluation, implying that a married couple cannot learn to better express themselves sexually in mutually satisfying ways. The fact that many have not done so does not support this pre-marital sex as the solution.
- **To be complete or whole, people need sexual mates.** *Unfulfilled desire* for sexual intimacy can easily be confused with a sense of incompleteness, particularly with the importance placed upon sexuality in the media. Wholeness comes through a spiritual relationship with Jesus Christ.

It would be nice to think that these myths are not embraced by people within the Christian community. Unfortunately, that is not the case.

Diane's track record with serious dating relationships wasn't very good. While in high school, she had been asked out a lot, in part due to her natural beauty and outgoing personality. However, those experiences left a bad taste in her mouth, for she often felt pursued as a trophy rather than a person with feelings, dreams, and dignity.

When she entered college, Diane was careful to get involved only with men who were professing Christians, treating seriously the biblical admonition to not be "yoked" with unbelievers. But Christians, she found, were not experts at love, though they should be. Even the men she met at church functions seemed more intent on conquest then on getting to know Diane personally. She found that dating was simply a prelude for sexual behavior, with the only unanswered question being, "How far is too far?" Diane resisted the pressure to be sexually active, though with some difficulty. She so wanted to be loved and treasured by a man. Finally, when she met a very nice, stable, intelligent law student who was sensitive in addition to attractive, Diane bit the hook. After a brief courtship, she rationalized that she would eventually marry this guy and agreed to a sexually intimate, cohabiting relationship.

The Bible clearly prohibits sexual relations between persons other than husband and wife. So, how do you explain the number of affairs, teenage pregnancies, and sexually-active singles within the Christian community? How do Christians like Diane lose their moral compasses? The verse printed below may provide an answer.

"See to it that no one takes you captive through hollow and deceptive philosophy, which depends on human tradition and the basic principles of this world rather than on Christ." (Col. 2:8)

Many Christians simply become deceived and believe lies about themselves, others, and even about God in order to do what *seems* right (Prov. 16:9), or try to ignore what they know is *not* right. A significant challenge faces Christian singles who want to live as Jesus lived—free of the pain of sexual sin. Here are some ways that Christians respond to the cultural temptations and become vulnerable to sexual sin.

Rationalizing. Many Christians rationalize or delude themselves to accommodate participation in extra-marital affairs. Previously married singles may justify sexual intercourse with dating partners since they have already lost their virginity. Some claim that petting, sustained arousal, partial nudity, and passionate lovemaking are warranted by the seriousness of a relationship and as long as they don't go "too far." Many singles struggle unsuccessfully to define an arbitrary "line" separating appropriate and inappropriate sexual behavior wanting to keep a clear conscience. Mutual consent by adults may be used to rationalize sexual intimacy, though it does not negate specific guidelines in God's word. Rationalization can diminish your awareness of anxiety or inner conflict. Eventually, your conscience can become hardened and insensitive, until your warning signals become so faint that painful consequences of the sin catch you by surprise.

Medicating. Conflict and discontent are often "fixed" by a mirage of intimacy in the bedroom. The sexual encounters serve only to "medicate" the relational wounds. But instead of healing, the sex only deadens the pain temporarily. Like Tylenol for a toothache, permanent relief requires getting to the heart of the matter. Sex, like alcohol, spending sprees, or pleasure trips can serve to escape pain that exists in relationships. But the pain needs to be confronted in love with an aim to bring about resolution and harmony.

Masking. Another danger of sexual behavior in relationships is that it can be used to *avoid* intimacy. Being sexually intimate in a relationship can seem easier than being honest and transparent. It may be easier for someone to be vulnerable sexually than emotionally (some individuals would prefer that you know their body than their soul). They may fear, for example, that you would reject who they are on the inside, so they keep that part hidden. Persons with a lot of shame in their emotional cups from childhood may identify with this tendency.

Addictions. If sexual behavior becomes compulsive or depersonalized, it can even become an addiction. Addicted persons will put valued "possessions," such as careers, family members, and even their lives at risk in order to continue the addictive behavior. For example, a youth minister might jeopardize his ministry by attempting to lure teenage girls into compromising situations for purposes of his sexual gratification. Sexual addiction is sustained by a lie that the sexual "high" will truly satisfy the soul. With the advent of the Internet, access to pornography has expanded. Research continues to reveal the damaging impact of pornography, but the big "loser" is the person who mistakes sexual arousal and activity for genuine intimacy and joy.

Personal Application

Vulnerability to Deception

Which of the cultural myths have been internalized by you or someone you dated? How did that myth affect your life?

_____
_____
_____
_____
_____
_____
_____
_____
_____
_____
_____

How have you experienced masking, rationalizing, medicating, or addictions in your previous relationships? What unresolved hurts might need to be confessed or grieved and comforted?

_____

_____

_____

_____

_____

_____

_____

The Unique Challenge for Singles
Capacity without Liberty

Single adults face a dilemma uncommon in most marriages unless one or both spouses has a debilitating physical or mental condition that limits sexual expression. Singles have a God-given, fully-functional sexual nature, but are denied an opportunity to fully express it unless they marry. The equipment works, but there is no place where God says it can be used. Single adults live in a state of limbo, not knowing how long this dilemma will continue, since marriage may or may not be in their future. It is normal for single adults to sense an attraction or desire for members of the opposite sex. It is also natural for them to have close personal relationships and want to express affection for one another. But singles must do this without engaging themselves sexually in the process. That can be a challenge!

Even as singles learn to meet one another's relational needs such as approval, security, respect, or comfort, sexual desires may be triggered unintentionally. Arousal leads to intense frustration if it is fed but not satisfied through sexual encounters reserved for marriage. It might seem better to have a switch that could turn you off sexually while single, as Rick Stedman suggests in his book, _Pure Joy_. Then, singles wouldn't have to work so hard to keep their thoughts and actions under the lordship of Christ. They could go about the process of developing spiritual and emotional intimacy by meeting relational needs and not have to worry about provoking strong sensual desire.

For singles, sexuality may be like a gift that you see under the Christmas tree but are not allowed to open, or a beautiful song that you are not permitted to sing out loud. Does this seem fair to you? Why would a loving God give you a capacity and desire for sexual expression that must be curtailed indefinitely? Is His intent to frustrate or toy with us? No. God is constantly at work for our good (Phil. 1:6). He is aware of our needs and ultimately provides what is best for us (Luke 12:6-7; Matt. 7:9). That does not mean that life on earth will be free of pain or frustration, however (John 16:33). God is preparing us for eternity, and His vision extends far beyond our own (Phil. 2:13; Jer. 33:3).

When we apply these truths to the issue of God's limitations on sexual expression, our faith may be challenged. It can be very difficult to rest in the knowledge that He is doing a greater work in our lives even while we are suffering disappointment, loss, or frustration. But the reward for trusting God at any point of His word, is holiness—conformity to the image of Christ Jesus (Phil. 1:6). We may balk when invited to fellowship in the sufferings of Christ, preferring instead to find our own way to secure satisfaction. But, just as Jesus did not demand His rightful place in Heaven, humbling Himself instead to carry out God's plan (Phil. 2:6-11), so we are challenged to accept the limitations he may place in our lives at any particular point in time.

Thus, living as a single and being a faithful steward of your capacity for sexuality is a part of Christian discipleship. You may often be faced with temptation to take matters into your own hands as Jesus was at the beginning of His ministry (Matt. 4:1-11). You will be faced with the choice of trusting God ultimately for your well being, which will require living by faith rather than sight (II Cor. 5:7). Some of the fruit of this walk may be the development of additional maturity, discipline, humility, endurance, and discernment. You may find that God is building within you a greater capacity to give sacrificially, putting the legitimate interests of others above your own. You will know more completely what genuine intimacy and oneness mean, for they are products of Great Commandment love rather than human passion. Though the world scoffs at such rewards, believers know that such faithful reliance upon the Lord leads to abundant life.

Can we walk this walk? Exercising restraint of your sexual urges requires maturity, sacrifice, and discipline, but most of all, faith. We must regard our gift of sexuality as God does—a resource that is beneficial when used as He intended, but harmful if applied otherwise. We must place the best interests of others (as determined by God) above our own. This means putting more value on the spiritual well-being of others than on our own desire for sexual gratification. Through this walk of faith, a single adult experiences God's Great Commandment love that gives first and doesn't keep score. The one walking by faith grows spiritually, the other person in the relationship is honored and loved as Jesus would love him, and God is glorified. However, genuine intimacy involving the spirit and soul may require more than most of us want to give.

Personal Application
Walking and Growing By Faith

What are some things that challenge your ability to remain sexually pure? _____

_____

_____

_____

What can you do to face these challenges well? _____

_____

_____

_____

_____

_____

_____

    As you have responded to God's call upon you to be a faith-
ful steward of your sexuality, recall how any of the following
character qualities have been developed in you: 1) deeper
faith, as you have trusted Him with your desires, not knowing for certain that they will ever be satisfied; 2) greater spiritual discernment of thoughts, feelings, and responses related
to your sexuality; 3) stronger reliance upon God's grace to
endure the "pain" of not fulfilling your sexual hunger inap-
propriately; and, 4) increased giving to meet the needs of others above your own.

_____

_____

_____

_____

Experiencing Great Commandment Love in Courtship

    When speaking to single adults about sexuality or dating,
we are occasionally asked to define the line between appropriate and inappropriate behavior. Sometimes it is beneficial to
share some specific instructions from Scripture or "spoon feed"
new believers. But Jesus calls us to a higher standard than the
"legal" boundaries. He calls us to practice Great Commandment
love.

> *And this is my prayer: that your love may abound
> more and more in knowledge and depth of insight, so that
> you may be able to discern what is best and may be pure
> and blameless until the day of Christ, filled with the fruit
> of righteousness that comes through Jesus Christ—to the
> glory and praise of God. (Phil. 1:9-11)*

1. Loving others well as God does

The art of Great Commandment living is a paradigm shift that has great significance for dating relationships, especially those with potential to become lifelong commitments. The central question to be addressed is, "How can I love this person well who has become so dear to me and to whom I am physically attracted?" We learn how to love well in romantic relationships by experiencing Bible verses about loving others the way God intended.

Love applies wisdom and discernment to remain pure and blameless (Phil 1: 9-11). Great Commandment love does not withdraw in fear from personal relationships. Instead, it brings godly knowledge, objectivity, and discipline along on the journey to ensure that the relationship honors God and accomplishes His purposes in our lives. The Apostle Paul exhorted us toward such love.

Love does not pursue evil, but rejoices with the truth (I Cor. 13:6). In the section of the Bible commonly referred to as the "love chapter," God makes it clear that His perfect love does not play with sin. Loving well means *giving* to meet emotional needs according to God's commands rather than *taking* sexual pleasure that God has declared off limits.

Love puts God above pleasure or themselves (II Tim. 3:2-4). There is passing pleasure in sinful behavior. However, if we maintain a perspective that trusts God to be looking out after our best interests, and if we remember that our sin hurts Him as well as others, we will be more motivated to resist temptation. God will be faithful to give us a way to escape (I Cor. 10:13).

Love does not cause a brother or sister to sin (Luke 17:1-2; I Cor. 8:9-13). Great Commandment love seeks what is best for others using God's standards of excellence. If we encourage others to sin, or even violate their consciences, we put obstacles between them and God. You can exercise personal responsibility so that you do nothing to limit your friend's or your own walk with God.

Love considers the interests of others as well as our own (Phil. 2:4). God calls us to be always mindful of the other person's best interests as He would define them. When applied to the area of sexuality, that means putting my partner's relationship to God in greater priority than satisfying my own sexual urges.

Love places great value on keeping our bodies pure (I Cor. 6:19-20). God exhorts us to treat our colleagues and ourselves as treasured possessions, whom He has bought with a price. Sexual sin affects the body. Inappropriate behavior puts guilt and shame in our emotional cups. The harmful effects of sexual sin are real even though awareness may be suppressed through rationalization, denial, delusion, or eventually, a reprobate mind.

Love encourages one another to grow spiritually (Heb. 12:25). Rather than hinder a friend's relationship with God through sexual sin, we need to be encouraging one another to love and good deeds, proactively fostering spiritual growth with practical application.

2. Sexual Stewardship—Managing Your God-given Sexual Desire

It is normal for all adults to experience sexual desire or even arousal. These sensations are not sinful in and of themselves. Sexual desire is a physiological urge that God designed into the human being. But the provision for its full expression and fulfillment is a marriage relationship.

Strong sexual desire or arousal is not a relational need that must be fulfilled in order to experience abundant life. If so, what would you say to the man whose wife was in an accident and has remained in a coma for several years? Should he put sexual fulfillment above being faithful to his wife? The bottom line is that you must learn to love your dating partner more than you love satisfying your own urges and desires. That is Great Commandment love in action.

Sexual desire and arousal are realities of life for most single adults. Learning to manage our behavior when sexual temptation is presented is not unlike learning to manage our tempers when people violate our boundaries. Now, let's study how to respond appropriately to sexual arousal.

Acknowledge arousal or strong desire (Rom. 7:14-8:1). It is not helpful to deny the existence of such feelings or to shame or condemn yourself when they appear. You must deal with these realities objectively. Though we do not know the specific issue that the Apostle Paul faced at the time he penned this passage, we know that he was frustrated with the struggle. But, the absence of condemnation lets us approach the problems and challenges freely and honestly, looking for practical ways to walk in God's light.

Flee temptation (I Cor. 6:18). Sexual urges are powerful. God's instruction is to flee the temptation that prompted the urges rather than test your power to resist them. This is especially true if you have become sexually aroused. You will need to remove yourself from the environment even though that may be somewhat embarrassing at the time. This is a discipline that will produce righteousness and character (Heb. 12:11). Afterwards, you may want to address the issue with your dating partner when the arousal has subsided.

Make yourself accountable to another (Prov. 27:17). We are all personally accountable to God (Rom. 14:12). But God can use others whom we trust to help us as we struggle in our Christian journey. Disclose your specific struggle with a trusted and discrete friend or group. Choose someone who is both discrete and courageous enough to confront you in love. Give that person or group permission to ask how you are doing from time to time in the struggle.

Address the matter with your dating partner (Eph. 4:15). This may seem uncomfortable, but if you are struggling with arousal in a dating relationship, you may need the other person's cooperation to avoid adding to the temptation. Your comment to your friend may sound something like, "I have been feeling uncomfortable at times in our relationship and need to explain this to you. I have been experiencing some strong desire and need your help so that I won't sin. I need to admit that these feelings exist and not act upon them. I need to sort out my feelings and responses." This disclosure removes intrigue and introduces accountability for the choices both of you make. Stuffing the feelings or acting upon them produces guilt or shame eventually. Such honest conversation can actually increase trust in the relationship as each person honors and respects the other. Acknowledge the arousal "signal," disclose it, and back away if necessary.

Maintain appropriate boundaries — let your 'yes' be 'yes' and your 'no' be 'no' (Matt. 5:37). Relational boundaries are like fences. They establish where one person or property ends and another begins. Relational boundaries are revealed when we say "no" to something. For example, if someone speaks rudely to me and I let them know I was hurt by that behavior, I have revealed the presence of an invisible boundary. In sexual contexts, boundaries can be established around the type or amount of touching that occurs, the subjects that are discussed, or the movies seen together. The primary guideline is to maintain the freedom to reveal where boundaries exist and the mutual concern to respect the boundaries that are disclosed (Rom. 12:10).

Meet needs for affection without prompting arousal (Rom. 16:16). There are appropriate ways for Christians who love each other according to the Great Commandment to express their affection. But there are some "tests" to assess the motive and method of such affection. The purpose of the touch should be to meet the need of the other person rather than to take something for oneself. The touch would not be intended to "light a fire" or arouse, provoking temptation or leading to a guilty conscience.

Our sexuality is a gift for which we can be grateful, even if we are told to "leave it under the Christmas tree" for an unknown period of time. Like our appetites for food or drink, it is a challenge to manage our desire for sexual fulfillment in order to honor God and His gift to us.

The Choice to Marry
Leaving One Family
to Form Another

A few years ago, I (Bruce) received an advertisement in the mail from a nation-wide dating service (it seems that these organizations do not always screen out the married households in their direct mail marketing). Since I was doing research on mate selection and leading a Bible study for single adults in our church, the ad got my attention. In the seven brief paragraphs on the flyer, one phrase kept reappearing in slightly different words:

> *". . . it just gets more and more difficult to find . . .*
> ***the right individual***.*" ". . . thousands of (our) members . . . have found **the right person**." ". . . (our) members succeed in meeting **the right people** . . ." ". . . many single people have a personal goal . . . to meet **someone special** . . ." ". . . you can learn more about how you can meet **someone special**." ". . . **the right person** is waiting to meet you."*

The truth is, it is not the 'right person' that is needed, but the 'right relationship.'

Professional dating services know that you have an inherent need for relationship. They know that it is not unusual for single adults to long for a healthy marriage partner as a solution for their loneliness. Romantic relationships are the vehicles for advancing toward that objective. Dating services also know that each person has certain criteria that limit the field of candidates for serious relationships, so they give you opportunity to express these criteria as part of the process. But few can provide valid information about the ability of each person to relate to others intimately on spiritual, emotional, and physical levels. Examining yourself in the light of God's Word is essential when considering choices about potential dating or marriage partners.

1. Replays of old Relational Struggles

Research suggests that our adult attachments present some of the same relational struggles that we encountered first in childhood. For persons married more than once, these relational struggles may be repeated over and over. For example, an adult male received a lot of criticism and disapproval in his first two marriages. His genogram revealed that he struggled as a child with a very critical and disapproving stepfather. Such inappropriate responses by parents and other influential people can distort the sense of identity in children and shape their interactions with others. These relational patterns may continue throughout life unless a conscious change is made in the perception of the individual and his responses to persons close to him.

God empowers us to make such changes. First, He offers a fresh start in our relationship with Him that was broken by sin. He responds to us perfectly and sends only valid and accurate messages about who we are, what we are worth, and how we are to interact with others. Though we are creatures of habit, he enables us to modify our habits, providing the strength and encouragement needed to do so. As we trust in the work of the Holy Spirit to conform us to the image of the Son, we leave a different legacy for those who follow us. The process for this change may be related to the biblical principle of "leaving and cleaving."

2. Leaving Before Cleaving

Dating among single adults has the potential to move toward a serious relationship, and ultimately marriage. Genesis 2:24 gives a clear picture of God's process for entering marriage: "For this cause a man shall leave his father and his mother, and shall cleave to his wife; and they shall become one flesh," (NASB). Before we can fully "cleave" to a spouse, or even relate freely to close friends, we must experience some of the "leaving" referred to in Genesis 2:24. The order of events is crucial—*leaving*, then *cleaving*. People often marry, having left their parents physically, but not having separated from them psychologically and emotionally. How would you know if this applied to you?

Ben was an intelligent young salesman who was ready to share his future with someone else. He believed that person was Maggie. She was a school teacher whose first marriage ended in divorce after her husband had left her for another woman. Maggie liked Ben's stability and dependability and he was drawn to her energy and determination. During the early part of their courtship, neither could find anything objectionable in the other. But after a year of steady dating, some serious conflict and distance developed. It often surfaced when Ben would visit Maggie at her apartment. When Maggie had work to do there, Ben would usually "veg out" in front of the TV. Rather than ask for help, Maggie would make disapproving faces or sarcastic remarks. Ben reacted to Maggie's criticism by withdrawing and turning his attention elsewhere, often working more and coming over less frequently. As time went on, frustration and resentment continued to build in their emotional cups.

Later, at a Great Commandment retreat, Ben and Maggie began to see that problems in their adult relationships were virtual replays of struggles each had encountered in childhood. For example, Maggie had been left to fend for herself a great deal, especially when her father left home when she was a teenager. Ben's mother had repeatedly scolded and criticized him and given little praise or affirmation. He had responded to the disapproval by withdrawing or avoiding her altogether. When Maggie was ignored as a child, she would say little, but vent her anger by slamming doors. The destructive pattern of interaction in their relationship was born out of the "unfinished business" of their separate childhood experiences. Unknown to them for years, those experiences had continued to influence their present-day thinking, feeling, and behaving. Neither had really left home emotionally.

Clearly, Maggie and Ben needed to become aware of how their childhood conditioning was impacting their adult relationships. As they learn more about their intimacy needs that can be met in appropriate relationships that honor God, they can be healed from the old hurts of childhood and freed to change their perspectives and patterns of interaction.

3. Date and Mate Selection

Failure to achieve a significant degree of freedom to express ourselves and make decisions independent of our parents can hinder intimacy with friends and marriage partners. Lack of such freedom can also affect whom you *choose* to have on your list of potential partners! In addition to physical attraction, our choice of dates and mates is influenced by constructs in our minds about who we are and whom we need. As we developed in childhood, we formed a mental picture in our minds of who we are. It was "painted" there primarily through the interactions of those closest to us in childhood. There is also a picture of what our potential mate needs to be. This, too, was influenced by the types of interactions we experienced as a child.

Unfortunately, these pictures often get painted with colors that are not accurate. For example, many of us got "defined" by others in ways that did not match how our Heavenly Father viewed us, resulting in a poor self-image. Our mental view of the people we depend upon can also get distorted. Often, the distortion comes about when we insist on "seeing" the central people in our childhood in an idealistic way—unable to recognize their shortcomings and how we were affected by them. Later, when we encounter potential marriage partners, we may unconsciously attribute to them some of the positive or negative traits of our parents. This mental process may explain why some of us seem to marry a person "just like Mom or Dad" or a combination of the two. Therefore, before "cleaving" and forming adult attachments, it is imperative that we sort out what our mental pictures look like, recognizing where they differ from God's reality, and allowing Great Commandment love to guide and direct us in these relationships. Otherwise, you may find two people who do not know themselves well, trying to relate to each other according to some very distorted pictures.

4. Free for Intimacy

How can you know that you have achieved a significant level of relational freedom or "leaving?" In general, your perspectives about the purpose and process of marriage relationships will be consistent with God's, you will have modified distorted perceptions of yourself and others, and you will have a deeper understanding of your relational needs that God will meet through relationship with Him and others. In more concrete terms, you will experience a greater degree of freedom to form and express your thoughts and opinions. You will sense greater empowerment to make judgments and act upon them. You will "own" or take full responsibility for living your life, and respect yourself as well as others. You will also be free to initiate or receive intimate encounters in an appropriate manner, maintaining and respecting God's boundaries at all times. (this list of relational abilities was adapted in part from a definition for "personal authority" in, *The Intimacy Paradox*, by Dr. Donald Williamson). It is time now to pursue a journey toward intimacy with God and others that honors Him and points people to the Cross.

5. The Purpose for Marriage

Achieving a sense of wholeness is not God's intended purpose for marriage. That goal may have been born from unmet needs in childhood. When infatuation with a dating partner has a tie to your self-esteem, beware. You may be expecting union with that person to complete you in a way only Christ can. Marriage was not intended to *make* us whole, but rather, *in marriage*, we are instructed to *function* as a whole. That has to do with how we work toward *harmony and unity* in all dimensions of our being.

Marriage is not the only path to a meaningful and fulfilling life. But that myth contributes to an unhealthy preoccupation with mate seeking, rather than a healthy desire that many singles will share. Pursuit of the Great Commandment leads to purpose for living that transcends our circumstances without denying them. God has called every believer to a life that contributes to His master plan for humankind. For many, that plan will include marriage, but you can rest in the knowledge that the timing and details of that part of your journey will be in His hands. For today, He may want you to experience a degree of comfort, encouragement, or acceptance from your friends who know your desires regarding marriage.

Most single adults in our society choose to marry at least once in life. And depending upon age and other factors, most people who divorce or lose a mate to death will marry again. Those who are considering marriage in the future may want to review the latter part of Chapter Four, *Fearless Friendships*, to further examine how developmental struggles in childhood can get replayed in adult relationships. In addition, we recommend that you complete all of the optional exercises in Chapter Six, *The Family Crucible*, in order to understand as well as possible how the relational environment in which you were raised can have a subtle, yet powerful, influence over your choice of a marriage partner.

Personal Application

Leaving Before Cleaving

Make a list of a few things you have longed for related to marriage. (For example, *I long to be married so that I might be able to express love for another in every aspect of my being; I desire to have children and raise a family some day; I want an attractive person to find me desirable; I hunger for someone to find me attractive and to demonstrate that sexually.*) Now, place a "✓" next to those desires that you think are part of your being created in the image of God. Next, place an "X" next to the ones that you think are illegitimate longings that have more to do with sinful desires or illegitimate pursuits of normal desires whose fulfillment is reserved for marriage.

_____ _____

_____ _____

_____ _____

_____ _____

_____ _____

_____ _____

_____ _____

_____

One of the ways that struggles in my adult relationships have paralleled those of my growing up years is _____
_____
_____
_____
_____

As I consider the degree to which I am currently free for relational intimacy with others, I suspect that some of the hindrances that remain may be due to unresolved feelings, such as _____ and _____ from my growing up years. I sense that God would want me to become more _____ and less in order to love Him and others well.

Encountering God in His Word
"Learning to Love Well"
Philippians 1:9-11

Printed below is the passage taken from *The Message*, a paraphrased edition of the Bible by Eugene Peterson. As you read it, consider carefully what it says to you about loving others well.

So this is my prayer: that your love will flourish and that you will not only love much but well. Learn to love appropriately. You will need to use your head and test your feelings so that your love is sincere and intelligent, not sentimental gush. Live a lover's life, circumspect and exemplary, a life Jesus will be proud of: bountiful in fruits from the soul, making Jesus Christ attractive to all, getting everyone involved in the glory and praise of God.

Given your own situation, whether you are pursuing courtship or friendship, study the passage above and ask God to reveal how He would want you to apply it in the relationships that He has ordained for you.

◆ Write in your own words what you believe it means to love another person well.

_____

_____

_____

_____

◆ *Circumspect* means to look about, to carefully consider all related circumstances before acting. How might you need to build this characteristic into your friendships or dating relationships?

_____

_____

_____

_____

◆   What changes would be needed for you to "use your head and test your feelings" in order for your love for others to be discerning and knowledgeable, and be able to discern what is best?

_____

_____

_____

_____

_____

_____

_____

◆ The word, *exemplary,* refers to a model worth imitating. How would you like your personal relationships to be an example for others that actually points them to God?

_____

_____

_____

_____

_____

_____

_____

> *God's love for us is conscious and intentional. He gives when we are not even grateful for the gifts.*

Group Dialogue

If you do not have a designated group leader, choose someone in the group who will serve to facilitate the discussion. Begin by briefly reviewing the discussion guidelines.

Discussion Guidelines

♦ Allow everyone an opportunity to share thoughts and feelings

♦ Avoid long story telling

♦ Be quick to listen with empathy

♦ Be slow to give advice

♦ Speak the truth in love

♦ Say what you mean and mean what you say

♦ Protect the confidentiality of every person

Discussion Suggestions for Chapter Eight

Note: Some group members may find it difficult to even talk about sexuality, particularly in a mixed-gender setting, so take extra care to avoid *requiring* anyone to participate as you encourage group discussion.

1. Allow group members to share about what they were taught about their singleness. For example, were they left with any feelings of shame or inadequacy as a result of being single now.

2. Go around the group, sharing what and how they were taught about their sexuality and sexual behavior in general. Encourage them to comment about the adequacy or inadequacy of the involvement of their parents or church in helping prepare them to deal with their sexuality.

3. Discuss ideas about why sexuality is often such a difficult area of life for everyone, whether married or single.

4. Ask the group members to discuss how the positive meeting of intimacy needs such as attention, approval, comfort, and respect might have an impact on the sexual dimension of their lives.

5. Discuss how sexual promiscuity, sexual addictions, and sexual offenses might be related to unmet intimacy needs in childhood and/or adulthood.

6. Close by praying together for courage to rely upon God to meet our most significant needs.

Journey-mate Encounters

- ◆ Set aside one to two hours for the meeting to give ample time for each person to share.
- ◆ Select a meeting location that minimizes distractions or interruptions.
- ◆ Read the chapter and complete all the written exercises *before* meeting to discuss them.
- ◆ Purpose to start on time and complete each exercise, staying focused on the material.

Suggestions for Journey-mate Encounter #8

NOTE: Because sexuality is so much a part of the core of our identity as human beings, the potential for vulnerability in this area is tremendous. Therefore, be sure to be respectful and gentle as you share with each other and use your emotional responding skills.

1. After completing the written questions in this chapter, take this opportunity to share thoughts and feelings about sexuality in general with your journey-mate(s).

2. If each of you is comfortable doing so and it is appropriate to do so, share your own thoughts and feelings about your own sexuality as a single adult, including hopes, fears, disappointments, and pain.

3. Many people have experienced hurt and pain related to their relationships with members of the opposite sex, whether as part of a dating relationship, former marriage, or childhood experience. Offer comfort to any journey-mate who would like to use this opportunity to grieve some of the losses or disappointments experienced. Remember that the depth of pain in these arenas can be extensive, but so can the potential for healing. These could include rejections, abuses, abandonments, decisions affecting unborn children, etc. Do not press an individual to disclose specifics if he or she is not ready to do so. Encourage such individuals to seek assistance with a professional or ministerial counselor.

4. Close your time together by expressing gratitude to God for the intricate and incredible design of human spirit, soul, and body that functions together for good when we are stewards according to His commands. Pray a word of encouragement for one another to experience Great Commandment love more fully and completely in the months to follow.

Hiding the Word in Your Heart
Philippians 1:10

Write the verse here: _____

_____

_____

_____

_____

_____

_____

_____

Repeat the verse from memory each day for several weeks. Using the space below, you may want to journal ways that God has allowed you to experience the verse as you have hidden it away in your heart. _____

_____

_____

_____

_____

_____

_____

_____

_____

_____

_____

_____

_____

_____

_____

Check the box at the right when you have committed the verse to memory. Continue to repeat the verse daily for at least three weeks.

Chapter Nine

———— ◆ ————

THE PURSUIT OF INTIMACY
Developing a Great Commandment Lifestyle

Where there is no vision, the people perish.
Proverbs 29:18 (KJV)

In Lewis Carroll's delightful story, Alice in Wonderland, the heroine follows the White Rabbit down the rabbit hole and embarks on an adventure unlike any other. As she wanders through the madcap maze of Wonderland, Alice encounters an assortment of outrageous, unpredictable creatures—the Dodo, the Caterpillar, the Mad Hatter, the March Hare, and Tweedledee and Tweedledum. But, perhaps her most telling encounter is with the Cheshire Cat sitting perched on a tree limb above her. As Alice faces a myriad of paths veering off in all directions, she inquires of the cat, "Would you tell me, please, which way I ought to go from here?" "That depends a good deal on where you want to get to," replies the cat. "I don't much know or care where—" replies Alice, a bit perturbed. Then, the Cheshire Cat responds insightfully, "Then it really doesn't matter which way you go, does it?"

Not only does Alice's conversation with the Cheshire Cat reveal her own situation, it reflects the current dilemma many of us face living in a fast-paced, rapidly changing society. In the counseling office, we commonly hear people complain that the patterns of their lives and relationships are stuck and frustrating. For example, a couple dating seriously for over a year might say, "We just don't seem to be getting anywhere." A thirty-something bachelor remarks, "I'm just spinning my wheels and getting prematurely gray in the process." A single-parent female comments sadly that there are no unmarried men out there her age worth pursuing.

Such complaints can usually be traced to a deeper concern—people have no idea where they are going, so they don't know how to get there or whether they have arrived! This dilemma is particularly true when it comes to our relationships. The Hebrew word for "perish" in Proverbs 29:18 is also translated, "go unrestrained...each to his own way." What a tragic but fitting description for many individuals, relationships, marriages and families in today's society. In this chapter, you will be challenged to do some serious thinking about your future, particularly with regard to relationships. We unapologetically encourage you to pursue a lifestyle of relational intimacy with God and others. Deepening your relationships, becoming more transparent and vulnerable, and learning to impart your very life to others will be challenging for you. It means purposeful change for most, and such change requires vision and energy. The support of journey-mates and friends will make this part of the journey more meaningful and productive.

However, don't be surprised if you are pulled into a counterfeit lifestyle. Consider Kurt.

Imagine. The alarm clock jolts Kurt into consciousness at 6:40 a.m. He hustles to get ready, scarf down a bagel as he scans the sports page for late scores, and lines his Honda up with a thousand other vehicles in a chain-linked freeway. He focuses his mind on the loose ends of his work from the previous day. Kurt enters the office, grabs the new contributions to his in-basket, and sinks into his chair trying to secure some order before the phone starts to ring off the hook. At lunch time, he rushes to the gym to work out and keep his trim physique intact. Most days, he works past six, finding that it does little good to leave early unless he wants to spend an extra half hour in traffic. Kurt works on an MBA at the university two nights a week, plays in a softball league another night, and leads a Bible study on Wednesday evenings at his church. He crashes on Friday nights from fatigue, watches television or studies most Saturdays, and keeps busy most Sundays at church. Though he has many acquaintances, there is little time for anyone to really get to know Kurt seriously or deeply. He has fallen into a fast-flowing rut. Just think what it would be like if he was also a single parent!

An exaggeration? A distorted caricature of today's working single? Hardly! This lifestyle applies to singles, married adults, and increasingly, senior citizens. King Solomon, the writer of Proverbs, was indeed wise when he wrote that what we need is vision. Perhaps today, more than ever, we, as individuals and as families, need a sense of direction and purpose, a guiding framework around which we can make our decisions. We need distinct objectives toward which we can stretch with all our strength and passion. The contrast is clear: perish or flourish; wander aimlessly or stretch forth purposefully. If we are not careful, the winds of change will direct our lives. Instead, we can chart a course that faces those winds with the God of the universe at the helm of our vessel.

Do not be deceived. Defining and pursuing a vision is not without cost. Time must be allocated and considerable thought put forth. Sacrifices must be made if goals are to be realized, saying "no" to one pursuit in order to say "yes" to another.

This concluding section of the book provides an opportunity for you to establish a direction for your life. You may have done an exercise like this with regard to your work and career, but it may be a new experience for you to develop goals about what you want your relationships to look like. Has it occurred to you that there is a need to actually *pursue* intimacy in relationships in a manner that honors and glorifies God? The basic concepts and skills for developing intimate relationships have been conveyed in the preceding chapters of this book. Now it is time to chart the next part of your journey toward intimacy with God and others.

Intentionality
Planning for Abundant Living

Abiding in Christ, so that your purposes are consistent with those of God, is the key to experiencing the abundance promised in the Kingdom of God. As we stated in Chapter Four, the abundant life available in Christ is always experienced in the present. Now, let's use another aspect of our God-given nature, intentionality, in order to position ourselves to experience more of His abundance during the remainder of our life on earth.

But why go to all this trouble? Are you thinking that this will be one more "to do" list that will simply gather dust and never be realized? Are you hesitant because you sense that you may not *want* to be accountable for some of your choices later? Can you see the value of community and trust-based relationships when we are seeking to change and grow? Let's take a moment to examine some of the blessings and benefits that come from intentional living.

1. Goal setting provides a framework for future decision-making.

Life consists of endless pressing decisions—where to invest your time, attention, effort, and money. Without established goals, confusion, contradiction, and conflict will abound. By setting goals, a person faced with a decision can simply ask, "Will this choice further accomplish my goals or hinder them?" Depending upon the answer, you can then proceed or decline. Goals also serve as boundaries for commitments. For example, Randy decided that he could work late or do ministry activities at church up to three evenings a week without jeopardizing his personal objectives and relationships. When the Associate Pastor of his church asked Randy to serve on the budget committee of the church, a group that met frequently in the evenings, Randy knew immediately that he must say "no" or clear something else from his agenda. Since he had already decided where his realistic limits and boundaries were, he was free of a nagging sense of false guilt that had plagued him before.

What are your thoughts about this aspect of goal setting? Complete the following statements to facilitate your thinking:

Failure to set goals in the past has hindered my decision-making by: _____

_____

_____

_____

An area in which I need goals to help maintain healthy boundaries is: _____

_____

_____

_____

2. Goal setting facilitates oneness in our relationships.

Amos 3:3 states, "Do two walk together unless they have agreed to do so?" Agreeing on where you are going and what you are doing is essential to oneness or unity in relationships. Cooperative goal setting on matters that affect one another can be very rewarding, but may require considerable effort. It requires patient listening as put forth in James 1:19, "Every man should be quick to listen, slow to speak, and slow to become angry..." With your close friends or within your small group fellowships you can begin making goals for your relationships by deciding to meet for lunch or dinner once or twice a month in order to maintain a sense of connection with each other. Other goals may involve recreational plans, joint endeavors, or distribution of responsibilities in the case of roommates.

Take a moment to reflect on your past experiences of goal setting in relationships, and then complete the following statements:

I remember a time that was important when I reached a mutual understanding and agreement with someone close to me concerning _____

_____

_____

_____

An issue about which I need to pursue more understanding and agreement in my relationships is _____

_____

_____

3. Goal setting reflects and reminds us of important priorities.

Many organizations, even churches, are spending considerable time and effort defining their mission, that is, their reason for being, and then specifying which activities are truly associated with that mission. In this way, they are able to recognize and eliminate extraneous activities that divert and drain the energy of the organization from that which is *most* beneficial. "Good" things are often the worst enemies of the "best" things. Goal setting serves as a frequent reminder of our accountability to priorities that matter to us. Clearly defined goals will help us consistently give our relationships with God and others the significance they deserve.

Consider how the presence or absence of clearly defined goals has affected your life to date by completing the following statements:

I have frequently gone overboard by giving too much time and attention to (For instance, my job, sports, hobbies, shopping) ___

_____

_____

A specific area of my life that I would like to give consistent priority to is. (For example, exercise, prayer, conversation with friends.) _____

4. Goal setting provides a sense of strength, security, and accomplishment.

When confronted with a populace that wavered between worshipping Jehovah God or other man-derived gods, Joshua exercised the decision-making power invested in him by God. Do you remember his declaration recorded in Joshua 24:15? He said, "...choose for yourselves this day whom you will serve,... But as for me and my household, we will serve the Lord." Do you hear the strength and security in those words? Joshua had set his heart on obedience and service to God. He had settled that issue and his purpose and objective in that matter was clear. We live in a world that presents an unprecedented number of options. Confusion is eliminated substantially when we consider who we are, where we are going, and what is most important to us. In addition, as we complete the goals that we have set forth, we experience a sense of progress and security instead of powerlessness. Though God has not chosen to give us control over all of our environment or other people here on earth, He has given us the capacity to choose and clearly intends for us to exercise it within the framework of our submission to Him.

Think about some of your past accomplishments and successes and finish the following statements:

I remember how important it was for me to complete or accomplish. (For example, paying off a substantial debt, obtaining a degree.) _____

_____

_____

When I have finished an important project or goal, I feel . . . (For example, satisfied, relieved to have it behind me, more mature.) _____

_____

_____

5. Goal setting is an example and witness to others.

We live in a time that is experiencing a leadership vacuum, with an insufficient number of quality role models, particularly with regard to faithfulness in trust-based relationships. The world is aching for more Joshua's who know what really matters, know where they are going, and have established goals for getting and staying there. Christians who fail to chart a course may be like lights that are being hidden beneath a basket. They have the truth of God's word in their hearts but have not incorporated it fully in their lives, in part due to a lack of a plan for getting there. When we think through the important areas of our lives and choose what we want them to look like in the future, making plans to move in that direction, we serve as positive witnesses to others. When we do this within the context of a church, family, marriage, or friendship, we demonstrate God's emphasis on relational community.

Reflect on your example to others as you complete the following sentences:

I have seen God use some of my convictions and goals to encourage or challenge others when I (For example, refused to cheat on my income tax because I had decided to trust God to provide for me without deceiving others.) _____

_____

_____

_____

An area I could be a better witness and example would be (For example, taking a responsible role at church.) _____

_____

_____

_____

_____

Charting Your Course

In this section, we will help you take stock of your life, reflecting on your past experience, present status, and future dreams. We invite you to make specific action plans for each of your goals for the next twelve months. Single adults who have completed this exercise during our field testing of this material reported significant benefits and enhanced motivation for the pursuit of life.

Your Personal Vision

...being confident of this, that He who began a good work in you will carry it on to completion until the day of Christ Jesus. Philippians 1:6

Take some time to reflect on your life's purpose and meaning. Write down your thoughts in regard to the subjects listed so that you can share these effectively later with a friend or group. If you are completing this material in a group setting, you may want to discuss your answers to the vision section before proceeding to the sections on goals or action plans.

Remembrances from the Past

1. What and who has God used in your life to give you perspective about yourself, your relationships, and your values? _

_____

_____

_____

_____

_____

_____

2. What attitudes, habits, and priorities have been changed within you in the last few years? Did God use any specific people, events, or Scripture to bring about these changes? _____

_____

_____

_____

_____

3. Describe the background and events surrounding how you came to establish a personal relationship with Jesus Christ. If this is something you are still considering or understanding, describe where you are in this journey. _____

_____

_____

_____

_____

4. What were some of the things you first learned or saw change in your life as you came to know Christ personally? __

_____

_____

_____

5. Think of other significant events or turning points in your life and note them here. Then pause to express your thanks to God for His working thus far in your life. _____

_____

_____

_____

Reflections on the Present

1. In what ways and areas are you now growing spiritually? __

_____

_____

_____

_____

_____

2. What circumstances does God seem to be using in your life to perfect Christ's character in you? What changes do you sense God desires to make in you? _____
_____
_____
_____
_____

3. In what ways and areas are you now developing as a complete, more well-rounded person?
_____
_____
_____
_____

4. In what ways are you now making relationships with family and friends a key priority in your life? _____
_____
_____
_____

5. Who knows you well enough to understand your pain, struggles, joys, and dreams? Whom do you know well enough to understand his or her vision and be supportive of it? _____
_____
_____
_____

Dreams for the Future

1. What dreams do you have for you spiritual, personal, and vocational life? _____
_____
_____
_____
_____
_____

2. What dreams do you have for you relationships with family and friends? _____

_____

_____

_____

_____

_____

_____

3. What are your vocational and financial dreams? _____

_____

_____

_____

_____

_____

_____

_____

4. What avenues of ministry do you dream about pursuing? _

_____

_____

_____

_____

_____

_____

5. Complete the following sentence: If all my dreams for the future could come true today, here's what my life would be like

_____

_____

_____

_____

_____

_____

_____

_____

_____

_____

The Proactive Application of Intimacy Principles

In spite of our advances in technology, little has been done to advance our track record for establishing and developing committed, trust-based relationships in marriages, families, or friendships. So, how do you as a single adult, face this scenario? Do you hang your head in despair, seeing the societal trends as overwhelming and impossible to escape? Or, do you enter the relational world with an emotional suit of armor, fending off every entree' for companionship for fear of being used or abused? We believe that just as God makes eternal life available to every person on earth regardless of the degree of spiritual depravation in his or her midst, God also empowers us to pursue and experience relational intimacy wherever we are.

A vision for living a Great Commandment lifestyle calls for proactive pursuit of meaningful relationships with God and with family, friends, ministry colleagues, co-workers, and neighbors. Such relationships remove our aloneness as we learn to relate appropriately with one another on an emotional level. An example of such a relationship is found in the Old Testament writings about David and Jonathan where we are told that they "delighted" in one another (I Sam. 19:1), and spoke well of one another (I Sam. 19:4). They were "knit together in the soul" (I Samuel 18:1), and loved one another as himself (I Sam. 20:17). This is an example of Great Commandment love experienced by two God-fearing warriors who, at the time, were single adults. The friendship with Jonathan went a long way to remove David's aloneness as he was being hunted down like a wounded animal by King Saul.

God provided additional instruction about trust-based friendships in the wisdom writings, particularly Proverbs. The Bible says that good friends are said to be faithful in adversity (17:17), value depth in relationships over quantity (18:24) and honesty over flattery (27:6). Friends are to be dependable (27:10), to care enough to challenge or confront (27:17), and to have utmost respect for the interests of the other (27:14). These, and other references to friendships parallel the intimacy principles introduced previously in this workbook. Such relationships demonstrate all components of healthy intimacy including, caring affection, vulnerable disclosure, and contagious giving. In relationships with the opposite gender, the priority is placed on spiritual and relational intimacy rather than sexual experience. Great Commandment love includes a choice to do nothing to encourage or lead another into sinful behavior of any kind.

Personal Application
Relationally Intimate Friendships

Consider your past and present friendships. Think of a relationship in which you experienced some degree of healthy intimacy like that enjoyed by David and Jonathan. What were some specific ways that your relational needs such as *approval, attention, affection, comfort, and respect* were met? _

_____

_____

What changed, if anything, causing the relationship to end or the needs to go unmet?_____

_____

_____

How do you feel as you think about the presence or absence of trustworthy, intimate friendships like that of David and Jonathan? _____

_____

_____

What do you think hinders you from experiencing more relational intimacy with friends of the same or different gender? *(For example, I fear rejection and thus share very little about myself with others.)* _____

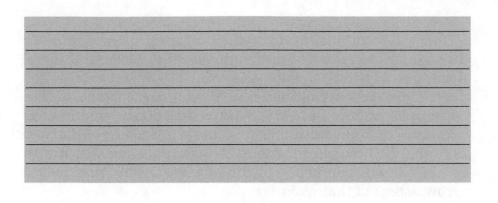

Moving from Fear and Control to Freedom and Faith

As we discussed in Chapters Five and Six, many of us were inadvertently programmed to experience aloneness by the time we became adults. We developed patterns that served to control or avoid personal relationships rather than experience them as part of our life in the Spirit of God.

Most of us have lived our lives in a frustrating cycle of fear and self-reliance, summarized below.

Break the Cycle of Futility

✓ **We are born with a basic need for intimacy with others.**

✓ **Our imperfect world fails to meet our intimacy needs.**

✓ **We develop our own ways to "secure" such needs.**

✓ **We rely on our ways instead of God's.**

✓ **We "succeed" to some extent.**

✓ **Our counterfeit solutions eventually fail us.**

✓ **Once again, we face our need for intimacy.**

You will recall that God wired all of us for relationship. In other words, He gave us an inherent need to have meaningful interaction with our Creator and with others created in His image. His design calls for people who are capable of free choice to experience intimacy in ways that honor Him and His word. But, even the word *intimacy* causes discomfort for many. Could that be because our society has virtually equated it with sex, thus limiting intimacy to the physical realm, and only a narrow aspect of that realm?

God has equipped us to practice and enjoy intimacy in every aspect of our being, and to do so without violating the boundaries of respect and purity that He ordained for us. There are meaningful and appropriate ways for single adults to experience intimacy with their journey-mates in spiritual, emotional, and physical dimensions. Yet, we often encounter people who have never experienced intimacy on a spiritual or emotional level. In fact, it is not uncommon today to find teenagers and adults who have been intimate sexually, but who know nothing about healthy forms of emotional intimacy. Many of these will marry and later become single again and again without tasting the joy of relational intimacy in all dimensions as God intended. Regardless of the number of people encountered, that is a lifestyle of aloneness.

Healthy intimacy is not something that comes naturally to human beings. It is much easier for people to stay focused on pursuing personal satisfaction rather than meeting the needs of others. Intimacy requires effort. It requires giving unselfishly to meet the needs of another. It means learning to know others, care for them, and be vulnerable. You learn to trust God to meet your needs even when you don't know how, or when, or through whom that will happen. You learn to discipline and deny yourself for the good of others rather than take or manipulate from them. Romantic involvements are meant to reflect the genuine concern and sacrificial love of Christ for His church, exercising discipline and restraint in order to present Her to the Father unblemished. In the same way, we are to keep the true interests of the other person, as defined by God, above our own. Such sacrificial love requires a relationship with God that includes humility, faith, and gratefulness. Our prayer is that you will develop deeper and stronger relationships with God and with the people He places in your path as you experience His truths about intimacy.

Being the People We Should Be

As we enter a new millennium, many are focused on trying to determine *when* Christ will return. But Scripture instructs us to focus instead upon being the people we should be *because* He will return (II Peter 3:11-14). For single adults, that means knowing who you are, a people created and called to love God and to love others with all your heart, soul, mind, and strength. Live with this identity of love, with integrity of lifestyle, and with an intention of service.

Contemplate the immeasurable love of God for you as you complete the following sentence:

> *As I consider the possibility that Christ is blessed by my presence with Him, and longs to receive my love for Him, my heart is filled with* _____.

Share that thought with someone you know, even if they have yet to learn of Christ's love that is available to him or her as well.

Encountering God in His Word

"God's Priority of Relationship"
Luke 10:38-42

As Jesus and His disciples were on their way, he came to a village where a woman named Martha opened her home to him. She had a sister called Mary, who sat at the Lord's feet listening to what He said. But Martha was distracted by all the preparations that had to be made. She came to him and asked, "Lord, don't you care that my sister has left me to do the work by myself? Tell her to help me!" "Martha, Martha," the Lord answered, "you are worried and upset about many things, but only one thing is needed. Mary has chosen what is better and it will not be taken from her."

This passage establishes a priority for "being with" rather than doing. However, it does not say that doing is unimportant. Many of our *doings* serve only to draw us away from that which is eternal and most significant even in the present—being with Jesus. How can we hear Him when the din of busyness is upon us? No relationship is likely to grow without conversation. What must we do to secure a margin of time for this relationship to be nurtured and developed? Earnestly pray for a stronger desire to know the Lord more deeply.

◆ Ask the Lord in prayer to bring to your mind some of the specific distractions that compete for His time with you. Ask God to help you see needs that these distractions relate to, and whether or not they present valid or counterfeit provisions for those needs. Journal your thoughts here: _____

_____

_____

_____

_____

_____

_____

_____

◆ In the Parable of the Sower (Mark 4:;7, 18-19), Jesus explains that the message of life, God's word, is often choked out by the "weeds" of this life, namely worries, wealth, and materialism. These do not take away the truth that has been received, but they do render it unproductive. How have the concerns of this life robbed you of the fullness of experiencing abundant life in Christ in the present? _____

_____

_____

_____

_____

_____

_____

_____

_____

_____

_____

God covets an intimate relationship with each of us. He needs to remain our "first love."

Group Dialogue

If you do not have a designated group leader, choose someone in the group who will serve to facilitate the discussion. Begin by briefly reviewing the discussion guidelines.

Discussion Guidelines

◆ Allow everyone an opportunity to share thoughts and feelings
◆ Avoid long story telling
◆ Be quick to listen with empathy

◆ Be slow to give advice
◆ Speak the truth in love
◆ Say what you mean and mean what you say
◆ Protect the confidentiality of every person

Discussion Suggestions for Chapter Nine

1. Share some of your own struggles trying to find time to pray and contemplate the character and person of God, and trying to live, working as though for the Lord.

2. Discuss the responsibilities that God has placed in your life that are in the "center of your plate," that is, they truly merit your highest priority in terms of time, resources, etc. Share what competes most often with these priorities.

3. Ask everyone in the group to write down three or four specific behaviors we would see you doing if you were truly pursuing a lifestyle of relational intimacy that glorifies God. Share these.

4. Consider the experiences you have had going through the *Discovering Intimacy* course with your group members. Write out answers to each of the following questions. Then go around the group sharing your answers to each question in turn.

   ◆ What would you have liked to experience more during the course?

   _____

   _____

   ◆ What occurred during the course experience as expected?

   _____

   _____

   ◆ What exceeded your expectations about the course experience?

   _____

   _____

5. Take turns affirming specific character traits of individuals that were evident during your times together. You may want to refer to Appendix G, *30 Selected Character Qualities*, for ideas. If time is limited, allow each person to *give* only one affirmation and allow each person to *receive* only one affirmation. Be sure to express appreciation for praise when it is received.

6. Close by praying for each person to take the next step in their life toward godly intimacy.

Journey-mate Encounters

◆ Set aside one to two hours for the meeting to give ample time for each person to share.

◆ Select a meeting location that minimizes distractions or interruptions.

◆ Read the chapter and complete all the written exercises *before* meeting to discuss them.

◆ Purpose to start on time and complete each exercise, staying focused on the material.

Suggestions for Journey-mate Encounter #9

1. Share your personal vision data that you completed on pages 267-270. Be sure to include your testimonies for how you each came to know Christ, the changes that God is bringing about in you at this time, and some of your dreams.

2. Discuss the overall impact of the *Discovering Intimacy* course on your life. How were you blessed, challenged, surprised, and encouraged by the material *and* by your journey-mate.

3. Share what you learned about each person's heart and soul that you will never forget. If you haven't already done this exercise in your small group, use Appendix G, *30 Selected Character Qualities*, to affirm and praise positive traits of your journey-mate. First, read through the entire list of character qualities. Then, circle four that you have seen demonstrated by your journey-mate during the course. Take turns sharing your observations by naming the qualities you selected, reading the definitions to your journey-mates, and telling them about a way you saw them demonstrate each trait.

4. Write down some specific plans for increasing the quantity and quality of relationships in your life. Share what will be especially difficult for you in pursuing these plans.

5. Discuss whether you and your journey-mates would like to co-lead others through the *Discovering Intimacy* course. This might be done by leading another set of journey-mates through it, or facilitating a small group class.

6. Close your time by expressing your gratitude to God for the work He has done within you during this course. Request further clarity of vision for what your relationship with Him and others should look like.

Hiding the Word in Your Heart
Proverbs 29:18

Write the verse here: _____

_____

_____

_____

_____

_____

_____

_____

_____

Repeat the verse from memory each day for several weeks.
Using the space below, you may want to journal ways that God
has allowed you to experience the verse as you have hidden it
away in your heart. _____

_____

_____

_____

_____

_____

_____

_____

_____

_____

_____

_____

_____

_____

Check the box at the right when you have committed the
verse to memory. Continue to repeat the verse daily for at
least three weeks.

Appendix A

$$\diamond$$

Intimacy Inventory for Single Adults

The term "journey-mate" refers to a person with whom you have/had a close, personal, caring, relationship. This might refer to a close friend of same or different gender, a serious dating partner, a fiancé, or a sibling. Circle the number that reflects your opinion for each item.

		Strongly Disagree	Disagree	Neutral	Agree	Strongly Agree
1.	My journey-mate is supportive and encouraging of my personal spiritual growth.	1	2	3	4	5
2.	My journey-mate and I seem to be good at giving one another undivided attention when listening or taking.	1	2	3	4	5
3.	My journey-mate is attentive and sensitive to my needs for affection and appropriate touch.	1	2	3	4	5
4.	My journey-mate and I seem to practice honest confession followed by genuine forgiveness when one of us has hurt the other.	1	2	3	4	5
5.	When I'm sharing my feelings, my journey-mate values them and is sensitive to provide understanding reassurance.	1	2	3	4	5
6.	I'm very comfortable communicating my need for affection and appropriate touch, as well as my boundaries, to my journey-mate.	1	2	3	4	5
7.	It would be characteristic for us to share together some of our long range dreams and hopes—even if they seemed silly.	1	2	3	4	5
8.	Sharing appreciation and verbalizing caring concern are two things my journey-mate is good at.	1	2	3	4	5
9.	My journey-mate and I seem to prioritize times of quality talking together.	1	2	3	4	5
10.	We seem to frequently recount the good times and blessings we have enjoyed together.	1	2	3	4	5
11.	I remember special times when my journey-mate and I shared together strong emotions like grief, sadness, joy, or brokenness.	1	2	3	4	5

	Strongly Disagree	Disagree	Neutral	Agree	Strongly Agree
12. I am very satisfied with my journey-mate's willingness to receive my need for affection and appropriate touch.	1	2	3	4	5
13. In many of the important issues concerning values and beliefs, my journey-mate and I often tend to agree.	1	2	3	4	5
14. Verbalizing to my journey-mate my needs and desires concerning our relationship would be normal for me.	1	2	3	4	5
15. I am satisfied with the freedom that my journey-mate seems to have to express affection appropriately.	1	2	3	4	5

Interpreting Your Score

Add your responses for Questions #1, #4, #7, #10, #13 and chart your score here:

Spiritual Scale:

0	5	10	15	20	25

Add your responses for Questions #2, #5, #8, #11 and #14 and chart your score here:

Friendship Scale:

0	5	10	15	20	25

Add your responses for Questions #3, #6, #9, #12 and #15 and chart your score here:

Physical Scale:

0	5	10	15	20	25

What insights or questions came to mind as you completed this inventory?

_____

_____

_____

_____

_____

_____

_____

_____

_____

_____

Appendix B

—— ◆ ——

Intimacy Needs Assessment Tool

While we all seem to have most of the same intimacy needs, the priority of those needs at particular times of life can be different for each person. Your greatest need may be for **affection**, while a friend's greatest need may be for **security**. One sibling may have an acute need for **comfort**, but another sibling's greatest need may be **encouragement**. **Appreciation** may be at the top of the list for you next door neighbor, while your tennis buddy needs **approval** more than anything else.

An important aspect of learning to love people well is taking the time to know them and to discover what their unique needs are. This questionnaire will help you assess your most important intimacy needs.

Name: _____**Date Completed:** _____

Instructions: Personally respond to these questions by placing the appropriate number beside each sentence. Then, use the "interpretation chart" to identify which needs you perceived as most important. Later, discuss your results with friends or journey-mates who have also completed it.

Strongly disagree	Disagree	Neutral	Agree	Strongly agree
-2	-1	0	+1	+2

_____ 1. It's important that people receive me for who I am - even if I'm a little "different."

_____ 2. It's very important to me that my financial world be in order.

_____ 3. I sometimes become "weary in well doing."

_____ 4. It's vital to me that others ask me my opinion.

_____ 5. It's important that I receive frequent physical hugs, warm embraces, etc.

_____ 6. I feel good when someone "enters into my world."

_____ 7. It's important for me to know "where I stand" with those who are in authority over me.

Intimacy Needs Assessment Tool
Page Two

Strongly disagree	Disagree	Neutral	Agree	Strongly agree
-2	-1	0	+1	+2

_____ 8. It is particularly meaningful when someone notices that I need help and then they offer to get involved.

_____ 9. I often feel overwhelmed, and when I do, I especially need someone to come alongside me and help.

_____ 10. I feel blessed when someone recognizes and shows concern for how I'm feeling emotionally.

_____ 11. I always like to know if what I "do" is of value and meaningful to others.

_____ 12. Generally speaking, I don't like a lot of solitude.

_____ 13. It means a lot to me for loved ones to initiate an "I love you."

_____ 14. I resist being seen only as a part of a large group - my individuality is important.

_____ 15. I am particularly blessed when a friend calls to listen and encourage me.

_____ 16. It's important to me that people acknowledge me not just for what I do but for who I am.

_____ 17. I feel best when my world is orderly and somewhat predictable.

_____ 18. When I've worked hard on a project, I am pleased to have people acknowledge my work and express gratitude.

_____ 19. I am unhappy at work unless I am surrounded by some co-workers who enjoy my company.

_____ 20. It's particularly encouraging to me when I realize that others notice my "pluses."

_____ 21. I sometimes feel overwhelmed and discouraged.

_____ 22. I want to be treated with kindness and equality by all, regardless of my race, gender, looks, and status.

_____ 23. The physical aspect of marriage is/would be very important to me.

_____ 24. I love it when someone wants to spend time with just me.

_____ 25. I am particularly blessed when my boss says, "Good job."

_____ 26. It is/would be very important to me for someone to hold me and love me after I've had a hard day.

_____ 27. While I feel confident about what I "do" (my talent, gifts, etc.), I always sense that I need other people's input and help.

_____ 28. Written notes and calls expressing sympathy after the death of a loved one, health problems, or other stressful stressful events are very meaningful to me.

_____ 29. I feel good when someone shows satisfaction with the way I am.

_____ 30. I enjoy being spoken of or mentioned in front of a group of people.

_____ 31. I would be described as a "touchy/feely" person.

Intimacy Needs Assessment Tool

Page Three

Strongly disagree	Disagree	Neutral	Agree	Strongly agree
-2	-1	0	+1	+2

_____ 32. When a decision is going to affect my life, it's important to me that I have a "say so" in the decision.

_____ 33. I am particularly blessed when someone shows interest in current projects I'm working on.

_____ 34. I appreciate trophies, plaques, and special gifts which are a permanent reminder of something significant which I have done.

_____ 35. I sometimes worry about the future.

_____ 36. When I'm introduced into a new environment, I immediately search for a group of people to connect with.

_____ 37. The thought of change (moving, new job...etc.) produces anxiety for me.

_____ 38. It bothers me when people are prejudiced against someone just because they dress or act differently.

_____ 39. It's necessary for me to be surrounded by friends and loved ones who will be there "through thick and thin."

_____ 40. I am particularly blessed by written notes and phrases of gratitude.

_____ 41. To know that someone is constantly praying for me is very meaningful.

_____ 42. I am particularly bothered by "controlling" people.

_____ 43. I am blessed by unmerited and spontaneous expressions of love.

_____ 44. I am pleased when someone looks me in the eye and really listens to me talk.

_____ 45. I am particularly blessed when people commend me for a godly characteristic I exhibit.

_____ 46. I never want to be alone when experiencing hurt and trouble; it's important for me to have a "soul mate" who will be with me.

_____ 47. I really don't enjoy working on a project by myself, I prefer to have a "helpmate" on every project.

_____ 48. It's important for me to feel a "part of the group."

_____ 49. I really respond to someone who tries to understand me emotionally and who shows me loving concern.

_____ 50. When working on a project, I would much rather work with a team of people than by myself.

Intimacy Needs Assessment Tool
Interpretation of Questions

Instructions: Add up your responses (-2, -1, 0, +1, +2) to the following groups of questions.

1.   1 _____
      19 _____
      36 _____
      38 _____
      48 _____
      Total _____
These responses relate to the need for ACCEPTANCE

5.   4 _____
      14 _____
      22 _____
      32 _____
      42 _____
      Total _____
These responses relate to the need for RESPECT

9.   10 _____
      26 _____
      28 _____
      46 _____
      49 _____
      Total _____
These responses relate to the need for COMFORT

2.   2 _____
      17 _____
      35 _____
      37 _____
      39 _____
      Total _____
These responses relate to the need for SECURITY

6.   5 _____
      13 _____
      23 _____
      31 _____
      43 _____
      Total _____
These responses relate to the need for AFFECTION

10.   8 _____
      9 _____
      27 _____
      47 _____
      50 _____
      Total _____
These responses relate to the need for SUPPORT

3.   11 _____
      18 _____
      25 _____
      34 _____
      40 _____
      Total _____
These responses relate to the need for APPRECIATION

7.   6 _____
      12 _____
      24 _____
      30 _____
      44 _____
      Total _____
These responses relate to the need for ATTENTION

List your three **HIGHEST totals.** These represent your current priority needs based upon your responses to the questions.

1. _____
2. _____
3. _____

4.   3 _____
      15 _____
      21 _____
      33 _____
      41 _____
      Total _____
These responses relate to the need for ENCOURAGEMENT

8.   7 _____
      16 _____
      20 _____
      29 _____
      45 _____
      Total _____
These responses relate to the need for APPROVAL

List your three **LOWEST totals.**

8. _____
9. _____
10. _____

NAME: _____

Scoring sheet revised 9/2000

Appencix C

---◆---

Increasing Your Emotional Vocabulary

Abandoned
Accepted
Aching
Accused
Adventurous
Affectionate
Agony
Agreeable
Aggressive
Aggravated
Alienated
Alive
Alluring
Alone
Aloof
Amazes
Amused
Angry
Anguished
Annoyed
Anxious
Apart
Apathetic
Apologetic
Appreciative
Apprehensive
Approved
Argumentative
Aroused
Arrogant
Ashamed
Assertive
Astonished
Attached
Attacked
Attentive

Attractive
Aware
Awestruck
Badgered
Baited
Bashful
Battered
Beaten
Beautiful
Belligerent
Belittled
Bereaved
Betrayed
Bitchy
Bitter
Blissful
Boastful
Bored
Bothered
Bound-up
Boxed-in
Brave
Breathless
Bristling
Broken-up
Bruised
Bubbly
Bugged
Burdened
Burned
Burned-up
Calm
Careful
Carefree
Careless
Caring

Callous
Capable
Captivated
Carried away
Cautious
Certain
Chased
Cheated
Cheerful
Choked up
Close Cold
Comfortable
Comforted
Competitive
Complacent
Complete
Concentrating
Confident
Conflicted
Confused
Conniving
Considerate
Consumed
Contemptuous
Content
Cool
Coy
Crabby
Cranky
Crappy
Crazy
Creative
Critical
Criticized
Crushed
Cuddly

Curious
Damned
Daring
Deceived
Deceptive
Degraded
Delightful
Demeaned
Demoralized
Demure
Dependent
Depressed
Deprived
Deserted
Desirous
Desirable
Despair
Desperate
Destroyed
Determined
Different
Dirty
Disappointed
Disapproving
Disconcerted
Disbelieving
Disgraced
Disgruntled
Disgusted
Distant
Distasteful
Distraught
Distressed
Distrustful
Dominated
Domineering

Doomed	Grim	Involved	Offended
Double-crossed	Grouchy	Irate	Open
Down	Grumpy	Irked	Optimistic
Dreadful	Guarded	Irresistible	Ornery
Eager	Guilty	Irresponsible	Out of control
Ecstatic	Happy-go-lucky	Irritated	Overjoyed
Edgy	Hard	Jealous	Overwhelmed
Efficient	Hassled	Jittery	Overworked
Egotistical	Hateful	Joyous	Pained
Elated	Healthy	Judged	Pampered
Embarrassed	Helpful	Kind	Panicky
Empty	Helpless	Lazy	Paralyzed
Enraged	Hesitant	Left out	Paranoid
enraptured	High	Lively	Passive
Enthusiastic	Hollow	Loaded	Patient
Enticed	Homesick	Lonely	Peaceful
Envious	Hopeful	Loose	Peeved
Esteemed	Horrified	Lost	Perceptive
Exasperated	Hostile	Lovable	Perplexed
Exhausted	Hot	Loved	Perturbed
Exhilarated	Humiliated	Loving	Petrified
Expectant	Hung over	Lovestruck	Phony
Exposed	Hung up	Low	Pleased
fascinated	Hurt	Lucky	Powerless
Fiendish	Hyper	Lustful	Pressured
Flattered	Hysterical	Mad	Proud
Foolish	Idiotic	Malicious	Prudish
Forced	Ignorant	Martyred	Pulled apart
Forceful	Impatient	Mean	Put down
Forgetful	Important	Meditative	Puzzled
Fortunate	Impotent	Mellow	Quarrelsome
Forward	Impressed	Mischievous	Quiet
Friendly	Incompetent	Miserable	Raped
Frightened	Incomplete	Misunderstood	Ravished
Frustrated	Independent	Moody	Ravishing
Full	Indifferent	Mystified	Real
Funny	Infatuated	Nasty	Refreshed
Furious	Innocent	Nauseated	Regretful
Generous	Insecure	Negative	Rejected
Genuine	Insignificant	Nervous	Rejecting
Giddy	Insincere	Noble	Relaxed
Giving	Inspired	Nonchalant	Relieved
Gossipy	Insulted	Nostalgic	Removed
Grateful	Interested	Numb	Repulsed
Greedy	Intimate	Obsessed	Repulsive
Grieving	Intolerant	Obstinate	Resentful

Reserved
Resistant
Responsible
Responsive
Reticent
Revengeful
Rotten
Ruined
Sad
Satiated
Satisfied
Scared
Scheming
Scolded
Scorned
Screwed
Secure
Seduced
Seductive
Self-centered
Self-conscious
Selfish
Separated
Shattered
Sheepish
Shocked
Shot -down
Shy
Sickened
Silly
Sincere
Sinking
Skeptical

Smart
Smothered
Smug
Sneaky
Snowed
Soft
Soothed
Sorry
Spiteful
Spontaneous
Squelched
Starved
Stiff
Stimulated
Stifled
Strangled
Strong
Stubborn
Stunned
Stupid
Subdued
Submissive
Successful
Suffocated
Sulky
Sure
Surly
Surprised
Sweet
Sympathetic
Tainted
Talkative
Tempted

Tender
Tense
Terrific
Terrified
Terrorized
Thoughtful
Threatened
Thrilled
Ticked
Tickled
Tight
Timid
Tired
Tolerant
Tormented
Torn
Tortured
Transcended
Trapped
Tremendous
Tricked
Triumphant
Trustful
Two-faced
Ugly
Unappreciated
Unapproachable
Unaware
Uncertain
Uncomfortable
Undecided
Understanding
Understood

Unfriendly
Unhappy
Unimportant
Unimpressed
Unloved
Unstable
Upset
Uptight
Used
Useful
Valuable
Valued
Violated
Violent
Volatile
Voluptuous
Vulnerable
Warm
Weak
Whipped
Whole
Wold
Willing
Wiped out
Withdrawn
Wishful
Wonderful
Worried
Worthy
Wounded
Zapped

Appendix D

———— ◆ ————

Unhealthy Thinking Questionnaire

In order to replace unhealthy thinking patterns, you must first identify which ones are in use in your relationships. This questionnaire will help you assess your own tendencies as well as those for a friend or journey-mate. Review the statements listed below and indicate which seem to be true for yourself. Next, indicate which statements seem to be true for your friend. Share your separate perceptions in order to work together to replace unhealthy patterns that impair your relationship with more valid ones.

True for me   **True for my friend**

_____ 1. I see things as pretty much black and white. _____

_____ 2. I tend to make mountains out of molehills. _____

_____ 3. I often take things personally. _____

_____ 4. Past disappointments seem to predict the future. _____

_____ 5. What I am feeling is more important than the facts. _____

_____ 6. I often think people make too much out of their problems. They should just get over it. _____

_____ 7. There's a place for everything and everything in its place. _____

_____ 8. Everything seems to be a big deal. _____

_____ 9. It's very important to sense others' approval. _____

_____ 10. I just know things won't get any better. _____

_____ 11. I can't really believe I'm loved unless I feel it. _____

_____ 12. I can handle almost any problem that comes my way. I don't really need much support from anyone. _____

Unhealthy Thinking Questionnaire (continued)

True for me   **True for my friend**

_____ 13. Being perfect in what I undertake is essential to   _____
              me.

_____ 14. I seem to overreact to relatively small irritations. _____

_____ 15. If someone in my family is upset, I must have been _____
              part of the reason.

_____ 16. I tend to write people off if they hurt or disappoint _____
              me.

_____ 17. If I feel unloved, it must be because no one loves _____
              me.

_____ 18. There's no reason to get so worked up or so   _____
              emotional.

Interpreting Your Responses

Now, using the chart below, find and circle each item number that you indicated as true for you on the questionnaire. Then, using a square instead of a circle, do the same thing for the items you marked as true for your friend. This exercise will give you an idea of the unhealthy thinking patterns that seem to be at work in yourself and your relationship with your friend.

	Polarizing	**Magnifying**	**Personalizing**
Item Numbers:	#1, #7, #13	#2, #8, #14	#3, #9, #15

	Generalizing	**Emotional Reasoning**	**Minimizing**
Item Numbers:	#4, #10, #16	#5, #11, #17	#6, #12, #18

Now, complete the following sentences:

According to this exercise, I have a tendency toward the following unhealthy thinking patterns:

_____

According to this exercise, my friend may have a tendency toward the following patterns:

_____

Discuss your conclusions with your friend, inviting similar feedback from him or her. Remember to listen and learn from each other, sharing your answers as *perceptions* rather than as *facts.*

Appendix E

——— ◆ ———

Childhood Questionnaire
Your Programming for Relationships

Relational struggles in childhood can have a profound influence on adult relationships unless they are recognized, understood, and addressed with love and wisdom. This questionnaire gives you an opportunity to examine some of your most significant relationships in childhood in order to discover sources of your current expectations for adult relationships. If you had more than one mother or father, give responses for every individual who was in a caretaker role for you.

Relational Modeling by Your Caretakers

Drawing from your memories of childhood, list the character traits of all the male and female parent figures with whom you grew up. Use adjectives such as *nurturing, pleasant, hardworking, easy-going, caring, talkative, reserved, critical, serious, manipulative, angry, abusive, violent, depressed, harsh, etc.* List both their positive and negative traits.

	Positive Traits/Strengths	**Negative Traits/Weaknesses**
Mother:	_____	_____
	_____	_____
	_____	_____
Father:	_____	_____
	_____	_____
	_____	_____
Other Caretakers:	_____	_____
	_____	_____

Childhood Questionnaire (continued)

Describe the way your parents handled conflict between themselves and within the family. (For example, *Mom would complain about things and Dad would either give in to her or act as though she hadn't said anything at all.)* _____

_____

_____

_____

_____

How did you know your parents loved each other as you were growing up? How did they show it? (For example, *My parents were openly affectionate, hugging a lot and offering each other help around the house.)* _____

_____

_____

_____

_____

How were emotions expressed between your parents and within the family as a whole? (For example, *Anger was the only emotion that I remember being expressed openly in our family. Otherwise, I think we just stuffed our feelings inside, until they kind of exploded, I guess.)*

_____

_____

_____

_____

_____

Put a check next to any of the following descriptors that apply to any of your caretakers.

	Mother	Father	Other Caretakers	
◆ True leader of the family	____	____	____	____
◆ Main disciplinarian	____	____	____	____
◆ Possessed a quick temper	____	____	____	____
◆ Comfortable giving affection	____	____	____	____
◆ Very hard to please	____	____	____	____
◆ The one I felt closest to as a child	____	____	____	____

Childhood Interactions

Describe how your mother would:

     ...praise you? _____

     ...criticize you? _____

Describe how your father would:

     ...praise you? _____

     ...criticize you? _____

As you were growing up, how did you *know* that your mother loved you? (For example, *My mother would often hug me and tell me that she loved me.)* _____

_____

_____

As you were growing up, how did you *know* that your father loved you? (For example, *He would buy me things—toys, clothes, books—especially when I was sick.)* _____

_____

_____

Describe how your mother and father each handled conflict that involved you. (For example, *My dad would lose his temper quickly and raise his voice, but my mom would usually just frown at me.)* _____

_____

_____

_____

_____

Self-assessment from Your Childhood

What were some of your best attributes as a child—things you liked most about yourself then? (For example, *I liked the way that I could compete in athletics; I was a very good student and enjoyed getting to go to Science Fairs and competitions; I like acting in school plays and did well at it.)* _____

_____

What were some of the things you liked least about yourself when you were growing up? (For example, *I always felt like a klutz around my classmates; I was afraid to stand up for myself; I didn't make good grades like the other kids; I had problems with my weight and got teased a lot.*)

_____

_____

_____

_____

When you were faced with hurtful, frustrating, or discouraging experiences, how would you have typically responded? (For example, *I would usually just go off by myself and think or read; I would think of a strategy and tackle it; I would try to get someone else to help me.*) _____

_____

_____

_____

_____

Check any of the following phrases that accurately describe your thoughts about your childhood:

_____ I was cared about primarily because of the things I did or accomplished.

_____ I often felt alone, like an outsider or observer compared to the rest of my family.

_____ I seemed to always be the "adult," even when my parents were around.

_____ I was loved for who I was, for my character more than for what I did.

_____ Our family *appeared* so normal to everyone else, but now I know it wasn't always.

_____ It was always extremely important for me to please others.

_____ It seemed to me that we always "walked on egg shells" around our home.

_____ My home environment was demanding, performance-based, with lots of rules.

Now that you are an adult and have observed other families, what do you think you missed most in yours? (For example, *Our family was so focused on achievement that I don't think anyone really knew me or what mattered to me most; My dad was very loving, but didn't stand up for himself or offer much guidance to me, something that might have helped me be less fearful in life.*) _____

_____

_____

_____

_____

_____

What thoughts and feelings did you experience as you were completing the questions above? (For example, *I felt grateful for the positive strengths that existed in my family; I felt really sad and a sense of loss that had never hit me before.*) _____

_____

_____

_____

_____

_____

How do you think your experiences and the modeling you observed may have influenced your relationships as an adult? (For example, *I remember that my father would criticize me a lot, as though nothing was ever good enough to please him, and I would withdraw into an emotional shell. It occurs to me now, that this was the same dynamic that developed with my ex-wife.*) _____

_____

_____

_____

_____

_____

When you have finished with this questionnaire, it might be good to share your responses with a trusted friend or journey-mate who is able to give good emotional responding, comfort, and understanding so that you may celebrate the good experiences together and mourn the disappointments.

Appendix F

———— ◆ ————

Genogram Symbols and Construction

What is a genogram?

A genogram is a diagram of your family tree which identifies not only who is or was in your family, but also the quality of relationships between family members. It provides a tool for helping families and individuals better understand and respond to the origins and dynamics of family issues.

We usually recommend that you draw the genogram as it was during childhood (ages 12-13 and younger).

Why do we recommend drawing a genogram?

Because the genogram not only includes the various family members, but also includes lines which signify the type of relationship among family members. The genogram is a good tool to help identify which needs were met and which needs went unmet, particularly in one's growing up years.

How do I draw my genogram? What symbols do I use to represent persons and relationships in the genogram?

1. Draw the important people, identifying who they are and how they were related to you and to each other. *Draw the genogram as it was during your childhood, ages 12-13 and younger.* **Use the following symbols for representing your family genogram.**

Gender: Squares represent males, circles represent females.

Marriage: A bracket connecting the two spouses.

Children: Draw a short vertical line from the marriage connection line with the square or circle at the end of that line. Children are always presented from oldest to youngest, with the oldest on the far left of the marriage connection bracket.

12/15/92

Death: Diagonal slash through either the square or circle which represents the person who died. It is often helpful to write out the date and year of death or the child's age when the family member died.

Divorce: Two diagonal slashes in the middle of the marriage connection bracket.

Separation: One diagonal slash in the middle of the marriage connection bracket.

Twins: A single line which forks into two lines, terminating in the respective gender symbols of the twins.

Pregnancy: A child in utero is represented by a triangle.

Abortion: A diagonal line drawn through the triangle.

Miscarriage: Same as above except with an "M" noted to the side.

Alcoholism: A family member who is an alcoholic or drug addict may be represented by an "A" to the side of that family member's symbol.

Other: Consider noting family disasters such as fire, earthquake, or other traumatic experience, such as sexual abuse.

2. **Identify the quality of relationships that existed between you and others who were important to you during your childhood (ages 12-13 and younger); for example, you and your parents, you and your siblings, you and other important extended family members.**

Also, represent the quality of relationship between other people who were important to you, especially if their quality of relationship affected you; for example, your mother and father's relationship with each other, their relationship with your siblings, their relationship; with their parents and in-laws, etc.

Use the following "lines" as symbols to represent your perspective of the nature of these relationships:

Estranged (depicted as a line with a "break" in it): A relationship which has been cut off, broken, or severed, such as two adult siblings who have not spoken to each other for at years because of a disagreement over their father's estate.

Distant (depicted as a dashed line): Significantly uninvolved—not much talk, seeing each other or doing things together. While distant relationship may occur with extended family members, they also may happen among family members living under the same roof.

Superficial (shown as a single, solid line): there is conversation, being around each other, and even doing things together, but not really deep knowing of each other. The relationship is really somewhat superficial.

Close (shown as double lines): This refers to a relationship that is intimate; close in a healthy way. It is a relationship in which intimacy needs are consistently met in ways appropriate to this relationship. Within marriage, for example, close means needs are mutually met. Between adults and children, the needs of the child are consistently met by the adult, rather than the child consistently meeting the needs of the adult.

Enmeshed (depicted as triple lines): This means close in an unhealthy manner. The two people involved are too close, and/or the child is used to meet the needs of the adult. The child may be used to meet the parent's needs for affection, attention, etc., which are going unmet within his or her adult relationships. A parent may attempt to live vicariously through his or her child, such as a parent who pushes a son to excel in a sport or other activity that the child does not really enjoy.

Conflicted (shown as a jagged line): This symbol represents a relationship which is characterized by tension and anger. The anger may be openly expressed and obvious, or it may be "covered up" or suppressed.

Genograms (continued)

What additional questions should I reflect upon and answer after I've drawn the genogram?

1. **Who met your need for** *attention?* **Consider:**

   What was your "world" as a child (what were you most interested in)?

   _____

   _____

   _____

   Who left their world, entered your world in a way meaningful to you?
   Who really knew you?

   _____

   _____

   _____

2. **Who met your need for** *affection?* **Consider:**

   Who conveyed "I love you" through meaningful, caring, non-sexual touching, such as hugs, kisses, holding? How did he/she do it?

   _____

   _____

   _____

3. **Who met your need for** *approval?* **Consider:**

   Who conveyed to you, "You are my beloved child, in whom I am well pleased," and you didn't have to do anything to earn or deserve this commendation? How did he/she do it?

   _____

   _____

   _____

4. Who met your need for _comfort?_ _Consider:_

When you were hurting, who would you tend to go to? _____
How did this person respond to you and your pain? Did he or she respond with true comfort, or with facts, advice, pep talks, or criticism? If it was genuine comfort, it should have sounded something like, "I really hurt for you," It saddens me that you were hurt like that." These are tender words with heart-felt emotions.

_____
_____
_____
_____
_____
_____

After you have reflected upon your answers to these questions, spend some time sharing your responses with a trusted friend, journey-mate, or small group. Be alert to opportunities to emotionally respond to each other with joy or sadness, as appropriate.

Appendix G

30 Selected Character Qualities

1. ACCEPTANCE - deliberate and ready reception with a favorable response; to receive someone unconditionally and willingly (Rom. 15:7)

2. CAUTIOUSNESS -gaining adequate counsel before making decisions; recognizing temptations and fleeing them (Prov. 11:14)

3. COMPASSION - feeling the hurts of others and doing all that is possible to relieve them (I Pet. 3:8)

4. CONTENTMENT - enjoying present possessions rather than desiring new or additional ones; being happy regardless of circumstances (I Tim. 6:6)

5. CREATIVITY - finding godly solutions to difficult problems; discovering practical applications for spiritual principles (Rom. 12:12,21)

6. DECISIVENESS - finalizing difficult decisions on the basis of God's ways, word, and will (Jas. 4:15)

7. DEFERENCE - limiting my freedom to not offend those God has called me to serve (Rom. 14:13)

8. DEPENDABILITY - being true to your word even when it is difficult to carry out what promised to do (Matt. 5:37)

9. DILIGENCE - seeing every task as an assignment from the Lord and applying energy and concentration to accomplish it (Col. 3:23-24)

10. DISCERNMENT/SENSITIVITY knowing what to look for in evaluating people, problems and things; saying the right words at the right time (Eph. 4:29)

11. ENDURANCE/PERSEVERANCE - maintaining commitment to what is right during times of pressure (Rom. 5:3-4)

12. FAITH - developing an unshakable confidence in God's Word and visualizing God's will and acting upon it (Heb. 11:6)

13. FORGIVENESS - choosing to not hold an offense against another, remembering how much God has forgiven us (Eph. 4:32)

14. GENEROSITY - recognizing that all possessions belong to God; learning how to be a wise steward of time, money, and possessions; being a cheerful giver (II Cor. 8:9, 9:7)

15. GENTLENESS - responding to needs with kindness and love; knowing what is appropriate to meet the emotional needs of others (Eph. 4:2)

16. GRATEFULNESS - recognizing the benefits which God and others have provided; looking for appropriate ways to express genuine appreciation (Eph. 5:20)

17. HOSPITALITY - sharing what we have with those whom we don't know; "love of strangers" (I Pet. 4:9)

18. HUMILITY - recognizing our total inability to accomplish anything good apart from God's grace; recognizing our fundamental "neediness" (Eph. 4:2)

19. INITIATIVE - taking steps to seek after God with our whole heart; giving first rather than waiting for others to give (Luke 6:38)

20. LOYALTY - adopting as your own the wishes and goals of those you are serving (Col. 3:22)

21. MEEKNESS - yielding our rights and possessions to God; being willing to earn the right to be heard rather than demanding a hearing (I Pet. 5:6)

22. PATIENCE - accepting difficult situations as from God without giving Him or others a deadline to remove the problem (I Cor. 13:4)

23. PUNCTUALITY - showing esteem for other people and their time by not keeping them waiting (Phil. 2:3-4)

24. REVERENCE - demonstrating to God and others respect for the authority and character of God (Prov. 1:7)

25. SECURITY - entrusting our needs and expectations to Christ based upon His eternal Word (I Pet. 5:7; Phil. 4:6-7)

26. SELF-CONTROL - identifying and obeying the promptings of the Holy Spirit; bringing our thoughts, words, and actions under the control of the Holy Spirit (Eph. 5:18)

27. SINCERITY - having motives that are transparent; having a genuine concern to benefit the lives of others (Rom. 12:9)

28. TRUTHFULNESS - gaining approval of others without misrepresenting the facts; facing the consequences of a mistake; telling the whole truth (Eph. 4:25)

29. VIRTUE - demonstrating personal moral standards which cause others to desire a more godly life (I Tim. 4:12)

30. WISDOM - seeing life from God's perspective; learning how to apply principles of scripture in practical situations (Col. 1:9-10)

About Intimate Life Ministries

Intimate Life Ministries (ILM) is a training and resource ministry, headquartered in Austin, Texas, whose purpose is to assist in the development of Great Commandment Ministries worldwide—ongoing ministries that equip believers in a lifestyle of loving God and others.

Intimate Life Ministries comprises:
- a network of churches seeking to fortify homes and communities with His love;
- a network of pastors and other ministry leaders walking intimately with God and their families and seeking to live vulnerably before their people;
- a team of accredited trainers committed to helping churches establish ongoing Great Commandment ministries;
- a team of professional associates from ministry, business, and other professional Christian backgrounds, assisting with research, training, and resource development;
- Christian broadcasters, publishers, media and other affiliates, cooperating to see marriages, families, and church fellowships reclaimed as divine relationships;
- headquarters staff providing strategic planning, coordination, and support.

For more information about the many services offered by Intimate Life Ministries for churches, denominations, or businesses, contact one of our team members at:

Intimate Life Ministries,
PO Box 201808,
Austin, TX 78720-1808
Phone: 800.881.8008 in the USA   01.926.421.004 in the UK
Fax: 512.795.0853 in the USA   01.926.435.704 in the UK
Internet: www.GreatCommandment.net or www.NeverAlone.net

About the Authors

David Ferguson and his wife, Teresa, are directors of Intimate Life Ministries, serving thousands of churches and ministry leaders worldwide with a message of how to deepen intimacy with God and deepen relationships in marriages, families, and the church. For the past twenty years, the Fergusons have been sharing that message in print and through ministry retreats, media, and speaking engagements around the world. David's graduate work in theology, counseling and the social sciences focused on the Great Commandment Principle and its impact on relationships, ministry, and culture. David has a masters of education from Southwest Texas State University and doctor of philosophy and doctor of letters degrees from Oxford Graduate School. He is a member of the Oxford Society of Scholars. David and Teresa have been married thirty-five years and have co-authored several previous books and numerous articles. They reside in Austin, Texas, and have three adult children—Terri, Robin, and Eric.

Bruce and Joyce Walker are on the staff of Intimate Life Ministries in Austin, Texas. Bruce is a Co-Director of the Intimate Life Enrichment Center and the Center for Relational Leadership which apply the Great Commandment Principles in the counseling, caregiving, and market place ministries of the local church. His doctorate in psychology and counseling from Southwestern Baptist Theological Seminary focused on the application of intimacy principles in single adult relationships. He also holds masters degrees in marriage and family counseling and religious education from the same institution. As a counselor, Bruce specializes in relationships and unresolved issues from childhood. Joyce's professional training is in secondary education from Oklahoma State University. The Walkers have one son, Drew.